tear here

UNIX Commands Quick

Account Manipulation

Directory listing	**ls -l**
Directory listing with dot files	**ls -la**
Make a new subdirectory	**mkdir** *directory_name*
Delete a file	**rm** *filename*
View the contents of a file	**cat** *filename*
View a file and pause at each screen	**more** *filename*
Your home directory	*~username*
Edit or create a plan file	**emacs** ~*username*/**.plan**
Edit or create a project file	**emacs** ~*username*/**.project**
Edit or create a signature file	**emacs** ~*username*/**.signature**
Change your password	**passwd**
Change your finger information	**chfn**
Change permissions on a file or directory	**chmod {u}{g}{o}{+ or -}{r}{w}{x}** *filename*

PGP Commands for MS-DOS and UNIX

(Mac users should select menu options that correspond to these descriptions.)

Encrypt plaintext file with intended recipient's public key	**pgp -e** *plaintextfile their_userid*
Encrypt and sign plaintext file as above	**pgp -es** *plaintextfile their_userid*
Encrypt plaintext file and produce ASCII output	**pgp -ea** *plaintextfile their_userid*
Add an ASCII digital signature to a plaintext file, but don't encrypt the file	**pgp -sta** *filename*
Generate public/private keypair	**pgp -kg**
Add another user's public key to your public keyring	**pgp -ka** *their_keyfilename*
Extract a public key from your keyring	**pgp -kx** *userid*
Extract a public key into an ASCII file	**pgp -kxa** *userid*
View the keys on your keyring	**pgp -kv**

Investigation

(Users must be logged onto same UNIX system.)

See what a user is doing	**w** *username*
See what a user has done	**lastcomm** *username*
See when a user has logged on and off	**last** *username*
Look up permissions on a user's home directory	**ls -ld** *~username*

UNIX File or Directory Permissions

Check the current permissions on a file	**ls -l** *filename*
Check the current permissions on a directory	**ls -ld** *filename*
Check the current permissions on your home directory	**ls -ld** *~your_username*

Permissions will look like this (the stuff on the left-hand side constitutes the permissions):

```
-rwx------   2 aaron         512 Feb 17 08:14 Filename
```

A closer look:

d	rwx	rwx	rwx
Directory or file	Permissions for **user** (you)	Permissions for **group**	Permissions for **other** (everyone)

For each set of three permissions (user, group, and other):

If you see...	This is what it means...
r	Read permission is on (can view file, copy file, download file).
w	Write permission is on (can rename file, modify file, delete file).
x	Execute permission is on (can run file).
–	Permission is off.

You can change the permissions of a file with the **chmod** command. You must tell it which set to change the permissions for (user, group, other) and which permissions to turn on or off. Parameters can be combined for convenience. For example:

chmod o-rw *filename*	Will disable read and write permissions for other.
chmod u+x *filename*	Will enable execute permission for user.
chmod -R og-rwx *~username/**	Will disable all permissions for group and other in all subdirectories within username's home directory.

The COMPLETE IDIOT'S GUIDE TO Protecting Yourself on the Internet

by Aaron Weiss

A Division of Macmillan Computer Publishing
A Prentice Hall Macmillan Company
201 W. 103rd Street, Indianapolis, IN 46290 USA

To Mom, Dad, Elliot...and Barney, the bush beagle. Also thanks to Richard Posner, whose foresight is better than most people's hind-sight.

International Standard Book Number: 1-56761-593-7

Library of Congress Catalog Card Number: 94-073043

98 97 96 95 8 7 6 5 4 3 2 1

Interpretation of the printing code: the rightmost double-digit number is the year of the book's first printing; the rightmost single-digit number is the number of the book's printing. For example, a printing code of 95-1 shows that this copy of the book was printed during the first printing of the book in 1995.

Screen reproductions in this book were created by means of the program Collage Plus from Inner Media, Inc., Hollis, NH.

Printed in the United States of America

Publisher
Roland Elgey

Vice President and Publisher
Marie Butler-Knight

Editorial Services Director
Elizabeth Keaffaber

Publishing Manager
Barry Pruett

Managing Editor
Michael Cunningham

Product Development Specialist
Melanie Palaisa

Production Editor
Kelly Oliver

Manuscript Editor
Barry Childs-Helton

Book Designer
Barbara Kordesh

Cover Designer
Karen Ruggles

Illustrator
Judd Winick

Indexer
Kathy Venable

Production Team
Steve Adams, Michael Brumitt, Charlotte Clapp, Lisa Daugherty, Chad Dressler, Amy Durocher, DiMonique Ford, Karen Gregor, Daryl Kessler, Tim Taylor, Michael Thomas, Jody York

Special thanks to Discovery Computing, Inc., for ensuring the technical accuracy of this book.

Contents at a Glance

Contents

Preface

Dear Reader:

The Internet is a safe place. There are not active terrors lurking behind each corner, as some newsmedia (whose names I will not mention) might have you believe. However, the Internet is a vast and open world, much like what everyone else calls "the real world." There are opportunities for people to compromise your security, and there are people who might choose to do so. Sometimes they'll have specific goals, other times they may just be on a joyride. While your Internet safety is not under constant survey and attack, there is good reason to practice caution; after all, most people lock their houses and cars, seal their envelopes, and keep their pet tigers caged.

Unfortunately, education on how to protect yourself realistically on the Internet—including what issues are of more concern and less—has been limited. Most users have seen brief disclaimers about keeping good passwords, perhaps with a couple of sentences explaining what exactly a "good password" is. Other users have picked up newspapers and newsmagazines or flipped around the cable box, only to see horror stories about the Internet that are (at best) out-of-context exaggerations and (more often) completely wrong.

This is not a scare book. You'll find no hype, no headlines, and no lurid sensationalism. What I hope you will find is a reasoned, reasonable look at a variety of security, protection, and privacy issues that face Internet users—veterans and novices alike—as well as what you can, and sometimes can't, do about them. Not every issue is of equal concern, and not every vulnerability is equally easy to protect against. Mixed together with relatively straightforward instructions and a strained attempt at humor, this book strives to be more than another boring-but-necessary read. Who said security can't be fun? Okay, I admit, it's not exactly a tickle-fest, but we'll do the best we can.

I can confidently guarantee that you'll find this book crammed, from front cover to back, with letters, words, and sentences. The kind folks at Que and I have tried to put them all into some sort of order—an order we hope will leave you with a better understanding and application of how best to protect yourself and your data on the Internet.

Aaron Weiss

aaron.weiss@pobox.com

Introduction: Reality Check

A quick glance at newspaper headlines and magazine features over the past year or so would scare anyone. After all, hackers on the Internet are stealing your credit cards, perverts are luring your children, and pornography is jumping off of the screen and onto your lap. In fact, one wonders why anyone would even want to use the Internet, given the press coverage it's been given. Well, it's not that bad.

The Internet—above and beyond the cables, wires, keyboards, and modems—is a collection of human beings. It's a society, one that exists without regard to physical and national boundaries. It's a wonderful society at that, offering many people opportunities they've never had before. But… every society has its troublemakers.

When you leave your house, drive to the supermarket, or go to work, there are things you are concerned about. In the real world, we all protect ourselves in a myriad of ways every day. We lock doors and close windows. We seal envelopes and write emergency numbers on a pad near the telephone. The Internet is really no different, except that many users don't know what to protect themselves from.

There are real concerns on the Internet: if an intruder breaches your Internet account, he could have access to all of your files, from data to research to e-mail. This means possible modification, deletion, or duplication. Furthermore, he could make changes to your account that weaken it so others can break into it too. Evildoers could masquerade as you and commit all sorts of heinous acts under your identity. In addition, an intruder could simply use your account as a stepping stone to bigger things, such as your service provider's entire computer.

Ultimately, the amount of risk that you choose to accept and to defend against is a subjective decision. Some people deadbolt their back door, other people leave the key in the lock. I don't propose to tell you how to run your life, off the Internet or on. But without even knowing about the security issues that you face, you're powerless to make any subjective evaluation whatsoever. In a lapse of idealistic delusion, I might even argue that this book shouldn't be necessary at all. But it is, and I think that you'll find most of the practices and procedures which will keep you relatively secure are not terribly difficult. The Internet is not an unsafe place, but some well-placed caution and a heads-up attitude can never hurt (unless you're a teenager, in which case you are exempt).

In writing this book, I had to make certain assumptions about you, the reader. The way I figure it, you're probably around 5 foot 8... no, just kidding... . What I mean is, even though this is a book oriented toward the novice user, I have to assume you have some Internet experience. After all, if you have never even used the Internet before, how likely are you to want to protect yourself on it? While I don't presume that you are extremely experienced, I do assume that you're at least superficially familiar with general introductory Internet material. I assume that you've sent some e-mail and maybe retrieved a file from time to time. Perhaps you've used Gopher, or more likely the World Wide Web. Again, you may not have months upon months of such experience, but the above words don't sound like Pig Latin to you.

How to Read This Book

Before diving right into the shallow end, there are some minor procedural points to make. First, you're going to need to know English. There's no way around that; it's the only language I know. Hold the book rightside up, and flip pages to the left to move forward, right to move backward. Beyond that, there's not much more to it... except for these things:

You will sometimes see text that is in a different typeface than the rest of the book, like this:

```
I am in a different typeface, and I mean something special.
```

The above is meant to be a representation of either what would appear on your screen or what you should type. So, if I say that you should enter the command `send pizza with cheese`, you should type it exactly that way—with one exception. Sometimes,

I don't know exactly what you have to type, so I need to put something in its place. For example, I might tell you to execute this command:

```
ls -l filename
```

Since I don't know what the name of the file you'll be dealing with is, I just wrote *filename*. Be sure to insert whatever is truly appropriate when you type the command. There are a number of instances throughout this book where similar situations arise. In some cases, I refer to things such as *user_id*, *your_user_id*, *keyfilename*, and so on. Realize that you're supposed to include whatever is appropriate for the context of those instructions. If you've read any other computer books at all, these are not unfamiliar conventions to you, because I'm copying them from every other computer book ever published.

Sometimes, I need to instruct you to hit "control sequences" to initiate a certain action in a program. For example, I might ask you to hit **Ctrl+A**. That means you hold down the **Control** key while hitting the **A** key. Note that when you are using UNIX, the case of the letter matters—a lowercase *a* is different from an uppercase *A*. So, if you're using a UNIX program and I tell you to hit **Ctrl+A**, I mean **Control+Shift+a** (since Shift+a generates a capital A). Alternatively, **Ctrl+a** in UNIX means Control+a.

But remember, if you're using a PC or a Macintosh, the case of the letter usually doesn't matter. If I tell you to hit **Ctrl+H** in Eudora on the PC, you don't have to be sure you hit a capital *H*. In that case, Control+h should be fine.

Some of the chapters have attractive screen shots, which are meant to help illustrate a particular example. But the screen shots were made on my computer with the programs that I use. You may be doing the exact same thing but have a different-looking screen. That's okay. The screen shots are meant as guides, not literal down-to-the-pixel commandments. Furthermore, I have a PC clone, not a Macintosh, so most of the pictures are of PC screens. However, most of the Internet applications that I discuss are quite similar on both the PC (running Microsoft Windows) and the Macintosh. There are a few Mac pictures—I'm not a total bigot.

Also, you'll find the following boxes will give some additional clues and may even entertain you:

These boxes provide some geeky stuff that isn't necessary to read, but can nonetheless be interesting. Try one, you might like it.

These boxes provide some mildly entertaining and moderately informative anecdotes, ripped from the trenches of the Internet.

Trademarks

All terms mentioned in this book that are known to be or are suspected of being trademarks or service marks have been appropriately capitalized. Que Corporation cannot attest to the accuracy of this information. Use of a term in this book should not be regarded as affecting the validity of any trademark or service mark.

Acknowledgements

If it weren't for the good people at Que, especially my editor, Melanie Palaisa, this book would just be handwritten scribbles in a spiral notebook. Thanks to Barry Pruett for wanting to make a real book out of this stuff, and to Melanie for helping to make a readable book out of it.

Without plenty of oxygen, I wouldn't have made it past Chapter 1, so I appreciate the window in my room and its ability to open outward, allowing air to flow in. It's even got a screen to keep bugs out.

Lastly, I'd like to acknowledge everyone on the Internet, for without them the Internet simply would not be. It's often tempting, when considering the Net, to think of the computers and hardware first, but in reality the heart of the Internet is made up of people, not coaxial cables. All of the Internet's qualities—positive and negative—are reflections of the characteristics of the humans who use it. That's my little "we are all one" speech. I have to go stare directly at the sun now.

Part 1
Over Your Shoulder, Behind Your Back

Well, okay, maybe that title is just slightly paranoid. Paranoia is like cinnamon—you want to have just the right amount. Too little leaves the applesauce wanting, but too much makes your nose flare.

New users are often shocked at how much of their activities and information is in full or partial view of others. It's like when you find out that the Macy's dressing rooms actually have two-way mirrors; it can be scary at first. You just have to learn how to put your underwear on while crouching (digitally speaking, of course).

This section will look at the various ways in which people can snoop, spy, peep, and poke at you, your Internet account, or your computer. Some are easy to protect against, some are not. Some are more serious matters than others. There's something for everyone, so bring the beach blanket, the folks, and a good book—no, actually bring this book.

There once was a man from Hubble…

The Least You Need to Know

This is a big book, and you probably won't want to read it all in one sitting. It's simply not that gripping. But before we launch right into everything, I want to make sure we're coming from the same starting point. One of the inevitable problems in discussing "the Internet" is that many people—especially newer users—don't exactly understand what the Internet is and what it is not. Popular press coverage has confused many of the technical terms involved and (as a consequence) has also confused the readers. So, for the purposes of this book, let's try to remedy that situation and get things straight. It'll help minimize confusion down the road, and it doesn't hurt at parties, either. (Well, yes it does, actually.)

What the Internet Isn't

The Internet falls under the umbrella of *online services*. An online service refers to any situation where you use your computer to talk to another one. Usually, this involves telephone lines and modems, although some people have special setups. There are other online services besides the Internet. Some examples include America Online, CompuServe, and PRODIGY, to name the biggies. Although you're also "online" when you use these services, they have some fundamental differences from the Internet. They are all privately owned companies, meaning there's a very specific organizing head. The owners of these services are the sole decision-makers about what sorts of information the service will provide—and what users may say or do. In this way, there are certain regulatory forces in place.

This book does not specifically address these types of "proprietary" online services. They have their own rules and their own user interfaces. Many of these services now offer users certain types of Internet access. But that access is still coming through the proprietary service. A number of the security issues discussed in this book (such as passwords, e-mail, and most of Part 4) still apply to users of these services. But specific instructions throughout this book are not written with these services in mind, so details may be different.

What the Internet Is

The term *Internet*, in the official sense and as used in this book, refers to a loosely organized network of computers all around the world. The Internet is not a static, unchanging thing; rather, it is continually dynamic, reflecting the network of computers connected together at any one time. What "binds" the Internet together is merely the fact that a whole bunch of computers know how to talk to each other. The physical technology they use to talk is not terribly important to the definition—most computers talk over phone lines, but some use specialized cables, and some even use satellite links.

Online Some people have been using the term *online* to refer to using any computer at all, while the more traditional meaning is when the computer is being used to connect to another computer. I prefer the latter, and that's how it is used in this book. In that case, *offline* does not mean the computer is shut off, it means it is not connected to any other computer. For most people, this distinction can be made by considering the modem. If it's presently using the phone line, then you're online. If the modem has hung up, you're offline.

Because the Internet is something like a "pick-up game" of basketball, there is no central authority. If you bring your computer and modem, you can play on the team. Some organizations and individuals have been given some responsibilities to help coordinate activities, like a team captain. But those positions are not carved in stone and are not the products of any type of "constitution" or other legally binding document. Because of this, nobody *owns* the Internet, nobody *controls* the Internet, and nobody *regulates* the Internet. The game works as well as its participants. To distinguish access to the Internet (as described previously) from that which proprietary online services provide, I will use the term *true Internet access*. Often, "true" access involves a local or regional service provider, not a national megacompany such as those online services mentioned earlier (with some exceptions, as there are some national providers who do offer true Internet access, such as NETCOM).

Without a fixed-in-place structure, there is no uniform way through which one accesses the Internet. While users of America Online all use the exact same software to access that service, this is not the case on the Internet. A variety of programs—and combinations of programs—can be used to coax your computer into participating on the Internet. We'll call the programs you use to access the Internet your *interfaces*. This book will make important distinctions, from a security standpoint, among several different types of interface you might use to access the Internet.

The first very common interface is called the *UNIX shell*. On the surface, this is a very simple interface: all you get is a prompt, such as a % sign or a $ sign, and you have to enter strange commands to do anything. Techno-geeks love this sort of thing, but those inexperienced with computing (and many folks who *are* experienced with computing) find it about as enjoyable as midnight dental surgery. Because this is a very popular Internet interface, and because it provides the widest array of personal security issues of any Internet account, this book will focus quite a bit on UNIX.

It used to be that a UNIX shell account was the only way to access the Internet. But when the proprietary services came along with their super-user-friendly *graphical interfaces* (which allow you to point at pictures and click instead of typing strange words), users flocked to them like game show hosts to a toupee shop. Graphical interfaces "pop up" windows on your screen; you can access and manipulate these with the mouse, in a fashion that makes more sense to many people than non-English commands. In response to the demand, an increasing number of Internet service providers began to concoct their own graphical interfaces.

Today the field is a mixed bag. Many users still use UNIX shell accounts. Other users use graphical interfaces, although there is no one "standard" graphical interface that service providers offer. Some providers offer an integrated *suite* of programs, designed to take care of all of a user's needs. One such example is The Pipeline USA, a service provider based in New York City. They are expanding their services and trying to offer The Pipeline USA graphical interface software to other service providers. Most providers offer a collection of programs, not necessarily designed as one integrated unit. Some popular examples of such programs are Netscape for World Wide Web use and Eudora for e-mail. This book addresses those users, too.

Lastly, many providers who offer UNIX shells have tried to compensate for UNIX's user-hostile rep and make users' lives a tad easier. They have created text-based menus; although these aren't graphical point-and-click interfaces, still they allow the user to choose functions from a list of choices. It beats being left in front of a flashing cursor without a clue. For the purposes of this book, I tend to group these "menu-based" interfaces with graphical interfaces.

And Now, the Top Ten List

One of the themes I try to drag into the open throughout this book (kicking and screaming, when I must) is that *not all security issues are of equal concern.* For example, it's possible I could be hit by a car when I cross the street, or a meteor could hit Earth. They're both risks, but I am more concerned about the car than the meteor (hence I look both ways when I cross the street, rather than up at the sky). So, now that this entire book has been analyzed by a team of Nobel-Prize-winning researchers using higher math, mind-boggling numbers, and slide rules, here is an overview of the top ten important issues and chapters in this book (in chronological order, not order of importance).

1. Everybody Knows Your Name

Unless you take active precautions, a surprising amount of information about you is available to much of the Internetted world. This can easily include your full name, home phone number, or address. Often, you can change any of this, if you know about it in the first place. Chapter 2 can help.

2. Your Personal Bodyguard: Passwords

The password to your Internet account is basically your front-door deadlock. With a wimpy one, you greatly increase the opportunity for someone to get in. Once someone is in your account, it's like having your house burgled—anyone can commit a host of nasty acts you wouldn't be pleased to come home to. Lock your account solid with Chapter 6!

3. Safe and Sound: Encryption

Your digital privacy is a right, not a privilege. The best way to protect this privacy is by learning—and, when appropriate, using—powerful data-encryption techniques so that no one can snoop around in your files. It's not just for the military anymore. Enroll in Chapter 7 for an introduction.

4. E-mail Up Close and Personal

If you send e-mail, and you probably do, you need to read this. Learn where your e-mail goes, who can see it, how to stop them, and other cool stuff. Four out of five doctors recommend Chapter 10.

5. The Nasty Virus

Digital terrorism hasn't eluded the Internet. If life isn't difficult enough, you have to worry about people trying to destroy your data simply because they don't have anything better to do. Learn about armaments and education in Chapter 11.

6. Permissions and Ownership in UNIX

Your UNIX system, if you have an account on one, is like a big king-size bed that a bunch of people share. There are mechanisms in place to make sure everyone keeps his hands to himself. Learn how to protect your files from fellow users' sticky fingers in Chapter 13.

7. Rlogin—Just Say No

Rlogin is a UNIX shortcut that many an unsuspecting user is too quick to use. If you use it improperly, you might as well just invite people to break into your UNIX account. Close that can of worms, courtesy of Chapter 14.

8. For Sysadmins Only

Whether you wanted this job or not, being a new sysadmin is a daunting task. It's like being groundskeeper, security, and janitorial staff of a mansion, rolled into one. Get a primer on important issues for running a UNIX system in Chapter 16.

9. Security Has Its Privileges

There's a veritable virtual bazaar on the Internet—buying and selling and trading. Lots of good stuff to be had for the discerning consumer who doesn't want to *be* had. Roll the capitalist wheel with confidence in Chapter 17.

10. The Copyright Conundrum

It's too easy to walk all over other people's intellectual property these days. There are some complicated and messy issues involved—on both sides of the fence. Understand how copyright affects how you use the Net, with other people's work and your own. Chapter 20 approved.

Getting to Know All About You

In This Chapter

- What your finger tells the world
- Signature file prudence
- An Internet phonebook?
- Hide-and-seek in Usenet

New users are often surprised at how much information—and what types—other Internet users can find out about them. But after all, on a network that connects millions of computers, it's sort of like the whole world sharing one big bed. For the most part, people will keep to themselves, but it's useful to know where, when, and how someone might just try to peek up your nightshirt. In our first real chapter of this book, we'll look at some ways that others can glean information relating to you or your *Internetting* habits.

Internetting There is no such word as "Internetting." I just made it up. I needed a verb. Feel free to use it with friends and family alike.

As explained in Chapter 1, there are three basic types of interfaces we'll be discussing throughout this book and this chapter. It's important not to confuse Internet resources with Internet interfaces. For example, the World Wide Web (sometimes called the WWW or just "the Web") is an Internet *resource*. That is, it's one way to explore and obtain information on the Internet.

One can, however, use a variety of *interfaces* to access the WWW. The popular programs Mosaic and Netscape are examples of graphical interfaces. Those are graphical interfaces for accessing the World Wide Web. However, there is also a program called Lynx, which is a UNIX shell interface for accessing the WWW. Often, the interfaces you use are determined by the type of Internet account you have. Users with accounts that support graphical interfaces will most likely *use* graphical interfaces to access Internet resources (as will those with SLIP/PPP and—less frequently—Ethernet). Users with UNIX shell accounts will use UNIX shell interfaces, which are text- and command-based. Because these different types of accounts (and their respective interfaces) pose different security issues, the distinctions between them will be highlighted when necessary.

Throughout this book there will be references made to the differences between "graphical" or menu-based interfaces to the Internet and UNIX shell accounts. UNIX shell accounts usually leave you with a prompt and a command line, at which you enter commands. Some forms of access have menus "on top" of a UNIX shell account, which means you can choose options from a menu, or you can go into the UNIX shell (command line) if you desire. Other types of services offer menu systems with no possibility of using a UNIX shell. And still other services offer "graphical" interfaces, meaning you navigate the Internet by using the mouse to point-and-click in windows that open on your screen. Menu-based or graphical systems tend to be more restrictive than UNIX shells, both in terms of power and vulnerability, and it is that difference which will be highlighted several times in the course of this book.

Pull Your Finger: The UNIX finger Command Tells a Lot

In the dark, cold, poorly ventilated laboratories of the 1970s, UNIX programmers—driven by either desperate boredom or far too much time away from human contact—came up with some pretty strange names for their programs. Now we're stuck with their legacy, an example of which we'll talk about now, called the *finger* command.

The common terminology in Internet parlance is to say, "Finger me," or "I fingered you." This is not obscene. Rather, it means the user asked for further information about another user. Specifically, by using the program called *finger*, which is available on all UNIX systems and is frequently available on many services that use graphical interfaces. When you finger someone, you receive a certain amount of information about the person—and (more relevant to this chapter) when someone fingers you, they receive some information about you.

Why would someone want to finger someone else? Well, it's a good way to find out whether another person is currently online, for one thing. You may choose to send them a message or attempt to talk to them over the Internet in that case. Some people offer information in their finger output, such as sports scores or standings. Lastly, it's just a general way to find out more information about somebody you might be interested in contacting for one reason or another. Let's finger a fictitious version of myself, and look at the results—note that I'm doing this in a UNIX shell for this example, but the output would be similar if you used another type of interface.

UNIX Shell Prompt Usually a character such as % or $ that represents the line on which you can enter shell commands. If your system has a menu, but not an option to change the password, there should at least be an option for going to the shell.

At the UNIX prompt, I typed:

```
%finger mw12@crux2.cit.cornell.edu
```

When I pressed **Enter**, I received the following display:

```
[crux2.cit.cornell.edu]
Login name: mw12     In real life: Aaron Weiss
Office: My bedroom  Home Phone: (555)555-5556
Directory: /usr/u/mw12      Shell: /usr/local/bin/tcsh
Last login Sun Mar 19 12:02 on ttyp9 from SLAX2.CIT.CORNELL.EDU
Project: Building a home with creamsicle sticks.
Plan: To conquer large tracts of Western Europe and buy a puppy.
```

The line crux2.cit.cornell.edu simply identifies the server that I log in to. On the first line of output (the second line down in the example just given), you see my *login name* (a.k.a. *username*). That's nothing new; you had to know it to finger me in the first place. To the right of that, you see my "real name"—that's something I may or may not want other people to know about. The next line lists my office and phone number, which may also be sensitive information. The finger command also reports on your login status. Were I presently logged in to the machine crux2.cit.cornell.edu in the example, it would have reported **On since ...** with a date and time. Since I wasn't logged in (which is about as rare as a raw sirloin), it reported when I was last logged in, and from where I logged in. Let's move down to the last two lines of the sample finger output; I never really understood what the purposes of the "project" and "plan" are. More often than not, people take it as an opportunity to flex their cleverness muscle for public spectacle. Some use it for "business card"-like reasons, providing any pertinent information they might want others to know.

The login information definitely makes it easier for someone to track you. Now, that doesn't mean people are out to track you, and it doesn't mean the information is not useful. For instance, I might finger friends to see if they are on (so I can talk to them), or find out when they last logged on (to see if they got home all right from our round-table discussion on the works of Aristophanes... yeah, that's it...).

Users of graphical interfaces can finger others also. Exactly how one would do so depends on the particular graphical interfaces you are provided with, but one common way is through your e-mail program. For example, the popular e-mail application Eudora offers you the option to finger someone. You would do so by selecting the menu option **Window/Ph**, or by hitting **Ctrl+U**. You'll then get a window with an empty input box labeled **Command**, at which you enter the address of the person you want to finger (just as in the UNIX example). Then you click on the **Finger** button to the right of the input box. The results will appear in the window below, as in the following figure:

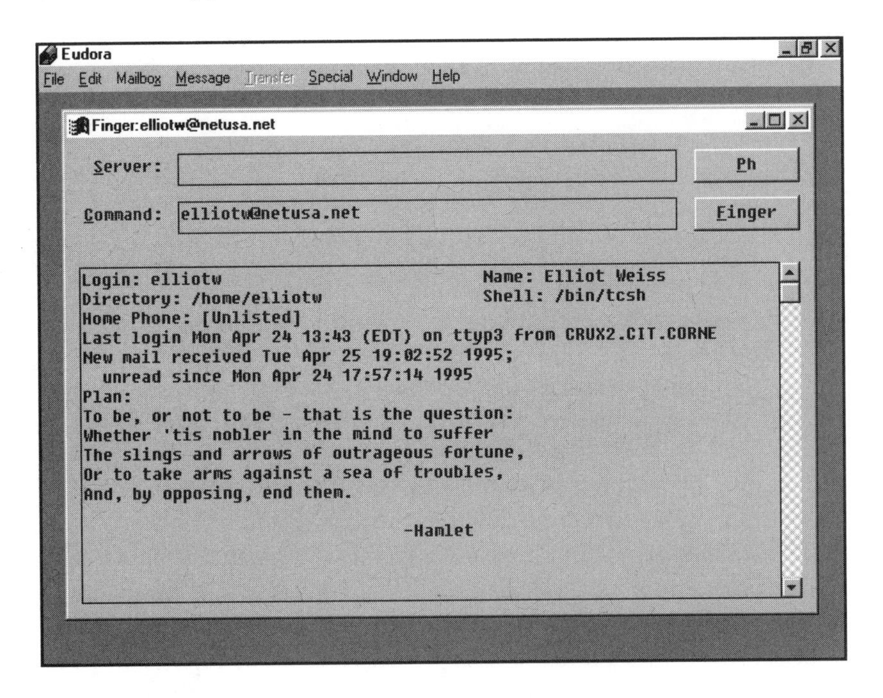

Here's how you would finger someone with Eudora, a graphical e-mail program that also supports finger.

If you have an account that supports graphical interfaces, however (such as SLIP/PPP), other people may not be able to finger you. If they do manage to, they may only receive limited information. When someone else fingers you at your e-mail address, your service provider's computer may report some information about you to them, but it may not be entirely accurate. For example, it might report a "last login" date that is incorrect. Some providers have a special system for users with graphical interfaces to submit personal profile information (such as the plan). If your provider offers you the ability to enter personal profile information, then others can finger you and at least find out some things. It's still less likely they'll get accurate login times, however. On the whole, users with graphical Internet accounts are less vulnerable to having information revealed about them than are UNIX shell users.

In a UNIX shell, you can change the entries for your real name, office, and phone number by entering the command **chfn** at the shell prompt. Here's what would follow, caught on special slow-motion film:

```
%chfn
Changing finger information for mw12
Name [Aaron Weiss]: Batman
Office number []: 10 Bat Cave Rd.
Office Phone []: 1-607-BATPHONE
Home Phone [ ]:
```

Between the brackets is what that field is already set to. As we see here, only my real name was set—to my real name. I then entered new entries for each. One can also just hit **Enter** to leave an entry unfilled, as I did here for the Home Phone field (unless the entry already is set to something, in which case you need to hit **Spacebar** once and then **Enter** to change it back to blank). This entire procedure gives you some control in tailoring what others will see when and if they finger you.

> **Service Provider** The organization that provides your Internet connection. For many home users, this is probably some commercial service whom you pay each month. Others access the Internet through employers or academic institutions, in which case these institutions (or a specific department therein) are the service providers. It's good to know who your specific service provider is—so you can yell and scream at them when they screw up. And, of course, compliment them when they do well. (I had to write that, you know.)

If your provider offers a graphical interface, those who use it will have some specific menu choice for configuring their personal information. There may be a menu for "Change personal profile" (or something to that effect); you'll have to consult your service provider or documentation. Some Internet *service providers* do not allow finger requests to their systems;

the idea is to preserve users' privacy. Other systems allow you to choose whether you're listed or unlisted. For these reasons, your particular situation may vary. Either way, whenever providing personal information, use your discretion—this information is before the eyes of the world. You might not, for example, want to give out your home phone number.

What's This About Hidden Files?

In UNIX, there are some files which are *hidden*: when you get a normal directory listing (using the command **ls** or **ls -l**), these files will not appear in the output. They're not really hidden, however, or at least not very well. The only thing that makes them any different from regular files is that their filenames begin with a period (.). A file named **document**, for example, is not a hidden file in UNIX, but a file named **.document** *is* a hidden file. Sometimes people call these hidden files *dot files* because the file name begins with a dot.

To see hidden or dot files in a UNIX directory, you have to add an **a** to the command-line options for **ls**. If you normally use **ls** to get a directory listing, for example, you would need to use **ls -a** to get that same listing with hidden files revealed. If you use **ls -l** normally, you would use **ls -la** to see all files including hidden ones. There is nothing else different about hidden files, other than the fact that their file names begin with periods. What's their use, then? Well, UNIX keeps a lot of configuration files in your home directory, and every one has a name that begins with a period. In one sense, dot files are a convention used to separate configuration files from everything else. It's not a rule, just a practice. Second, you have many configuration files in your directory—imagine if they were always displayed in a directory listing—the output would be huge and a pain to deal with. So the common **ls -l** command doesn't show the dot files; if you want or need to see them, just tack an **a** onto the **ls** command line.

You can also change the information displayed in your project and plan. As with your office and phone number, services using menus or graphical interfaces will have their own methods of setting your project and plan. On a UNIX system you merely have to create a text file named **.project** that contains your project information and a text file named **.plan** that contains your plan information. (Note that period in front of the word. That's very important. UNIX likes periods.) Both files do need to be in your *home directory*—for example, if your username were **bob** and you used **emacs** as your text editor, you would type **emacs ~bob/.plan** at the shell prompt to create and edit your .plan file. Additionally, both files need to be "world-readable" (see Chapter 13). Always remember that everything you enter in any of this information sits before the eyes of the world, so if you make a plan that reads, "This is my plan. I am a man. I'm a fan of Stan. I don't eat much flan," not only will you look stupid, but you'll also be unoriginal, since that's *my* plan!

What you choose to use your plan and/or project for, if anything, is really a personal decision. Many people never create them at all, in which case users who finger them just receive the message "No Plan." Other users leave personal information, and yet others just make stabs at wit. Some people use their plan to offer information to the public. For example, there was once a user who put the Top 20 Nielsen ratings for television shows each week in his plan. Users who were interested in such could finger him and find out. People use plan files for a variety of similar informational uses. Your plan can be as long or as short as you want, but your project can only be one line, so the plan is more widely used.

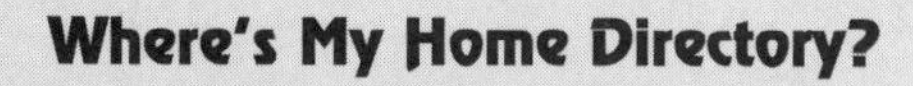

Where's My Home Directory?

Some of the files I'll be talking about creating (or manipulating) take a little bit of know-how in UNIX file management. First, you have what is called a *home directory*. This is the main directory in your UNIX account, where all your subdirectories reside (you can create new subdirectories with the command **mkdir *dirname***). You can check what directory you are currently in at any time by entering the command **pwd** at the UNIX prompt. The output of pwd might look something like this if your username were **bob**:

```
%pwd
/home/bob/docs
```

This output means you are in the "docs" directory in the account of "bob." Note that your UNIX system may not say "/home/bob" exactly; it could be "/usr/bob" or "/usr/home/bob," or similar variations on that idea. Any time you want to return to your home directory, type **cd ~*bob*** (replacing *bob* with your actual username). You won't see anything exciting happen when you enter this command, but you can check that it worked by typing **pwd** again:

```
%cd ~bob
%pwd
/home/bob
```

The tilde (~) in UNIX has a special meaning. It means "the home directory of the username that follows." So **~bob** means "the home directory of username bob." Whenever you want to specify your home directory, you use ***~username*** in the command line.

Also note that some UNIX systems provide, in addition to the example finger output shown, the status of the user's e-mail folder, such as whether there is any new mail still unread, or when the last message was read. This can be a convenient way for you to check your e-mail on another account without logging into it, but it's also another tip to someone else as to your behavior.

Regarding the information listed for your directory and shell, that is not information you can alter. There is some opinion that reporting your directory to the world is not such a great thing, as potential intruders then learn exactly where on your provider's computer your account sits. Because you cannot alter the reporting of that information, this lies in the hands of your service provider. Related matters will be discussed in Chapter 16 (but don't skip that far ahead now—there's all manner of good stuff before that).

In the end, keep in mind that someone may be able to learn a good deal about you by fingering you, but that you have the power to regulate at least a portion of the information they will receive.

Your Signature Is More Than Just Penmanship

With no end of opportunity for self-aggrandizement, the Internet also offers the option of creating what is called a *signature file*. Like the .plan and .project files, your signature file is a text file that contains anything you want it to. The signature file is most often appended to the end of e-mail that you send, and usually to Usenet postings, as well. Because of this, any information that you include in your signature file truly gets around. Whereas someone has to take the effort to finger you to read your plan and project, everyone you send e-mail to—or who reads your public posting to Usenet—reads your signature. Again, some users use the signature as a business card, with "official" sorts of information. Many users just draw (or shamelessly plagiarize) pretty ASCII pictures, and some take the opportunity to list everything they own as a symbol of personal wealth and therefore worth. Any and all of the above are fine from the security perspective (personal standards are another issue entirely), as long as you keep in mind that the information you are divulging is seen by potentially millions of people.

Signature Your signature is a little blurb that appears at the bottom of the e-mail you send or the messages you post to Usenet. It may contain more personal information, methods by which someone can contact you, or a quotation from a favorite book. Or anything else. You don't *have* to have one, but many people do, and they've become an art form on the Internet in their own right.

UNIX shell users can create a signature file the same way they created a plan and a project, except this time the file has to be named **.signature**. Again, the file must be in your home directory. Users of other types of systems are on their own—just kidding—but again, creating your signature in menu-based or graphical systems will be done via one of the options your service provider offers you. Graphical e-mail applications may or may not have options for including signature files, whereas under UNIX, your signature will generally be automatically included if the file **.signature** exists in your home directory.

Your signature is not a major threat to health and home insofar as Internet security goes, but it's just another route by which you can divulge information about yourself to the world. As such, it's worth taking care what information that will be.

"I'm in the Book"—Online White Pages

Even if you choose not to reveal your office location, phone number, and similar kinds of facts in your finger information, someone else might already have done it for you. Some organizations offer public "e-mail directories" that Internet users can access, often via finger or Gopher. Academic institutions, especially, have such directories, where students and staff are listed—sometimes with office or even home addresses and phone numbers. Once again, I don't mean to incite paranoia (if I wanted to do that, this would be a campaign rather than a book). But you should know that your name—and possibly more—is out there for others to gain access to, in this case possibly provided by your organization or institution. For the most part, this is a good thing, as it allows people on the Net who might be looking for you to locate you, such as colleagues, students, or old friends.

> **Gopher** Gopher is an Internet resource for retrieving information, like FTP and the World Wide Web. You can use Gopher to traverse tree-like hierarchies of information, wherein you can run searches or retrieve files. You can access Gopher either through a Gopher client interface or a World Wide Web browser. Most users with any experience on the Internet at all have run into Gopher at one point or another.

Some institutions have mechanisms that allow you to alter the information in the public e-mail directory. For example, at Cornell University, if someone telnets to the address **qi.cornell.edu**, he can enter his University ID and password, and then alter the information that is reflected in the directory. Other places might have similar Telnet-based systems, different systems, or nothing at all. Best to talk to whoever is in charge of computing services at your organization or institution to learn more about the information in the public directory (if there is one). If they don't know, kick them—and if that doesn't work, kick them harder (below the shins is best). In the end, it's your right to determine what happens with your personal information.

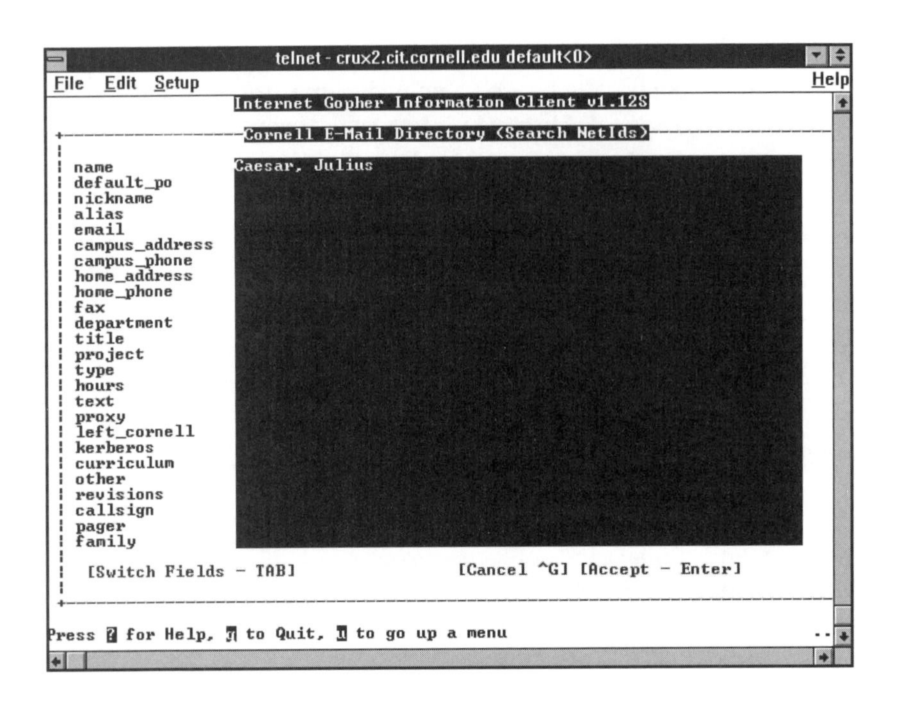

An example of a public e-mail directory. This one is accessed using Gopher. As you can see, it allows the user to search for someone based on a wide array of criteria.

As you can see on the left side of the preceding figure, with a search directory like this a user can search for someone else based on a whole cupful of criteria. You can search for someone based on name alone, e-mail address alone, or even just an address or phone number. These directories can be powerful ways of tracking someone down—which has its definite uses, both virtuous and less so. Not everyone can be looked up in directories such as the one shown here; only if your organization offers such a thing to the public (which most often will be a university and sometimes a business) can people try to track you down this way. Most private service providers don't give the public this type of access to their users.

Plastering Your Face All Over Usenet

The signature at the bottom of a Usenet posting isn't the only information about you strewn across the globe. Don't forget all that stuff at the top of the post!

Most obviously, the header of your Usenet posting contains an Internet address that is very likely to be your e-mail address. So by making a public posting, you are providing—to the whole conscious, reading public—your e-mail address (which can often be used to finger you). Now, of course, this isn't an accident. After all, if your post *didn't* contain your e-mail address, how would anyone respond to you? It helps to identify you, making you a participant in a discussion with more self-identity than just a random hollerer. On the other hand, you might not want anyone to find out your e-mail address in a particular post, or, if you sneak in some office time posting to newsgroups outside your business area, you may want to remain *anonymous*. Additionally, there are a variety of personal reasons you may not want to reveal your true identity in a newsgroup; these range from self-protection to emotional issues.

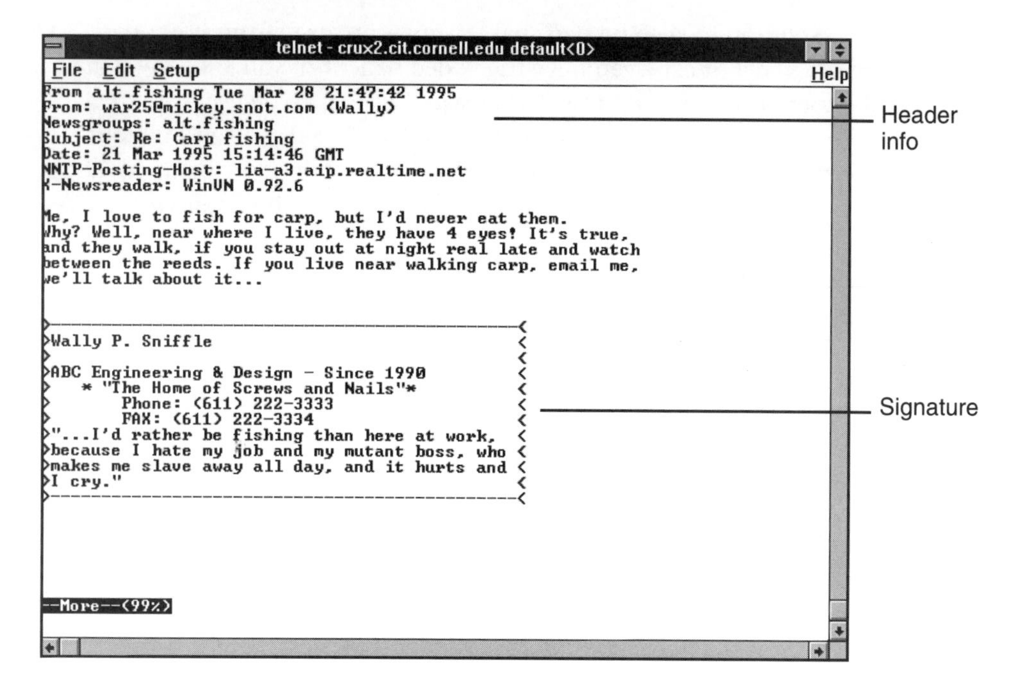

A sample Usenet post. As you can see, at the top and bottom there is information that someone might find useful in getting to know more about you.

In the sample Usenet post shown here, the top few lines are what is called the *header*. They contain background information about the post that someone might find useful. The first line describes the newsgroup in which—and time at which—the post appeared. After that is the address of the poster, which is very probably his e-mail address. Beyond that are some more arcane details about the post, but it's the poster's address that is the most useful to someone else. Of course, you usually *want* people to know who you are, in part so they can identify and respond to you. There are times, however, when you don't want to be seen in all your glory. We'll discuss how to achieve that later in this chapter.

At the bottom of the sample is the signature. In this case, Mr. Sniffle has a very large signature—Usenet convention is to keep the signature to four lines or less, to save network traffic and storage space. Aside from its size, he provides a lot of personal information in the signature, such as a phone and FAX number, and workplace. That's certainly his right, but it's something you should think about first. Some people may be more comfortable than others in giving that sort of information out to the general public.

Who Was That Masked User?

There is a solution to keeping personal information away from other people when posting to Usenet. It can even have the added benefit of still allowing you to receive e-mail responses to your posting. The answer is called an *anonymous re-mailer* (hey, it's better than "finger"). Sending anonymous e-mail to other users will be discussed in more detail in Chapter 10, but now let's chat about making anonymous Usenet postings.

Anonymous Re-mailer
When you want to send an e-mail message or make a Usenet post without revealing your identity or real e-mail address, you can use one of these. You send a message to the address of a particular anonymous re-mailer, and it strips away all identifying information about you. Once done, it then forwards the message to your intended destination, following the instructions you included with the original message. It's a way to preserve your privacy, when and if you want or need to, and those times do arise.

An anonymous re-mailer is a service you send a message to, with instructions about what to do with the message. The service wipes out all information identifying you, and then passes the message on to the destination. Often the service gives your message an ID that a reader of Usenet can respond to; the service will forward the reply back to you. In this way, readers of Usenet have no idea who you are, but they can communicate with you. Let's take a look at one of the most popular anonymous re-mailer services, known as **anon.penet.fi**. There are other anonymous re-mailers and other things you can do with them, which will be discussed in more florid detail in the aforementioned Chapter 10.

With the **anon.penet.fi** anonymous re-mailer (sometimes called an *anonymous server*, and that's what I'm going to call it from now on), you must set up a password with the server before you can make a Usenet posting. This provides extra security for you, preventing others from faking your original e-mail address, finding out your anonymous ID, and other nasty things.

Why a Password?

If someone manages to fake your actual e-mail address, which is possible, he could send mail to the anonymous server as if he were you. Not only could he find out your anonymous ID, he could use your anonymous ID to make their own Usenet postings or e-mail (and possibly harass others) under the guise of being "you." Needing a password to access the anonymous server reduces the risk of this happening.

To create a password for yourself at the **anon.penet.fi** server, go into the application with which you send e-mail and create a new e-mail message addressed to **password@anon.penet.fi**. The subject line doesn't matter; you can leave it blank or write anything you want for it. In the body of your e-mail message, enter what you want your password to be. (Be sure to spend some quality time with Chapter 6 before making up a password.) Send off that message, and a few hours later you should receive confirmation of your new password from the server.

To make a posting to a particular newsgroup, you have two options. Here they are, in order of the result of a flip of this coin I found in my pocket (which has gone through the wash three times and now appears newer than the original minting).

Anonymous Posting with anon.penet.fi: Method 1

Start your e-mail application and address the message to **news.group.name@anon.penet.fi**.

For example, if you want to make an anonymous post to the newsgroup **alt.fetish.lint** (there is no such newsgroup… yet), you would address the e-mail to **alt.fetish.lint@anon.penet.fi**. In the **Subject:** line of your e-mail, enter whatever you want the subject of your post to be, for example: **Looking for movies with lint scenes**.

Now, this next part is very important. On the *very first* line of the body of your e-mail message, you must enter the line exactly as it appears here (typing in the proper text of your actual password, created earlier in this chapter, to take the place of *yourpassword*):

```
X-Anon-Password: yourpassword
```

Make sure there is no space before the X, make sure there is only one space between the colon and the first character of your password, and make sure there are no trailing spaces after your password (hit **Enter** immediately following the last character of your password). Make sure you follow the capitalization of the X-Anon-Password phrase as written here, or you can make it entirely lowercase or entirely uppercase.

On the line just below the X-Anon-Password line, hit **Enter** again. This will create a blank line between the X-Anon-Password line and the start of your desired Usenet post. Then begin typing your post as usual, as you want it to appear in Usenet. Following is how this example message might appear (though it may look slightly different, depending on what e-mail program you use).

```
To: alt.fetish.lint@anon.penet.fi
Cc:
Subject: Looking for movies with lint scenes

X-Anon-Password: i9%rr3=bo

Hi,

I'm looking for any movies with good lint scenes, maybe with people picking
lint off of sweaters or from their pockets. I especially would like scenes of
lint rollers being used on garments that are covered with lint-- the more
lint the better. And of course, bellybutton lint is the best, if there are
any good, flabby scenes of that I'd really like to know!

Thanks!!
LintLuver
```

Before you complete the message and send it off, let's consider your signature for a second. For many people, the signature file is automatically appended to the end of an e-mail message. You don't really want this to happen if you're making an anonymous post—especially if your signature file contains any personal information. The best thing to do is be sure to remove your signature from the e-mail before sending it off to the anonymous server.

Some e-mail programs (such as PINE) may insert your signature directly into the body of the message. In that case, you can cut it out of the message manually before sending it off. Other e-mail programs (such as Eudora) don't show you your signature, but they append it after you choose **Send**. In that case, you have to find a way to tell the e-mail program *not* to append your signature file to the outgoing message. In Eudora, you can do this by clicking on the box that says **Signature** (just above the e-mail composition window) when creating a new message, as in the following figure. When you click on that box, you'll see that there is an option called **None**. Choose it; that way no signature file will be appended to this e-mail message when you send it off.

Other e-mail programs may have slightly different ways to disable your signature. Search the menus; it should be there on any decent e-mail program.

Oops! If you mess up anything in your syntax, the server will just mail you back an error message. It's not the end of the world—you can just fix your error and re-send the message—but to save time, try to follow the syntax properly the first time. The server can sometimes take a few hours to respond with diagnostic messages such as errors. It's very lazy. (Just kidding; it's very popular and therefore quite busy.)

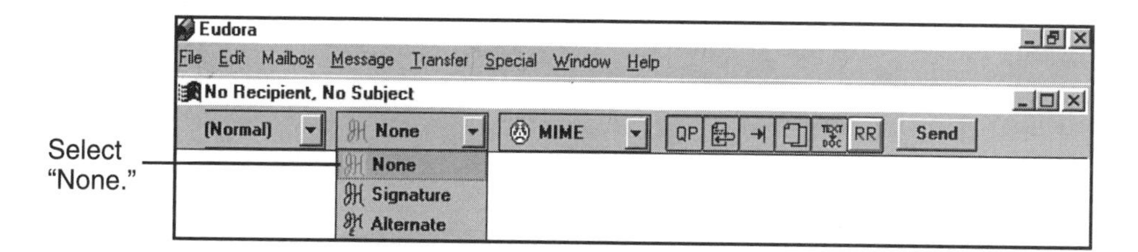

Here's how you can tell Eudora not to append your signature to a particular e-mail message, so as not to undermine the whole point of "anonymous."

The anonymous re-mailer at **anon.penet.fi** has a built-in way of attempting to remove your signature, in case you forgot. Because many people's signatures begin with a row of dashes, the penet server will look for a line that begins with at least two consecutive dashes (they must begin at the leftmost end of a line). It will then excise everything below that line. If your signature does not begin like that, penet won't excise it. Furthermore, if you accidentally include a row of dashes in your message for whatever reason, penet will cut out everything below the point where it finds them. The moral: it's safest to remove your signature (or prevent it from reaching penet in the first place), and don't include any rows beginning with dashes in your message. More than once have I seen a message posted anonymously to Usenet which contained something to the effect of "The following story is about such-and-such," followed by a line of dashes that the poster included as a separator, followed by nothing because penet deleted the rest of the story.

The only problem with this method is that it doesn't allow you to *crosspost* to multiple newsgroups simultaneously. Enter method #2:

Anonymous Posting with anon.penet.fi: Method 2

In this method, you should address your e-mail to **anon@anon.penet.fi** rather than the newsgroup name as in the previous example. Again, write your subject line as you want it to appear on Usenet. As before, make sure the very first line of your message contains:

```
X-Anon-Password: yourpassword
```

Keeping in mind all the caveats regarding appropriate syntax, enter the next line exactly as:

```
X-Anon-To: news.group.name1,news.group.name2,news.group.name3
```

Make sure only commas separate the newsgroup names, not spaces; be sure to spell the newsgroup names correctly. If you enter a newsgroup that **anon.penet.fi** cannot find, you will receive an error message in return. Rules regarding the body of your message are the same as in the previous method (such as your signature file and dashes). Remember to hit **Enter** after the X-Anon-To line so as to leave one blank line before the start of your message. Here's what a complete e-mail to anon.penet.fi might look like, with a message to be crossposted to 2 newsgroups, continuing with the example drawn earlier:

```
To: anon@anon.penet.fi
Cc:
Subject: Looking for movies with lint scenes

X-Anon-Password: i9%rr3=bo
X-Anon-To: alt.fetish.lint,rec.arts.movies
Hi,
I'm looking for any movies with good lint scenes, maybe with people picking
lint off of sweaters or from their pockets. I especially would like scenes of
lint rollers being used on garments that are covered with lint-- the more
lint the better. And of course, bellybutton lint is the best, if there are
any good, flabby scenes of that I'd really like to know!
Thanks!!
LintLuver
```

The Point of All This Being...

...that by using the methods just mentioned, you can make anonymous postings to Usenet that do not carry your signature or your e-mail address, while still allowing readers to communicate with you. I am not recommending that you must or must not use these procedures every time you make a public posting. What I do want to stress is that there are options for preserving your privacy on the Internet, which you may choose to exercise at your discretion.

The bulk of this chapter has in one way or another dealt with the issue of your privacy. People sometimes wonder why they should be so concerned about their privacy if they have nothing to hide, especially regarding such practices as anonymous posting. Ultimately, your personal information is your personal property. (A longer rant on that topic awaits you in Chapter 7.) Knowing the ways in which others can learn about you should be empowering rather than fear-inducing, if I may take a moment to channel Oprah Winfrey. On tomorrow's show—poodle makeovers!

The Least You Need to Know

There's a certain amount of personal information about you on the Internet that anyone can access. Much of it is under your control; the first step is to recognize what's out there, and the second is to modify it per your desires. Unless you wear transparent jeans, you probably care how much others know about you, and taking reasonable steps to protect your privacy is only rational.

- The information reported about you via the finger command may include your real name, office and/or home phone numbers, new mail status, login times, and anything else you want it to.
- Your .plan, .project, and .signature files all allow you to write things about yourself that will be available to the world, so be aware of what you include in them.
- Your signature file and e-mail address can easily be circulated en masse when you make Usenet postings, so if you are concerned about posting a particular message or in a particular newsgroup, use an anonymous re-mailer to make an anonymous posting.
- Overall, your privacy is your property, so stay aware of the sorts of information others can find out about you, and keep track of what you're allowing to circulate in accordance to your desires.

Chapter 3

Spies Like Them

In This Chapter

- Watching you work
- You're leaving footprints, so cover your tracks
- E-mail: For whose eyes only?

Why would someone want to watch your moves on the Internet? Pretty much for the same reason someone would want to spy on you anywhere else, really. Perhaps they find you irresistibly attractive, or (more likely) you have something they want. It might be related to a project you're involved in, or just your account itself. Or someone might have more traditional, real-world crimes in mind, and want to use the Internet as a tool in scoping you out. Once again, the type of Internet account you have comes into play. Users of graphical interfaces are far less vulnerable to many of the spy attacks posed in this chapter, except for those relating to e-mail. UNIX users, pay closer attention. UNIX systems are like a Porsche in some ways—they're fast and they're best suited for buffs, and attract more attention from others than do graphical interfaces or Chrysler K-Cars.

Previously we looked at some common ways folks can glean some info about you. Beyond that, it's also possible to sneak some peeks at your actual activities on the Internet. Amazingly, it doesn't even take an inordinate amount of skill to track your login behavior, your current activities, or even some of your previous activities—especially on

UNIX-based accounts. Even so, UNIX shell accounts are more vulnerable to such spying than graphical interfaces. Furthermore, even if you often fire off e-mails left and right, you can't necessarily be sure that only two pairs of eyes see them (or more, if you write missives to insects). It's not that there are hordes of people staking out your Internet account night and day, but if someone does, unfortunately you can't even see (the cybernetic equivalent of) a '78 Gremlin parked in front of your curb for a week.

He Knows When You've Been Sleeping... (Hackers Monitor Your Account)

To continue a theme that you'll find heavily trodden throughout this book, UNIX shell users have the most to be concerned about when it comes to privacy. In the first chapter (technically the second, if you must be that way) we looked at personal information revealed from the finger command.

Again with the Finger

Remember when I fingered my username in Chapter 2, there was a line that related the user's login status? Let's call that line back for a refresher...

```
Last login Sun Mar 19 12:02 on ttyp9 from dfw.net
```

TTY The port on your host's computer which you are connected to is called the *tty*. Knowing which tty you are on can lead someone to figure out where your computer actually is, with many limitations and conditions. I don't know how it's pronounced.

Time for some quick anatomy. The first portion of this line is relatively obvious in meaning—**Sunday, March 19**, and **12:02** all refer to calendar events derived from the position of the Earth in relation to the Sun. **ttyp9**, on the other hand, does not. Rather, the short answer is that it denotes which *tty* you logged in to. Very helpful, huh? Basically, the tty is the port on the host computer (your service provider's) that you were attached to. Your host will be able to support a finite number of simultaneous connections; each one is assigned to a tty port.

So what does your tty port tell a potential spy interested in your Internetting behavior? Technically, it can tell someone where you are physically located, if they know where that tty port is connected to. Practically, it usually doesn't tell very much. That is, if you have a computer that is physically connected to tty port q1, for example, someone with inside knowledge might know where your computer is located.

Note, however, the two important conditions in that sentence: *if* you are physically connected to your host, and *if* someone has inside knowledge. Considering the second condition first, only someone who works with the host computer is likely to know anything about its tty ports. That doesn't mean they can't use that knowledge to track you, but it certainly limits the number of possible spies to current and/or former employees of that department (or people who know them).

More importantly, the great majority of readers are not physically connected to their host. There is no wire going directly from your computer into your host. When you dial in by modem, for example, you get assigned whatever the next available tty port is. Even most users on Ethernet connections are not connected directly to the host in question—they telnet in to it from their own computer (usually). Hence, they too are assigned the next available port. So, by sight alone, the tty port that finger reports you as connected to doesn't tell a sleuth very much (unless you have a physical, unchanging connection directly to the host). In special circumstances, however, your tty port *can* be traced back to you if absolutely necessary, even if you're using a modem. This activity (discussed more appropriately in Chapter 4) is extremely rare.

Back in the Days...

In the old days, before I stopped eating rubber cement, people used *terminals* (keyboards with monitors) connected directly to a mainframe computer, and each terminal constituted a tty port. Nowadays, the computer you use is essentially the "terminal" (though much cooler and more powerful), and your service provider's computer is the host in place of what used to be a mainframe. Lastly, the connection is courtesy of your modem and phone company, or whatever other means you use to connect to the Internet.

The rightmost portion of the line, which reads **from dfw.net**, can be more significant. It reports where you connected to your host from. If you dial in to your service provider with a modem, this portion of the finger output may be left blank; you don't really have a "from" other than your phone number, and the host doesn't trace your call! If you had a computer with a dedicated Internet connection, however (such as you might find in an office at work or school), its address would be displayed—and that could give someone enough information to figure out

Host Computer
The computer that you connect to with your own. Usually this means your service provider's computer. It kindly "hosts" your computer's connection because you kindly fork over the greenbacks each month.

where your computer is located. Furthermore, if you have multiple Internet accounts and you telnet from account A to account B, the address of account A would appear in the finger output. Consider the previous example output once again. You see that it says I logged in **from dfw.net**. Well, I have a UNIX account with a service provider whose address is **dfw.net**, and from that account I telnetted to my other UNIX account at **crux2.cit.cornell.edu**. This tells someone who might finger me at my crux2 account that I also have an account at dfw.net. That may or may not interest them, but if they're trying to follow my Internet behavior, that could be a big lead for them, knowing that I have another "home" on the Internet on which to spy.

"Last"—A UNIX Story

Believe me, there are plenty of good reasons to use UNIX! But with the increased power of the system come increased abilities for all manner of behavior, good and not-so-good. Take notice of the "last" command. This command allows a user to ask the UNIX system to tell him to give a log of when a particular user has logged on over a period of time. This includes when, for how long, and from where. It's very important to note that one can only "last" another user *on the same UNIX system*, so it's not information that is available to the general public, but it may be available to the others who have accounts on your same service provider (unless your service provider has somehow disabled this feature).

At the UNIX shell prompt, let's enter the command **last mw12**, where "mw12" is the username we want to get a report on (that's me). Here would be the output:

```
mw12 ttyp0   CU-DIALUP-0431.C Tue Mar 21 13:53    still logged in
mw12 ftp     crux5.cit.cornel Tue Mar 21 13:21 - 13:21    (00:00)
mw12 ttyq2   CU-DIALUP-0431.C Tue Mar 21 12:49 - 13:53    (01:03)
mw12 ttype   CU-DIALUP-0430.C Tue Mar 21 12:02 - 12:13    (00:10)
mw12 ttyp1   CU-DIALUP-0430.C Tue Mar 21 11:07 - 11:59    (00:52)
mw12 ttyp1   CU-DIALUP-0527.C Tue Mar 21 10:28 - 10:56    (00:27)
mw12 ttyp1   CU-DIALUP-0207.C Tue Mar 21 08:57 - 10:22    (01:24)
mw12 ttyp0   CU-DIALUP-0114.C Mon Mar 20 21:55 - 22:29    (00:34)
```

I know, I know—what the *heck* is all that? Be glad it's only an excerpt—the full output might list upwards of a month's worth of logins or more! Time for another anatomy lesson; I hope you still have your gloves on. (Smell that formaldehyde!)

In the first column we see the username in question. Since we asked for the report on user **mw12** that's what we got. In the second column we see the familiar tty port.

Note that in line two it says **ftp** rather than a tty port. That's because the user (mw12) connected to this account with an FTP session rather than by logging in via Telnet or dial-up. In the third column, we see the address of the computer from which the user logged in. The fourth column lists the date and time of login, and the time of logout, and in the fifth column we see a calculation of how long that was. Note that in the first line the user has logged in, but has not yet logged out—and that is reflected in the output. Okay, so the natural question that any reasonable individual is asking at this point is, "Why in a bat's butt are you telling me all this?" I'm glad you asked, although you could be a little less rude about it next time...

From a vulnerability point of view, the output of the last command is an excellent way for a spy to learn about your Internet habits. He might, for example, want to try to break into your account, and he wants to know when you do and do not use it. There's no way for you to alter the information reported in the "last" command; that is your service provider's domain. You can, however, use the "last" command on yourself from time to time to check that your account has not been broken into. If someone managed to steal your password (Chapter 6), for example, and logged in to your account from some other computer, you would see in the last output a login at a time (and from a place) that isn't yours. Personally, I don't last myself very often, but if something changes in my account that I don't remember doing, I will run last just to be sure no one else got their grimy little chicken-grease-coated fingers in it. Assuming no unusual entries were found, I can rest assured that it's just my brain that's not working properly. (In addition, now you're aware that your logins and logouts are being recorded.)

Cool Trick If you enter the last command with no username specified, it will show all the logs for every user who has logged in during the record-keeping period. It's a big mess. If you want to get a last report that will scroll beyond the screen, whether for an individual or everyone, you can pause the output after each page using the command **last username | more**.

They Know Too Much

Actually, a clever intruder could remove the record of his entry so it wouldn't show up in the last record. In that case, he's a smart one, and probably has other tricks up his sleeve, too. But at least you know you can watch for the dumb ones.

...And He Knows When You're Awake (and What You're Doing)

Those UNIX programmers certainly thought of everything, even if it was poorly ventilated down there in their dungeons. Not only can other users on your system track your login behavior, they can even watch what you're doing. But at least, in some circumstances, you can try to hide.

There is a program in UNIX called "w" (named in what was clearly an inspired moment) that pulls the covers off everyone on a particular UNIX machine. As with last, this command only works for users logged on the same machine. If you enter **w** at the UNIX shell prompt and hit **Enter**, you will get a list of everyone who is currently logged in, and what programs they are running. The command **w username** will report the information for only that particular user. If you're reading e-mail, someone else on your system can know about it. They can't tell what e-mail you are reading, just that you're running the e-mail program. Perhaps more embarrassing (and more common?), a user can be seen downloading pictures with, shall we say, "blue" filenames. For the sake of protection and mere privacy, you may want to take steps to prevent others from so easily watching you. Unfortunately, there's no real standard way of hiding your "w" information.

Here, for example, is the output of the **w** command on a user on the same UNIX system I use:

```
%w scc3
  5:41pm  up 6 days, 15:36,  19 users,  load average: 1.40, 1.28
User     tty from            login@  idle   JCPU   PCPU  what
scc3     p7 132.236.178.17  5:05pm     5                 gopher
```

We see where user **scc3** is logged in from, at what time, and how long he's been idle, but that's all information that finger would have told us, too. All the way on the right, though, it says **gopher**, meaning that's what scc3 is doing. He's using Gopher. The **w** command basically reflects what the user entered at the shell prompt when entering a command—so if scc3 had entered "gopher bobs.gopher.site," that's what it would say in the output. You may see **w** output like this:

```
User     tty from            login@  idle   JCPU   PCPU  what
scc3     p7 132.236.178.17  5:05pm     5                 -tcsh
```

Where you see **-tcsh** in this output, it might instead say **-csh**, or **-zsh**, or **-bash**. These are all names of UNIX shells. If you see something like what's here, it means the user isn't doing anything. They're logged on (otherwise **w** wouldn't report anything), but just sitting there. Perhaps they're asleep, perhaps they're dead. Some people who work at

UNIX machines all day don't ever log out, so you may see idle times in the hours or days over the weekend, or since they were last at work. Something to remember if you're the boss.

A Crude Way to Hide

If you are downloading files with filenames that you'd rather not have others see, you could simply rename the files before downloading them. If you have a program in your account that you want to run, but don't want others to know you're running it, rename it (remember that the **w** output will reflect the name of the program you're running). So, for example, if you want to run a program named "foo" but don't want anyone to know you're running "foo," rename it "bar" and then run it.

Foobar? The words "foo" and "bar" have significant insignificance in computing. Basically, they just mean "variable whatever," like "x" and "y." So if someone suggests that you "copy file *foo* to file *bar*," they mean the same thing as if they said, "copy file x to file y."

A Slightly-Less-Crude (But Far From Perfect) Way to Hide

Another possibility you might explore to hide yourself is the UNIX "screen" program. Some service providers do not allow the use of this program on their machines, so you had better find out first whether using screen is okay, or else you might get a nasty e-mail. The screen program is too complicated to describe in full detail here, but it's worth your time to look into it if you spend a lot of time using a UNIX shell. In brief, screen allows you to create multiple "windows" in your UNIX account (normally you're limited to the one screen you have when you log in). To hide your activities from the prying w command, you'll want to use screen to create another window, and then launch your desired program within that window. Note that you'll want to tell screen to make that new window "logged off," so that it won't show up to the w or even the finger command.

Unfortunately, you have to create a special configuration file for screen so it knows to keep you hidden. The good news is that making said file isn't horribly difficult. Remember that UNIX configuration files often begin with a dot—and that holds true in the case of screen. The configuration file you will need has to be called **.screenrc**, and reside in your home directory. There should be one line that contains "`deflogin off`" in the file. If you already know how to make such a file, go ahead. If not, it's quite easy. At your UNIX shell prompt, enter the following (replacing your actual username where I write *username*):

```
echo "deflogin off" >> ~username/.screenrc
```

That's it—now you have the necessary configuration file for the screen program to keep you hidden when you run it.

Hey, Man
When you want to learn more about a command in UNIX, remember the word "man," which is short for "manual." If you know the name of the command that you're interested in, enter **man *command*** at the shell prompt. If your UNIX system knows the command, it will spit out the manual pages for using that command. If you're not sure of the exact command you're looking for, try **man -k *keyword***. UNIX will try to find all the commands that have something to do with the keyword, and it will show you the commands it knows that match. And people say UNIX isn't user-friendly!

To run screen, just type **screen** at the shell prompt and hit **Enter**; you'll be brought to a new prompt. From here, you can do your normal thing such as reading e-mail or Usenet news. If someone tries to find you, however, it won't appear that you're logged in to the system.

There are two caveats here. First, you cannot download files from within the window created by the screen program. If you try, it will just generate download errors and burp garbage onto your screen. Second, because you are not logged in (as far as your host knows), you cannot use online talk programs for talking with other individual users, such as the commonly used talk and ytalk. Normally these programs allow you to type in real-time "conversations" with another user on another system, but they have to believe that you're logged in—so you can't use them from within the screen program. If you want to leave from inside the hidden confines of the screen program, just type **exit** at the shell prompt; you will be returned to your previous shell prompt (from before you ran screen), and you will be restored to a "logged in" state.

Screen can do a lot more than just hiding you—among other things, it can allow you to open multiple "screens" and execute several programs at the same time. But that is outside the scope of this book. For much more information on screen, type **man screen** at the UNIX shell prompt (of course, if your system doesn't have screen, then none of this song-and-dance will work; you'll just get errors to the effect that your host has no idea what the heck "screen" is).

Looking Into Your Past with lastcomm

For really digging deep, there is the UNIX command "lastcomm." With this, you can get a recent history of the commands executed by a particular user, a particular tty, or the users who executed a particular command. Versatile!

Here is a sample of lastcomm output, representing the history of commands for a specific user:

```
%lastcomm mw12
lastcomm     X      mw12    ttyr0   9.55          secs    Tue     Mar 28 15:21
head         X      mw12    ttyr0   0.00          secs    Tue     Mar 28 15:21
perl                mw12    ttyr0   0.75          secs    Tue     Mar 28 15:20
more                mw12    ttyr0   0.02          secs    Tue     Mar 28 15:20
lastcomm     X      mw12    ttyr0   12.00   secs  Tue     Mar 28 15:16
f                   mw12    ttyr0   0.12          secs    Tue     Mar 28 15:16
lastcomm     X      mw12    ttyr0   11.30   secs  Tue     Mar 28 15:15
w                   mw12    ttyr0   0.22          secs    Tue     Mar 28 15:15
perl                mw12    ttyr0   0.88          secs    Tue     Mar 28 15:15
more                mw12    ttyr0   0.02          secs    Tue     Mar 28 15:15
```

In short, you've just seen a list of commands that mw12 has executed, the tty mw12 was on when doing so, and duration and time statistics. As I said, one could execute the lastcomm command for a tty port rather than a user, in which case the commands executed from that tty port would be reported. If one runs lastcomm with a specific command name, then a list of the times and users who executed that command recently would result. As with the last command, you haven't any control over the output of this command. Also, note that commands executed in the hidden screen (explained previously) *will* show up in the lastcomm output. Touché!

The lastcomm command should basically be thought of in the same category as the w and last commands. More tools with which to spy—not overly powerful in and of themselves, but if a user on your UNIX system uses these in combination, a stranger can begin to get a pretty good picture of your behaviors if he or she is so determined.

E-mail Voyeurs

Presumably, when you send e-mail to someone, you only want the intended recipient(s) to read it. So the question naturally arises: Who else can read my e-mail?

For a start, anyone who has access, authorized or unauthorized, to your Internet account can read your e-mail—and I'm not only talking about UNIX anymore (so wake up!). This is why a secure password is very important, but you'll have to read Chapter 6 to learn about that. Your system administrator can read your e-mail, although that doesn't mean that he should. But he could.

System Administrator
Often called a *sysadmin* as a term of great endearment and affection, the *system administrator* is the individual who lords over your host computer and is responsible for keeping it up to speed, securing it from intruders, and providing you with necessary programs and applications. He is who you complain to when you have a problem with the system, and in return he will curse, spit fire, and bemoan the day of your birth, but ultimately will respond to your query. Actually, sysadminning (is there such a word?) is a very tough job, with heavy demands from many users, so be nice—really.

If someone breaks into your service provider's machine and has the same access privileges that your system administrator has, then he of course can pillage your e-mail, too. Securing your provider's computer from such intrusion is your provider's responsibility.

On the destination end of your e-mail, anyone who has access to the account of the intended recipient can read it, too, once it arrives. So it's important that they have a good, safe password, as well. (Chapter 6—did I mention that?) Symmetrically, the system administrator at the destination end can also access the e-mail that you sent. Again, this is not to say that sysadmins *do* read users' e-mail, nor *should* they, but the technical fact is that they have the *capability*.

In addition to these concerns, your e-mail does not travel directly from your service provider's machine to its destination. It passes through a series of computers along the way, where an unscrupulous administrator or intruder—at any of them—may violate your e-mail as it passes through. For more information on the journey that your e-mail takes, see Chapter 10; for details on how to hide your e-mail from anyone's prying eyes, cuddle up with Chapters 7–9 about encryption techniques.

The Least You Need to Know

There are several ways that lookers might see some of your more sensitive parts. Unfortunately, the amount of control you have over these peepholes is limited (though it beats zero). Recognizing their existence, however, at least provides you with knowledge about the situation, and (to continue with this unsubtle and obvious metaphor), you can at least adjust your hemline when and if it begins to ride up.

- The results of a finger command can yield some valuable information about your login behavior and whether you have other accounts.
- For UNIX shell users, the "last" command reveals some detailed information on your login behavior over an extended period of time.

- The "w" command captures you in mid-action, like so many highway deer, showing what you're engaged in at the moment. Finally, the "lastcomm" command adds to the arsenal of ways with which to chart your Internet habits.
- There is plenty of opportunity for others of ill morals (or suspect agendas) to read the e-mail you send out, if they have the right access. Therefore, plain (non-encrypted) e-mail cannot be considered secure.

Chapter 4

The Advantages of a Dumb Terminal

In This Chapter

- Playing dumb has its advantages
- Uploading and downloading files with a dumb terminal
- What your tty tells them, and what it doesn't

One might say that walking with stilts offers the ability to see over everyone else's head, but the risk of falling is greater. Conversely, a pair of $1.99 flip-flops are comfortable and have little risk, but they make it hard to run a marathon. What does this incredibly overreaching analogy have to do with the next two chapters? The manner in which you access the Internet with your computer affects your vulnerabilities in different ways. In this chapter, we'll talk about the most common form of Internet access: the *dumb terminal*.

Did You Just Call My Computer Stupid?

Well, no. And yes. If you connect to your Internet service provider (sometimes called an "ISP" by people who call it that) by dialing it up using a modem, a phone line, and a terminal program, then you're using your computer as if it were a *dumb terminal*.

Remote Computer The computer you connect to. In this case, your service provider's computer is the remote computer, because you connect to its faraway site from your personal computer. (It probably *is* far away, though it could be only two inches away and still be considered the "remote" computer.)

To help illustrate the role your computer plays as a dumb terminal, imagine the scenario between your computer and your service provider. You probably launch your terminal program, dial your service provider's phone number, make a connection, and log in. What's really happening? When you dial the phone number, your computer reaches your service provider's computer (which is probably bigger, faster, more expensive, and just generally cooler). Your service provider's computer answers the phone and asks you who you are. Assuming you logged in properly, it then lets you in. From that point on, every keystroke you type is just shuttled by your computer to your service provider's. It is your service provider's computer that can actually communicate on the Internet. So, when you type **mail** (for example), your computer in front of you does nothing except send the characters "m-a-i-l" over the phone line. Your service provider's computer interprets the letters, and in this case it runs the e-mail program. Then it sends each character the e-mail program generates back over the phone line to appear on your screen.

Basically, your terminal program's job is to send characters to the *remote computer*, receive the characters that are sent back, and show them on your screen. The remote computer (your ISP) does all the work—in essence, it "speaks" to the Internet on your behalf. Like Moses and Aaron. Thus, in this scenario your computer is called a "dumb terminal" because it's not doing very much. It's acting as if your keyboard and monitor were connected to a really long cable directly to your service provider's computer, rather than your own.

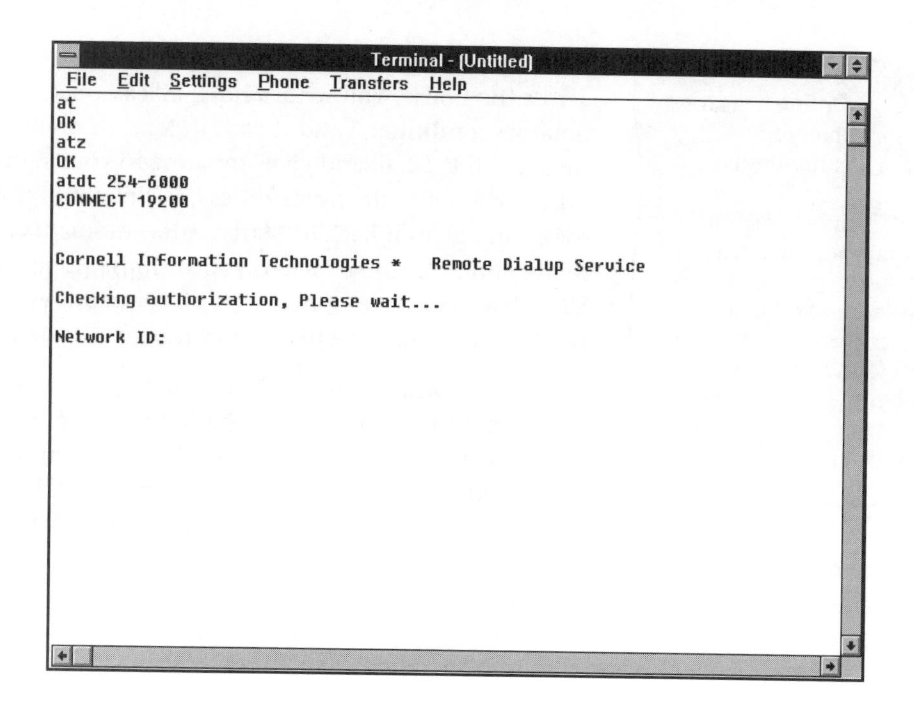

This is a terminal program called "Terminal" that comes with Microsoft Windows. In this example, the computer is being used as a dumb terminal.

At present, it's safe to say that the method just described is how quite a few, if not most, Internet users access their accounts. It's popular because it's cheap, and requires very few computing resources on your end. After all, since your particular computer doesn't do much besides send and receive characters, you can use just about anything with a keyboard and a modem as a dumb terminal. Hence, one can connect to the Internet with any sort of computer ranging from a Pentium down to a Commodore 64, or lower, when using it as a dumb terminal. (Of course, if you have a powerful computer, you may not want to waste all that brainpower by using it as a dumb terminal, in which case you want to read the next chapter. You may be excused.)

So, by calling your computer a "dumb terminal," we're not saying that it's stupid—it may be very smart—but it's acting dumb when it is accessing the Internet. Like some people you probably know... .

Data Checks In, But It Doesn't Check Out

Imagine that you own a dog named Marty. Marty is very obedient, but that's about it. Because you and your spouse are both extremely lazy, you only communicate with each

Online Means that your computer is connected to another computer. Commonly this refers to being on the phone line, as is the case when you dial in to your service provider. It's also why your friends get busy signals all night long when trying to reach you, and they soon stop being your friends.

other by writing notes and giving them to Marty to carry across the house. You write a note, "Please make boiled potatoes for dinner," and stick it in Marty's mouth. Marty runs down the hall and gives the note to your significant other, who reads the note, writes, "We're out of potatoes," and gives it back to Marty. A few moments later, Marty comes trotting back to you with the response. Since Marty can't read, he doesn't interpret or even care what the note says, he just carries it between the parties.

This is what your dumb terminal is, albeit far less cute and furry. Because of this basic limitation, it's quite safe from a security point of view. After all, you cannot instruct Marty, for example, to bite your mate, because Marty doesn't listen to instructions. In the same way, someone on the outside cannot instruct your computer to do anything when it's a dumb terminal because it's not listening. It doesn't interpret data, it just sends and receives it. Now, remember that your Internet account is not located on your computer—it's located on your service provider's computer, so it's vulnerable to all the possible insecurities discussed throughout this book. But anything that is on *your* computer can't be touched by anyone on the outside, even while you are *online*, when you are using it as a dumb terminal.

With One Exception...

Upload/ Download There's an important distinction between uploading and downloading. When you *upload* a file, you *send* the file from your computer to the remote computer. When you *download*, you *receive* a file from the remote computer. If you mix these up, you'll sound like one of those people who always says, "So-and-so is coming *up* to visit this weekend," no matter where so-and-so is coming from, which always bugs me.

You may be using the terminal program on your computer to *download* and *upload* files to the Internet, in which case you realize that there are ways to pass data between your computer and your provider's without typing it. That doesn't make me a liar, it makes this a technicality, but an important one: when you download a file, your computer is still not interpreting the incoming data, it's just packaging it into a file rather than displaying it on your screen.

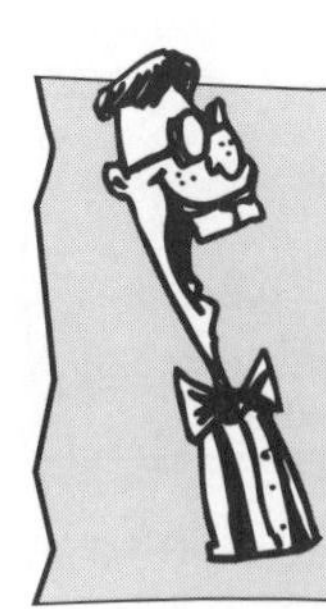

Garbage Barge

Sometimes when a download goes awry, the incoming data will not be packaged into a file and your terminal program will try to show it on the screen. If you were downloading a binary program when a problem occurred, you'll invariably see lots of garbage and gook with lots of funny characters and beeps and burps. This is a bad thing. Try to download the program again.

When you download a file from a site on the Internet, however, it could possibly contain a virus. Downloading files that may be infected is one risk you always face, even with a dumb terminal. That topic, however, is more appropriately addressed in Chapter 11, which is about viruses. This one isn't.

The Thrill of the Trace: TTY Concerns

Back in Chapter 3, when introducing ttys, I mentioned that for dial-up users they didn't provide spies with much information except for one thing. Then I made you wait until Chapter 4 to find out what that was. This is all very exciting, I know.

Your service provider's computer is connected to a certain number of modems for accepting incoming calls. When you dial in with your modem, it connects to one of the modems connected to your provider's computer; this modem is then assigned a tty port. (It's similar to how your modem is connected to a serial port on your computer; if you had multiple modems, you would have multiple serial ports for incoming calls.) That means someone who knows the configuration of your provider's hardware can trace which modem you are on, based on the tty port that the "finger" or "w" commands reveal. Knowing which modem you are on, one could possibly trace the call coming into that modem and find out where you are. BUT!!—that's not as scary as it sounds. Not very many people know your service provider's particular hardware configuration (except the people who work there). And not just anyone can trace a phone call—actually, only the phone company can do that. So the fact that your modem connection can theoretically be traced from your service provider back to your modem's location is not a realistic worry in regard to spies. However, let this be a little warning to you that if *you* are the spy, or engaged in some other illicit activity and the service provider has caught on, they *can* trace you back to your location and break down the door and film the whole thing in cinema verité for prime-time television viewing.

Fireside Reading

In fact, there is a now-famous account of such a tracing. A German intruder had made his way through a number of high-level U.S. computer systems, and after a long and bizarre series of events, was eventually traced, several times, to determine his exact location. In the end, he was nabbed. That's the short version. The long version is contained in a book that I literally read in one sitting, called *The Cuckoo's Egg* by Clifford Stoll (Doubleday, 1989). Even if you're not a computer enthusiast, the book is a great espionage and mystery story (normally I don't even like that kind of book). And it's all true.

The Least You Need to Know

This was a short chapter, as you can see. In a sense, that's a good thing, and not only because I got to write less. When you access the Internet using your computer as a dumb terminal, the information on your computer just doesn't have many vulnerabilities. There are limitations, however, on the Internetting you can do with a dumb terminal—so there are many reasons why one would choose *not* to use a dumb terminal; we'll get to these in the next chapter.

- When you dial up your service provider using a terminal program, your computer acts "dumb" so it cannot interpret any data, and therefore cannot be commanded to do anything by anyone on the outside.
- Downloading files, though, does pose the potential risk of catching a computer virus, which is another discussion in and of itself. It's another chapter too—11, to be specific.
- If you're the one engaging in naughty activities, your call can be traced back to you. But the difficulty in doing this means only officials on the lookout for you can realistically do this, not other curious spies.

Chapter 5

Taking the Direct Route—SLIP/PPP and Ethernet

In This Chapter

- TCP/IP and the social computer
- Nomad or homebody—dynamic versus static IP addresses
- Client and server security
- Scent of a packet—sniff, sniff
- Wall of flames, protection by fire(wall)
- Operating systems aren't created equal

Lucky people get to access the Internet via a SLIP or PPP. Extremely lucky people (called "extremely lucky people" in net-speak) have some sort of "hardwired" connection to the Internet, very often by Ethernet. What is all that? Why are they so lucky? Will I always be this short? Those questions and more (plus some information on security you might find interesting, too) will be addressed in this chapter.

Your IP Address and You

Remember, way back in Chapter 4, when we talked about connecting to a remote computer (which was your Internet host) and using your own computer and a modem as a dumb terminal? Well, some people's computers can actually communicate on the Internet without having to send the characters to another computer (which a dumb terminal needs to speak on its behalf).

Talking the Talk—TCP/IP

Computers that can "talk" to one another on the Internet speak a language called *TCP/IP*. (Technically, TCP/IP is a networking *protocol*, and we'll look at some other protocols that are used within TCP/IP later on.) TCP/IP is not to be confused with the traditional use of the term "computer language," which refers to programming languages such as BASIC, Pascal, FORTRAN, and so forth. Human beings use those languages to instruct the computer. TCP/IP, on the other hand, is used *between* computers so they can instruct one another. When your computer is capable of "speaking" TCP/IP—which takes the right software and connection—it can participate fully on the Internet rather than through a third party. Then it's happy.

Talking the Talk There are several popular software packages that allow your computer to speak TCP/IP. For the Windows users, the most popular package is probably Trumpet Winsock, which is available at the major PC FTP sites. In addition, there are commercial packages that contain their own TCP/IP implementations for your PC, such as NetManage's Chameleon or Spry's Internet-in-a-Box.

Mac users rely on MacTCP, which is a commercial product. It is included with some Internet books for the Macintosh, so check the software that comes with them while browsing the store shelves. Beginning with Apple's System 7.5, MacTCP is included.

Getting your computer to learn how to speak TCP/IP isn't too difficult—there are software packages available for all major computer systems for that. But, TCP/IP can only be used over certain types of network connections, and that's the real obstacle.

People who work at academic institutions and some businesses often have it easy, and not only because they get free photocopies. If the school or business is networked to the Internet, then many if not all of the computers in offices have what is called a *direct* connection. That means their computers can speak TCP/IP and have the proper connections to do so. They don't use modems—their computers are directly connected with wires, probably called *Ethernet* cables. The advantages of this over using remote-dial-up dumb terminals are:

- Full TCP/IP capabilities. This means you can do lots of neat stuff that you can't do over a dumb terminal, but it also means you may be vulnerable to extra security concerns, too.
- Extremely fast transfer rates. Data can often transfer over Ethernet cables at several times the speed of even the fastest modems—which makes them very nice to use. If you've never played with a computer Ethernetted to the Internet, sneak your way into a computer lab at a nearby campus and try one out. You may never leave. (I do not condone sneaking, even if I did say to.)

The problem with direct connections such as Ethernet is that you can't get them at home. Technically, I suppose, you could, but let's put it this way: it would cost more than braces for four children.

If you pay for service from a service provider, you may have also had the option of subscribing to a *SLIP* or *PPP* account. These generally cost more, and have more limited hours/per month available to you than UNIX shell accounts. SLIP/PPP is a way of allowing a computer to speak TCP/IP over a modem rather than via Ethernet. This allows users who do not or cannot have Ethernet connections to enjoy the same TCP/IP capabilities. But it doesn't make your modem any faster than it already is—you get TCP/IP at the speed of your modem, not Ethernet speed. Still, it's a good compromise.

The Right Connection

Note, for the purposes of this discussion, SLIP and PPP are two different ways of doing basically the same thing, so from now on I'm writing it as SLIP/PPP to save space. Whichever one you use, the same information in this chapter applies to you.

A new type of connection called *ISDN* is beginning to gain popularity, as its cost comes down. It will allow you full TCP/IP communications as well, but is much faster than a traditional modem.

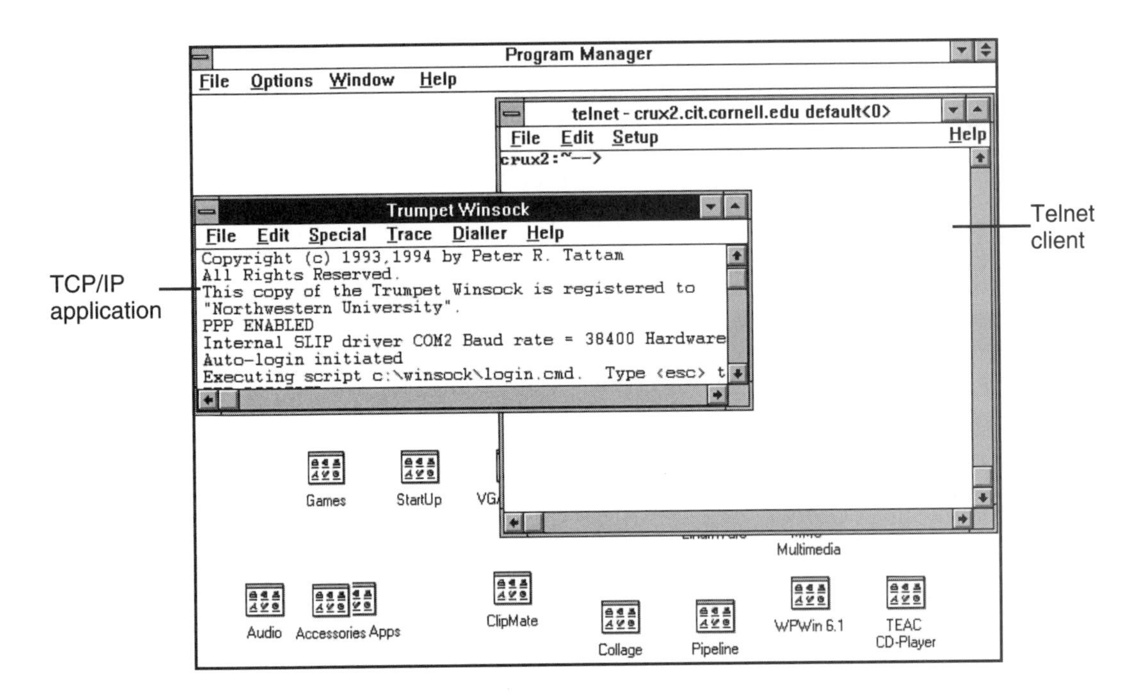

An example SLIP/PPP setup. The TCP/IP application enables the computer to speak to the rest of the Internet, and the Telnet client allows the user to log in to remote terminals.

A key distinction, for our discussion, between TCP/IP and dumb terminals is that unlike the dumb terminal, TCP/IP *can* interpret the incoming and outgoing data. This means that under certain circumstances (to be outlined later), outsiders can send commands to your computer and tell it to do things. In many cases, this is a good thing—it allows you to provide information and services to the outside world from your computer. Unfortunately, it also means that some people might tell your computer to do things you don't want it to do, like give them information that was supposed to be private.

The security information presented in this chapter applies to all TCP/IP connections equally, whether they are over Ethernet, SLIP/PPP, ISDN, cable TV (some places can do that), or long pieces of string (nobody can do that).

IP on the Run—Dynamic Versus Static

When you communicate with TCP/IP, you get an *IP address*, which is basically an address for your computer. You've probably seen these before; they're numbers like **130.150.21.4** and sometimes they're names, like **conform.disney.com** (the names just get translated to numbers, but they're easier for us humans to remember).

There are two common flavors of IP address that you might have: dynamic or static. Having a *dynamic* IP address means you get a new IP address every time you connect. This is common for SLIP or PPP users. *Static* IP addressing means you always have the same IP address. As with all things in life, each of these has pros and cons, particularly when it comes to security. Which type of IP address you get is determined by your service provider and what they offer. Some offer both dynamic and static, with static IPs costing more (sometimes a lot more).

Having a static IP has the nice feature of giving your computer a stable address. That means you can run things like an FTP server, World Wide Web servers, and so forth—and people out there in the world will know the name of your computer and can connect to it for data that you are offering. For that same reason, this arrangement is also a potential risk. After all, one might say you're a sitting duck. Because your machine always has the same IP address, people can learn about it, investigate, maybe try to spy or break in, and so forth. If you want to set up your machine as an information server, though, you really need a static IP. This means that you should have heightened attention to the various security concerns detailed throughout this book.

With a dynamic IP, it's like your computer is in the Witness Protection Program. Every time you connect, you've got a new address, so no one can pin you down. On the other hand, you can't very well start your own FTP site, because what address would you tell people to connect to? Sure, you could say, "Come visit my FTP site, at address w.x.y.z from 5:00 p.m. to 12:00 p.m. tonight," but that's a real nuisance. While it's harder to provide information to the outside world with a dynamic IP, it leaves your computer less at risk from intruders.

One Compromise Solution...

Have a static *name* address but a dynamically *numbered* address. In other words, maybe you have the named address **talon.claw.flc.com**, but your true numeric IP address is dynamic. Then, whenever someone tries to communicate with the above name, it gets translated to whatever your current IP address is at the time. Ultimately, though, this is no more or less secure than having a true static IP, since you do have a stable referent to your computer. But, if you want a static IP and are with an ISP who can't implement one, this is a possible workaround. It's not something you can do, however; your service provider would have to offer this service. You might try begging; that can help, especially when combined with gifts of money and chocolate.

The Client: Its Vulnerabilities

If you want to read e-mail, you run an e-mail application, such as PINE in UNIX, or Eudora on Macs and PCs. If you want to browse the World Wide Web, you run a Web browser, such as Mosaic or Netscape. If you want to FTP files to your computer, you run an FTP application. You see where I'm going... What all these programs have in common is that they are retrieving information from another computer—a remote computer, if you will. These applications are called *clients*. When running a TCP/IP connection, all of these clients can be run *natively* on your own computer, rather than remotely. One advantage of this is that data you retrieve can come directly from the Internet to your computer (or hard drive), rather than to an ISP's computer, from which you would then have to download the data. Another advantage is that you can choose any client you want to use, rather than be limited by what your ISP provides. For example, there may be multiple FTP clients available for your computer, which may suit your personal tastes differently.

Run a Program "Natively"
This means it can be executed directly on your computer. In the dumb-terminal scenario, it was your ISP who ran the client, and merely returned the results to you. In the TCP/IP scenario, when you run a client natively, it interacts directly between your computer and another computer on the Internet, with no middleman. Sadly, as far as Internet access goes, cutting out the middleman tends to cost more.

By its very nature, the client is not likely to be a horrible security risk, because it's not giving out information—it's receiving it. I should mention, however, that this doesn't mean that the client cannot send back any information at all—it can, and it does. For example, if you are using an FTP client to download files into your computer, then just as downloading with a dumb terminal, the possibility of a virus being in one of them always exists. (And as I said in Chapter 4, that is Chapter 11 territory.)

It's also possible that a client might find out something about you without your knowledge and send that somewhere seedy. For instance, maybe a hacker has modified the client so that it records what you entered as your password to an FTP site, and then it tries to e-mail that password to someone. The client looks innocent and pure, but has been deviously altered to swipe and deliver passwords to the hacker. If you get your clients from major well-known sources, such as popular FTP sites for your machine, commercial purchases, or any other major distribution routes, this shouldn't be a major worry. But if you take clients from strangers, then who knows what's been done to them? At the risk of sounding like an information booth at a mall, I'll redirect you to Chapter 15 for more gory information on these sorts of tricks.

Even aside from the tricky dickies, there is some information that even proper clients will pass on. For instance, when you use an FTP client to make an *anonymous login* to a public FTP site, you are supposed to enter your e-mail address as your password. You may do that manually, or if you've got a slick FTP client, it may do that for you automatically. Either way, that's some information about you that is being passed on to others. Many FTP sites will keep a log of everything you do while on them, to protect themselves.

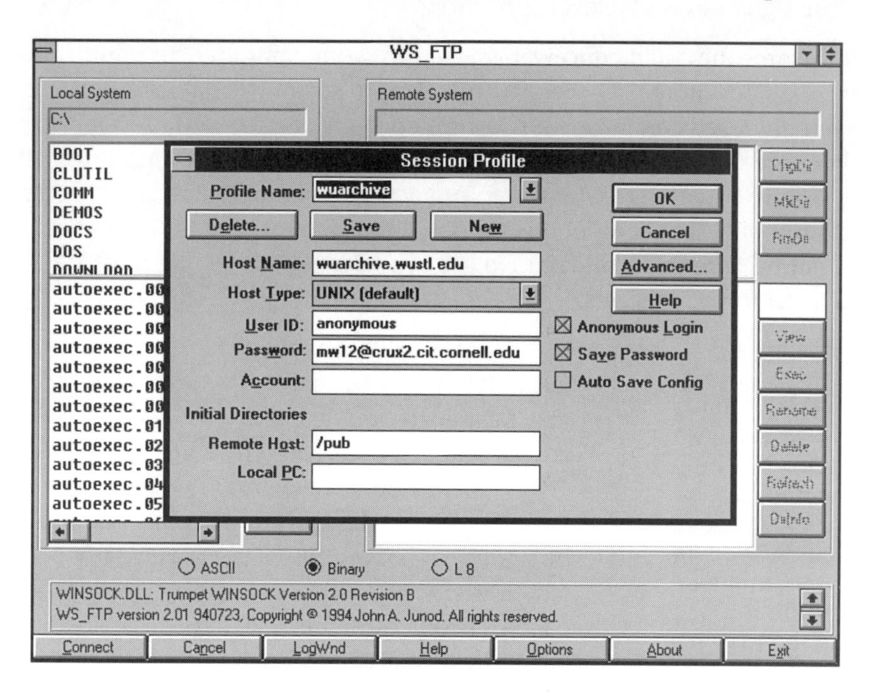

Here's an FTP client. Notice the window that opens up when I try to connect to an FTP site. It contains entries for my username and password—information that will be sent back across the network, and is therefore a possible insecurity.

Also consider that in many instances, when you use some sort of client, you have to enter some private information to gain access. For example, you may have to enter a password to get into a private FTP site (when using an FTP client), or a UNIX account (when using a Telnet client), or a POP mail account (when using an e-mail client). So, even though the majority of information will be coming into your computer from outside when you're running a client, some information (such as your password) is going the other way. This is noteworthy, as we'll see in the next section.

Are Those Fresh Packets I Smell?

In the dumb-terminal scenario, your connection is a "private" one, between your computer and your ISP. That's because it uses traditional phone lines; when you make a phone call, only you and the receiving end communicate over that channel. Unless, of course, someone violates that relationship and breaks into the line, using a wiretap or intercepting signals over wireless connections.

While someone could conceivably intercept your computer communications this way "for kicks," it's more likely they would want to spy on you specifically. Such is not the case in networked computing environments such as the Internet. Here the communications lines are shared; your data flows along with other people's data—over the same channels—on its way to its destination. In practice, your data is addressed to a specific computer, and only that computer is supposed to receive it. Normally, that's how it happens, but because this is all taking place in shared pathways, the potential is there for someone to "sniff your packets."

Packet In hip Internet banter, a *packet* is a unit of data. When you transfer data, it's broken up into lots of little packets, transmitted across the network, and re-assembled at the receiving end.

I'm not talking about a strange autoerotic practice (although it may be that, too). Rather, it means someone may be able to catch your data as it flows up the stream and look at it. When you type your password into your Telnet client, those characters are flowing through the network; some joker can go in and see them, and then he's got your password! It's not particularly easy to tell whether someone has been sniffing your packets. Of course, if something horrible happens—say, someone breaks into an account of yours—there's evidence that someone did something, although it doesn't necessarily mean that they got the information by sniffing. But, packet sniffing is a pretty good way for a hacker to get in between your client and the outside world and violate your data.

One way to protect against packet sniffing is to encrypt data before it comes in or goes out of the computer. While it's feasible to encrypt files and e-mail them (Chapters 7–9, be patient), encrypting and decrypting every piece of data you send or receive is not a project for the casual user. Ultimately, this type of low-level encryption is going to have to be implemented by service providers, but this is not yet widespread.

Although it is sometimes possible to detect sniffing, it requires a good deal of networking know-how, and, frankly, if you can understand how to operate sniffers and sniffing detectors, you probably don't need to be reading this book.

Another possible form of protection from packet sniffing is the *firewall*, which gets its own section in this chapter, but not until after the next section (those are the breaks).

The Server: Its Vulnerabilities

Another nice capability of running TCP/IP rather than a dumb terminal is that you can set up your computer as a data server. Since the client receives information, the server doles out information, upon request by a client. In fulfilling my lifelong dream to work for the Educational Testing Service, here's an analogy:

client:server :: ?

(a) comb:hair
(b) patron:waiter
(c) obsequious:perspicacious
(d) fruit:fly

The correct answer is (b). In that scenario, you have the receiving party, the patron (or *client* in computerese), making a request from the offering party, the waiter (or *server*), in this case the request being for food rather than information. Running TCP/IP, especially with a static IP address, allows you to open your own "restaurant" on the Internet. By running a server, you can be in the position of offering information to others, which can be purely for fun (information about your favorite TV show) or business (information about your product line). Running a server, however, also opens up a potentially huge can of worms as far as security goes.

After all, when you're letting people patronize your computer, you've got to put safeguards in place to prevent them from stealing the silverware. There are numerous different types of servers, depending on the manner in which you are offering your data:

- FTP servers for file transfers
- WWW servers for offering hypertext World Wide Web-based information
- Telnet servers for allowing outsiders to run programs that reside on your computer

On top of that, there are different servers for different types of computers—UNIX machines have different servers from PCs, which have different servers from Macintoshes. Sorry, but so many possibilities make it entirely impossible for me to cover the details of safeguarding your particular server.

But, rather than get into server-specifics, let me fly some generalities past you.

If you are running a UNIX machine, definitely read Chapter 16 on system administration. But *don't* rely on it solely, by any means. UNIX is a very powerful, but very complex, operating system—and it wasn't developed with security issues at the forefront. If you are responsible for the security of a UNIX system, either spend some real time learning about the issues presented in Chapter 16, or cast off the responsibility to someone who already understands it.

Most readers will not be running their own UNIX systems, which is a good thing. If you have a Mac or a PC with some sort of TCP/IP access (Ethernet, or more likely SLIP/PPP), you can run servers as well. Although the Mac/PC environment is not as fraught with potential configuration and security complexities as UNIX, it's still important to set up your servers properly. As obvious as this might sound, that means, above all, *read the documentation*. Whichever server you obtain is going to come with configuration instructions and security instructions. Read them, understand them before running the server, and follow them. Again, it sounds like an obvious thing to say, but it's often very tempting and exciting in computing to try to fly by the seat of one's pants with applications and rely on the manual later. Ordinarily, that's fun (and probably a good learning experience), but when we're talking about securing your computer against hackers, the adult in me says to work by the book. Opening a server is essentially opening a channel directly into your computer, so if you don't completely understand the documentation, find someone who does to help you out. Poorly-configured servers are a major area of security breaches. It's only logical; if you leave the front door open with no one watching it, what else can you expect?

High and Hot—Firewalls

Some organizations aren't entirely thrilled at having to deal with all the issues raised in this chapter and throughout this book. Or, they may have information that is too sensitive to risk these possible intrusions. If you have Internet access through such an organization, you may have to deal with something called a *firewall*. In short, a firewall acts as a security guard to any data coming in or out of your organization's internal network. It can be set up to act with a variety of degrees of paranoia and muscle—it might stop all incoming data, for example, but allow outgoing data. Or it might allow certain kinds of data to go in and out, while stopping others—it all depends on the perceived needs of your organization, and how they designed the firewall.

If you access the Internet from behind a firewall, it's a good idea to learn what sort of security the firewall provides. For one thing, that can give you a measure by which to judge the security issues in this book, and their relevance to your situation. Smiling at whoever runs your networking-related department and asking very nicely should work.

Nonetheless, however your firewall is configured, assuming it doesn't block 100% of traffic in or out (in which case, you may as well unhook the network from the Internet altogether and save the firewall costs for pizza), there are some things it can't protect against. At the risk of monotony, recall the virus. Yep, they can make it through a firewall, because they can probably occupy some form that is allowed through the firewall (more on the forms they can occupy in Chapter 11). Anything similar to viruses—anything that does its damage by making its way onto a machine inside your network and then running—has only to get through the firewall. For example, imagine a client that has been tampered with in an effort to capture your password; all it need do is get through the firewall in a way that is allowed (maybe you are allowed to transfer files in from the outside world), and it can do its damage. Well, then, suppose someone offers you a file, and you accept it. Once you receive it and it's behind the wall, it's ready to do its thing when you run it. That means the caveats in this book against taking files from strangers (Chapter 15) and in favor of avoiding viruses will apply more to a firewall situation than, say, people stealing your password and logging into your account; outsiders probably wouldn't be able to log in through a firewall. Again, the effectiveness of this strategy depends on what your particular firewall is set up to allow and prevent.

Platforms—Not Just for Shoes Anymore

Previously, I've made some allusions to differences between computer platforms. Because different operating systems have different degrees of security protection, there are differing degrees to which platforms are subject to security concerns.

The general rule of thumb (if it isn't blazingly obvious already) is that UNIX is the biggest problem child as far as security goes. It's not because UNIX is bad—in fact, UNIX is extremely powerful and extremely flexible. That also makes learning it more difficult. And, because of its complexity, there are that many more possible ways clever people can try to get through its safeguards. It's like having a mansion with 250 rooms and 1000 windows—it might be a great place to live, where you could do virtually anything you wanted—but it also has that many more ways for someone to break in, and you may need a grounds crew to maintain it.

On the other hand, common "home computer" operating systems such as System 7 (on the Macintosh) and MS-DOS or Windows (on the PC) do not have near the vast power and flexibility of UNIX. They are more like suburban homes than mansions—comfortable, you can live there contentedly, but you can't build a swimming pool in the North Wing. The learning curve is flatter, though, and you can probably tend to the grounds yourself most of the time. That includes locking the doors; it's easier to safeguard a system such as a Mac or PC. Many vulnerabilities that exist in UNIX are not so widespread on Mac and PC systems.

Platform The thing that the computer sits on top of is probably a desk. A *platform* means a type of system, generally defined by brand. That is, a PC-clone is one type of computer platform, a Macintosh is another. Although the definition gets squishy here, we'll consider UNIX to be a third type of platform.

The conclusion that's most reasonable from all this isn't that any computer platform is watertight. With increased complexity comes increased power and increased vulnerability. So if you do most of your Internetting from a UNIX machine, basically every last detail in this book is worth remembering. If you spend a lot of time on Macs and PCs, then many of the behavioral issues in this book still apply to you—such as virus checking, passwords, encryption, e-mail safety, and so forth. But some of the stickier issues (such as running servers, or having people sneak into accounts on your computer) are less likely to be major issues. Then again, though you're also less likely to be using Macs or PCs for such functions as keeping user accounts or running servers, it's not unheard of. With the proliferation of SLIP/PPP, more and more "home computer" users are beginning to set up their own servers.

That Squishy Definition of "Platform"

Actually, there's a reason for the squishy definition of platforms: it depends on whether you are including both the computer hardware and software. Any computer has two major components—its hardware and its operating system. The operating system is software, but is most often bundled with hardware. For example, System 7 comes with Macintosh hardware, and is called a "Macintosh" computer. MS-DOS often comes with PC-clone hardware, and hence the combination is called a "PC." UNIX is an operating system, so it's really software. But it can be run on a variety of hardwares. You can, for example, run a version of UNIX on PC hardware. So, when we talk about "platforms" we're really talking about the operating system more than the hardware that tends to come along with it.

The Least You Need to Know

Learning to speak TCP/IP confers some great advantages upon your computer, but also some increased security risks. These security risks vary from application to application and from one computer platform to another.

- ➤ A static (non-changing) IP address will allow you to be a strong presence on the Internet if you so desire, but it also makes you something of a sitting duck.
- ➤ Generally, it's fairly safe to run clients (which request and receive information from remote computers), unless you end up with a tampered client.
- ➤ One concern, though, is packet sniffing, where outsiders could "listen in" on the little information that your client does send out to the network, such as user IDs and passwords.
- ➤ Running a server is like opening an Internet restaurant, where you can play host to people from all over the world and share your data with them. But it also opens a channel directly into your computer, so be sure to fully understand all the issues when setting up your own server, and rely heavily on the documentation—it's no time to put the manual back in the box and wing it.
- ➤ If your organization uses a firewall for security purposes, find out what type of data it does and does not allow to flow into and out of the organization, and interpret the issues in this book accordingly.
- ➤ Different computer platforms have different security concerns, and you should know what platform you use and how its vulnerabilities stack up against everything discussed in this book.

Part 2
A Pound of Prevention

For many readers, this part will be the real Thanksgiving feast of the book. It's heavy and filling, and you may have to collapse on the sofa after reading it. Indigestion may follow. Unlike a gluttonous orgy of stuffing your face with food, this part is necessary, although the former is more fun.

The following chapters present issues and techniques for protecting your data and files. Locking, storing, hiding, and immunizing are just a few of the things you'll learn to do. From passwords to e-mail to the World Wide Web, the majority of Internet action is covered here. Understand these chapters well, because otherwise the rest of the book loses a lot of its use (use for reading, anyway. It'll still work for other things, like combustion).

Who lived in a giant bubble…

Chapter 6

Passwords—On the Frontlines

In This Chapter

- Passwords, hyah, what are they good for?
- Choosing with care
- Change is good—for keeping them on their toes
- Don't ask, don't tell

There's something big, burly, and perhaps even a bit smelly sitting in front of your Internet account, and it's not your co-worker. But to potential intruders great and small, your password is your own personal Billy the Bouncer, and it can be either your greatest vulnerability or strongest line of defense. With your password in hand, absolutely anyone can access any and all data in your Internet account, including programs, work files, and e-mail. It's not pretty. Ahead, we'll look at how to best secure your account (and your peace of mind) with a well-considered password.

Keep Out!

At least there are several means of securing your house—you can lock the doors, the windows, and the garage; install an alarm system; and buy a twelve-foot-tall Great Dane. Not so with your home on the Internet. As far as a computer is concerned, once someone logs in to your account with your password, they are you, no further questions asked. They can read anything you can read, download anything you can download, and delete buffet-style.

Lock, Stock, and Barrel

At the expense of convenience, you could take more secure measures. For example, you could keep any important data in your account *PGP-encrypted* (consult Chapters 8 and 9 for the dirt on PGP), and have your private key stored somewhere other than that same account. Then you would decrypt any file you wanted to read and encrypt it again before logging out. This would be quite secure, but would also require a lot of effort unless your data is extremely sensitive and your vulnerability quite high.

Technically, there are other ways into your account besides logging in with your password, but those involve holes and *backdoors* that your service provider is responsible for securing (some of which are revealed in Chapter 16). Certainly, no self-respecting burglar is going to forego trying the front door of an unoccupied house. The same goes for all manner of hacker and cracker. Bar none, the first route an intruder will try is "cracking" your password.

Peter Piper Picked a Password

Because it is the strongest defense you have against intrusion—and I stress this to the point of hernia—it is *extremely* important that you pick a crack-proof password. There are two major ways that a hacker will try to determine your password, and a well-chosen one can protect you against both.

Don't Get Personal

It is generally a very bad idea to pick a password that has anything to do with yourself personally. The easiest method for a hacker, especially a novice one, to determine your password is simply to guess at it. Now, that's not going to be very easy for them to do, and you certainly don't want to make it any easier for them. The password "blue," for

CHT. 8-9 PGP ENCRYPT
CHT 16. BACKDOORS

ackdoor A ackdoor on a omputer system just that—a ay in through a ess-commonly used route hat may not be as carefully ecured. Technically, a *hacker* s someone who explores for he sake of curiosity and self-education. This may involve breaking into private systems, and harm may be done even if none was intended. A *cracker* is one who breaks into systems with specific malicious intent, commonly to steal information or spy on someone. The difference may seem minor, but they get all uptight about it. In this book I will use the term 'hacker' to refer to either sort of intruder, in the hopes of avoiding a he/she thing.

Some very determined hackers will manage to steal the password file from your service provider's computer. Should that happen, fortunately, all is not lost. The file that contains your password is not easily readable by a human being—the passwords are coded and encrypted. A hacker can, however, feed a computer a "dictionary" of many thousands of words—and the computer will guess each of them in turn until your password is cracked. These dictionaries can be very advanced; they account for prefixes and suffixes, abbreviations, and compound words—the whole Hooked on Phonics gambit. What this means, in effect, is that any word or simple modification thereon is quite crackable by these computer dictionaries.

FYI... My password is not "blue." Nor is it "blue42."

Wrong Way

Passwords are encrypted in a one-way manner, so that the encrypted password cannot be reversed to reveal the real one. The computer checks whether your password is correct when you log in by encrypting what you type in and comparing that to the encrypted code in the password file. If the two match, then you entered the correct password. It's neat.

The Right Choice

No birthdays, no dog names, and no words at all. So what *does* make for a secure password? Voodoo? Nope—randomness. The hacker's mind can only make human guesses, and the computer dictionary can only find lingual words or patterns. The less meaning and pattern in your password, and the more random the distribution of characters, the safer.

It is usually recommended that your password be at least eight characters long, and contain a mix of upper- and lower-case letters and non-alphanumeric characters (such as # or @ and so forth).

Don't Worry, Be Random

For example, the password "ab12cd34", while not a word per se, is not a good choice because it contains a pattern that's relatively easy to discern. In contrast, "w9$;=aMg3}" is a good password. Usually, passwords are case-sensitive, so the difference between upper- and lowercase characters is important. Hence, "w9$;=aMG3}" is a different password from the one just mentioned, due to the capitalized "G." In theory, both of these are good passwords. In practice, of course, they are no longer very good because they have just been suggested in this book! But the important point is that they contain no meaning and no pattern.

As illustrated above, sprinkling your password with non-alphanumeric characters is a good idea—not only at the beginning and/or end. However, I sense some disgruntlement out there. After all, it's all well and good to be secure, but how are you supposed to *remember* "w9$;=aMG3}"? Unless you're one of those savants who appear once a year on daytime talk shows, this may not be so easy. An alternative is to use mnemonic memory tricks to create passwords that appear random but aren't. For example, take a music lyric, or make up a phrase, such as, "Fred, my boss, is a total jerk." Now take the last letter of each word—in this case, **dyssalk**—mix up the case a bit in a memorable way—DYssalK—and throw in some non-alphanumerics, say, after every third letter—DYs/sal;K[. Note that I chose those symbols based on a logical keyboard pattern which—if you look at your keyboard (and if you don't use some sort of mutant-freak keyboard)—you'll see. None of these tricks would be recommendable on their own, but in combination you can often generate a fairly random password.

The Great Debate

There is split opinion out there, among those who have opinions on such matters, about using mnemonic devices in constructing your password. One argument is that you can devise a reasonably secure mnemonic password that is easy to remember yet hard to crack. The opposing argument is that when you let people attempt to create memorizable passwords, they will fall into the trap of creating passwords that a computer can guess. The former camp counters that gibberish passwords force the user to write them down, which is even more insecure. They battle the whole thing out in naked mud fights on Friday nights.

Many systems have limits on the minimum and maximum length of your password. In addition, some systems do not allow certain (or any) non-alphanumeric characters, and some are not case-sensitive. If your system doesn't notify you of password length parameters—or doesn't accept non-alphanumeric characters in passwords—you should yell, scream, and stomp about it. Or find a new service provider. Ultimately, it's the security of your data at issue.

Passwords 101: Quiz 1

What do you think of these passwords? Which ones are good and which are bad? Check below for answers.

1. MomNDad0812
2. w1nd0w$
3. e-o2G;oCh%?
4. e=mc2
5. s;418:$[]b
6. 9I=1\t]p'm/n(
7. All of the above

Key:

1. Very bad—it's basically a compound word plus a number.
2. This one might look good, but actually it's not. The simple "look-alike" substitution used to replace numbers for similar-looking letters can be checked for by the cracking dictionary.
3. A good one, generated randomly by a UNIX password generator. Tough to remember, though.
4. Bad—it's an easy mnemonic, but it's too short. Even if the dictionary doesn't look for this obvious formula, a brute force search will probably crack it because there are only five places.
5. Good. Generated randomly by closing my eyes and banging on my keyboard a few times until I came up with a fairly well-distributed string. If you're going to do this, do it on a practice screen until you come up with a password that meets the criteria. And don't break your keyboard.
6. Also good. Looks random, but it's not; this is a mnemonic: "I like to pick my nose." I took the first letter of each word, inserting a non-alphanumeric character between each letter. To get those characters, I followed a keyboard pattern (it's a pattern on *my* keyboard, yours may vary a little) and capped the password with a 9 on each end—the tailing 9 was shifted to make an open parenthesis.
7. Sneaky, eh? Technically, they're all bad now, since they've been printed here for all to see. Avoid printing your password in a book.

Variety Is Spicy—and Secure

As with your underwear, you should change your password every so often. Some systems will force you to change your password periodically. This is a laudable practice. If your system does not enforce such a policy, make it a practice to do so yourself. You can usually change your password as often as you like, but it's okay to be reasonable. I change my password every few months, when the mood strikes. Of course, if your current password violates any of the guidelines in the previous section, then it should be changed, as they say in upper Brooklyn, *immediatement*!

For the UNIX in You

If you are like many users, you access the Internet through a dial-in UNIX-shell account. When you originally signed up with your service provider, you either chose a password or were assigned one. Either way, it's a good idea to change that one shortly after you get onto the account, because the original password may be written down on an application somewhere in the service provider's records. Service providers who offer menus to their UNIX systems often have a choice for changing your password. Whether you do or do not have a menu available to you, you can change your password from the shell prompt by typing **$passwd**.

You will then see a prompt that says

```
Old password:
```

At this prompt, type your current password. You will not see what you are typing on the screen! Some systems will not show anything at all, some will show a * or other character in place of the letter you actually type. Be sure to type very carefully. When you hit **Enter**, the next prompt will say

```
New password:
```

Here you enter what you would like your new password to be. Again, your typing will be masked, so enter it carefully. After hitting **Enter**, the computer will prompt you to verify what you just typed:

```
Retype new password:
```

You must re-enter the new password that you just entered at the previous prompt, to be sure that you entered it correctly. If what you entered at the "New password:" prompt does not exactly match what you entered at the "Retype new password:" prompt, your old password will not be changed and the procedure will abort.

Fingers Tripped? If you think you may have mistyped your intended new password, try hitting **Ctrl+c**, which should abort the process immediately and return you to the shell, no harm done. If that doesn't work, just enter something at the Retype prompt that definitely will not match and it will abort the process.

Users of menu-based or graphical interfaces to the Internet will have a service-provider-designed way to change passwords. If your Internet access came with software, then that software should have a built-in option for altering your password. In the best-case scenario, your Internet access software will have an intuitive interface for entering a new password. If it does not seem to have any such option, definitely contact your service provider, because the ability to change your password is a very important one. Users who have SLIP/PPP accounts but no service provider-provided software may have to also contact their ISP about changing their password. If your service provider makes it a hassle for you to change passwords, seriously consider finding a new provider if possible. To repeat the mantra of this book, your privacy is your property, and should not be kept from you.

If you make it through this whole process successfully, you should be notified that your password has been changed. Before deciding how to note your new password, however, read the nearby sidebar about protecting passwords.

And Now the Bad News...

It's virtually impossible to protect your password 100 percent. If a hacker fails to guess or use a computer-generated dictionary search successfully, he can always try a "brute force" search. That means he runs a program that will try every possible combination of every character until it finds a match. In theory, this will always work to crack a password, but it takes a *lot* of computing power and an extremely long time, so only the most determined hacker is going to go to such extremes.

Shhh! Can You Keep a Secret?

The final step in protecting your password is hiding it. The number one best place to keep your password is in your cerebral cortex (it's just above your cerebellum). This is the advantage of creating mnemonic-based passwords, as long as they retain randomness. Sometimes things fall out of the brain, however, and it can be very hard to find them once they slip down the spine and into your kidney. Some users prefer to generate completely random passwords and try to memorize them with brute mental force. If you must write your password down somewhere until you're confident in your retention, the closer to your person that you keep it, the better. Minimize the chances that anyone could come across it. A Post-It note on one's monitor is not such a good idea. A Post-It note in one's underpants would make a better, if more chaffing, hideaway. Alternatively, perhaps your wallet would make a reasonable compromise. Don't tell it to anyone that you don't absolutely trust, and don't let anyone else log in to your account for you. Nonetheless, it's safe practice to destroy all references to your password wherever they may be as soon as you're sure that it's locked tight into your brain.

There may be several instances in your Internetting where you have to come up with passwords. Besides your main account, you may need a password for other accounts, or for access to other types of services. Remember the password we created to use the anonymous re-mailer back in Chapter 2? In the coming chapters, we'll be looking at a form of data encryption that may require you to choose a password. In all of these cases, everything in this chapter applies—this advice is not limited to passwords for UNIX accounts.

> **IMHO** While it's common practice to advise people absolutely to never tell a single soul your password, I think it's reasonably safe to share it with, for instance, your significant other. On the other hand, if you have a break-up, change your password immediately!

The Future's So Secure...

Never willing to stop and rest, tech-heads have been brainstorming new possibilities for passwording that will eliminate a lot of the risks that today's passwords face. There are an array of up-and-coming *one-time password* technologies, although it's too soon to say which will gain widespread, mainstream usage. One example of such a system is known as S/Key. With this system, both sides know the password, but it doesn't have to be transmitted from one side to another through the network. Instead, the host issues a "challenge" which the user combines with his known password in some way, and comes up with a result. That result is sent to the host computer, which can verify that the correct password was used to generate the result. Importantly, the challenge is different every time, so it's not something an outsider could "steal."

Another system, called OneTime Pass, doesn't use any complicated algorithms at all. It just providers the user with a list of passwords, and the user uses them in sequence, crossing each one out after use. And yet other systems have different means by which they try to authenticate the user, similar to S/Key, without having to have one key piece of information pass between the systems.

These two passwording systems represent the extremes from very complex to very simple approaches, and, unsurprisingly, other proposals fall anywhere in between. The next chapter, an introduction to cryptography, should offer some food for thought on ways that this type of authentication might be done.

The Least You Need to Know

Armed with everything previously beaten into you, you should be able to secure your account from front-door entry by would-be intruders *and* mix metaphors in opening sentences.

- Your password is your strongest line of defense against invasion, so pick a secure one!
- Choose a password that is at least eight places long, with a random distribution of upper- and lower-case letters, numbers, and symbols.
- Changing your password every few months will keep yours from getting stale, but don't get so far ahead of yourself that you can't even remember your own password.
- Memorize your password as quickly as possible, and don't keep written copies of it anywhere that someone might find it.

Chapter 7

Tales of Encryption

In This Chapter

- Filling in the gaps—some background
- Who me? Why privacy is everyone's business
- Always with the legal mumbo jumbo
- Practical options

For most people who ever ate sugary cereal as a young 'un, encryption is a familiar trick. All of those secret decoder rings were not for nothing. Perhaps, at the time, it was a surreptitious training program to help boost defense against the Red Hare (or was that the Red Scare? I get them mixed up)—but whatever the intent, encryption for the masses is coming into its own in the age of networked communications. Your ability to encrypt your data is the cornerstone of the future virtual society—it guards the intersection of privacy and protection. That's why the next three chapters will be about encryption. This chapter will give you some background and provide some general information about encryption. The remaining two chapters will educate you to the use of some specific applications. There will be no exam, and no Spring Break.

What It Is, Man

From the earliest time, human beings didn't trust each other. Encryption, in fact, is a very old practice. I'm sure there's a BBC documentary about it somewhere. So, at its most basic, the goal of encryption is to disguise some information from outsiders' eyes, so that only the intended recipient can make sense of it.

For example, take a look at this "before" shot of a line of text:

```
Hi! I'm a line of "plaintext" which means that this text is plain.
```

Then we use our miracle encryption system (only $19.95!)—and now, look at the "after" shot:


```
hEwCtbdGE386fBsBAgCQc9uN+0LoCiOyrwvTVbxqlPOkIoOqjduV8RfaokdEAIz/
oRsALZbe590M/lfvlHk5vvAh/I42vaNoADMVJEzLpgAAAFb4h1F7p0vu9m5vPSfN
LFoafILn2s3HP6akUUeADAe7ZlPbxWJ+AqK7SiA23euvDS3B8Pd5b51CZMX+JB5e
HGjcZxe8OUwh7PtBADg+9b9CXRzt9wDJCA==
=2smR
```


Impressive, I hope you agree.

Perhaps the most common form of encryption, and the style that you are most familiar with, is known as *secret-key cryptography*. In this process, you make up some transformation to the original data which is the *secret key*. Here's a third-grade example: You transform every letter to three letters down the alphabet. So, "mother" becomes "prwkhu." That was a very simple secret key; it can be much more complex than one simple transformation. But secret-key encryption has one major weakness: no matter how complex your algorithm, both parties have to know it. Which means that it has to be communicated from one party to the other. That opens up a catch-22: optimally, you want to use a secure means of communication to tell the other party the secret key, but the whole point of your encryption scheme is to *create* a secure means of communication.

Enter *public-key cryptography*. One day, perhaps after an intense game of bocci ball, some guys decided that rather than cook up a barbecue, they'd order pizza in and try to solve this secret key dilemma. What they came up with was the following: Each party has two *keys* (which means the same as "codes"), one used to encrypt the data, and the other used to decrypt the data. One of these keys can be "public"—that is, anyone can know it. It will be used to encrypt the data. The other key is "private," meaning that only one person knows it. That one person can use the private key to decrypt data which has been encrypted with their public key.

In real life, it works this way: I want to send some private data to Morton. I find Morton's public key, and I use it to encrypt the data. I then send this encrypted data to Morton. Upon receiving it, he whips out his private key and decrypts the data. Notice that the private key—the one that ultimately decrypts the data—never has to pass from one party to another. Ingenious, huh? The public key can be stored in a public database, or made available in some other way, so that anyone wanting to send encrypted data to Morton just has to find out his public key. But only Morton, with his private key, can decrypt it. Of course, it's still up to Morton to secure his private key, so the onus of personal responsibility is not entirely removed.

This public-key encryption forms the basis of most widely used cryptography systems on the Internet today, and we'll explore some of the very gory details of it in the subsequent chapters.

A Digital John Hancock

Although we've been talking about public-key encryption as it pertains to encrypting data, it has some other very useful applications. Due to the secure nature of this form of cryptography, one can use it to *authenticate* an individual—that means to assess confidently whether an individual is who he or she claims to be. Although authentication can be done using secret-key systems, one particular application of authentication using the public-key system is the *digital signature*.

A digital signature allows one to create a "signature" at the end of a document, even though the content of the document may or may not be encrypted itself. But the signature is verifiable by the receiving party, and can be used to prove that the document was sent (or created) by the claimed party and has not been tampered with since. This gives digital signatures the one-up on handwritten signatures, because penmanship can be forged, while digital signatures cannot. One interesting side note about all this is that because the digital signature is non-forgeable, the originating party cannot later say, "No, I didn't send you that, someone forged my signature." Forced honesty, it is.

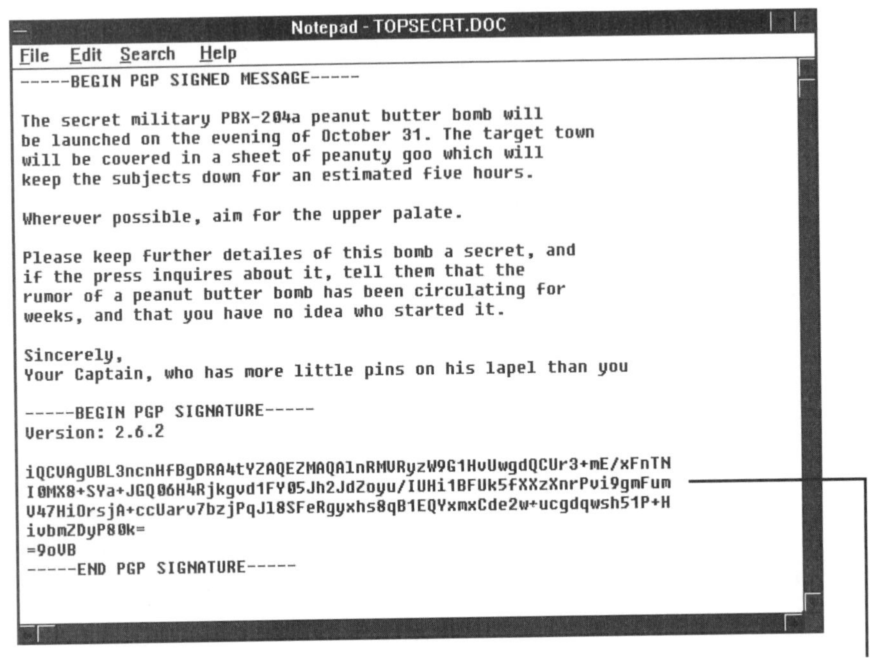


```
-----BEGIN PGP SIGNED MESSAGE-----

The secret military PBX-204a peanut butter bomb will
be launched on the evening of October 31. The target town
will be covered in a sheet of peanuty goo which will
keep the subjects down for an estimated five hours.

Wherever possible, aim for the upper palate.

Please keep further detailes of this bomb a secret, and
if the press inquires about it, tell them that the
rumor of a peanut butter bomb has been circulating for
weeks, and that you have no idea who started it.

Sincerely,
Your Captain, who has more little pins on his lapel than you

-----BEGIN PGP SIGNATURE-----
Version: 2.6.2

iQCVAgUBL3ncnHfBgDRA4tYZAQEZMAQAlnRMVRyzW9G1HvUwgdQCUr3+mE/xFnTN
I0MX8+SYa+JGQ06H4Rjkgvd1FY05Jh2JdZoyu/IUHi1BFUk5fXXzXnrPvi9gmFum
V47HiOrsjA+ccUarv7bzjPqJl8SFeRgyxhs8qB1EQYxmxCde2w+ucgdqwsh51P+H
ivbmZDyP80k=
=9oVB
-----END PGP SIGNATURE-----
```


This digital signature can be verified with the proper software, proving that the originator of this message is who he says he is, and that this document has not been altered since the signature was calculated.

Carved in Stone

One reason that *the digital signature is non-forgeable* is because it is created based on both the originating party's private key and the content of the message. The receiving party then analyzes the message content, the attached digital signature, and the originator's public key. If, through a complicated series of mathematical loop-de-loops, it all turns out hunky-dory, then that is verification that the original party did indeed send the message and that it has not been altered from its original form.

But I Have Nothing to Hide

A common question that arises when discussing all this encryption stuff is, "Why would I want to do this? I don't have CIA secrets, and I'm not selling black-market blenders for the underground!" We touched on the basics of the answer back in Chapter 2. Privacy is not a right solely possessed by the criminals. Whether or not you choose to use them, as a society, these forms of privacy protection are fundamentally important to the viability of the Internet, or any form of networked communications. Without any means of self-protection, you would remain vulnerable without any other choice, and such a society would not thrive. (If you've ever seen the film "Caligula," you can imagine what such a society would be like.)

If you know how to seal an envelope, then you should know how to do the same on the Internet. Going through the effort of all that (as described in this chapter and those that follow) may seem a very paranoid endeavor. Remember, though, that it's your choice how often (and under what circumstances, and to what degree) you will assure your privacy. There is good news on the horizon, though. Part of the reason it seems to take a lot of effort to encrypt your data right now is that encryption has not yet been integrated into the network at a very fundamental level. That means you have to do all the work. But encrypting everything automatically as it goes out of and comes into your computer is certainly within the computer's capabilities, and is merely a matter of widespread implementation on the part of service providers and other Net industry organizations. Over the next few years this will probably happen, and although everything described in these chapters will still be necessary and will still go on, much of it will be automated.

Undecided, the Jury's Still Out, Patent Pending

There is a messy tangle swirling around the issue of encryption. For one thing, governments don't tend to be thrilled with people being able to hide information from them. This has led to a confusing and unresolved situation. In some nations, encryption is flat-out illegal, such as in France. In the United States, cryptographic systems are patentable, but not exportable without special licenses, as they are considered to be munitions. The legal status of some of the cryptographic products and the people involved with them is still undecided in a number of circumstances. There's a lot to be sorted out in this area that governments are not terribly enthusiastic about, although lawyers probably are. Of course, if an encryption algorithm were not exportable outside of a particular country (such as the United States), you can imagine that this poses a problem concerning its usefulness on the Internet. Since the Internet is global in scope, its users would be expected to need encryption systems that are compatible regardless of physical national boundaries. Not to sound too subversive, but the reality is that what happens on the Internet does not necessarily reflect what governments, or their laws, would like. One popular form of encryption, which we'll be discussing in detail shortly, has managed to make it across the great ponds, and for the most part is interchangeably usable by everyone. The ability of governments to say or do something about these things has yet to be tested in any meaningful way.

For these reasons, some of the cryptographic packages available may have notices that you use them "at your own risk." In a way, this is an attempt to cover for the fact that the legal issues around them haven't been resolved. By the same token, a couple of packages that will be highlighted in this book are on much more solid ground than others. If I might play digital Nostradamus for a moment, let me overextend myself:

When I was in college, there was a yearly ritual at the end of Spring classes where thousands would gather on the hill and "party," which, invariably, is a euphemism for consuming large amounts of alcohol (often by means of funnels or other cavernous containers). Of course, in the United States, people under 21 years old are not allowed to drink by law, and in a college environment, a majority of the student population is under 21. Nonetheless, perhaps for a variety of reasons, the university administration chose to allow the en masse underage drinking in an "unwritten" manner, while providing security and facilities to help keep the situation safe. Some of the issues arising on the Internet, cryptography being one of them, remind me of this situation, although with encryption, one's clothes are much cleaner the following day. If enough people are doing it—data encryption is widespread, popular, and accepted on the Internet—the lawmaking bodies in the "real world" will ultimately have to figure out how to accommodate the practice rather than force existing laws onto it. They won't be happy, and governments will probably whine and moan about it, but in the end I suspect that what is considered "at your own risk" right now will win out in the end, preserving our privacy. (Otherwise I'm moving to Mars.)

Popular Picks

There's more than one encryption technique you have the option to use. In fact, there are many, but just a few that have widespread and popular use on the Internet. So, in the interest of conformity (not that conformity should normally be very interesting, but this is an exception), we'll stick to the Net-popular.

rot13: Protects Innocent Eyes

One of the simplest forms of encryption used on the Internet is knows at *rot13*. It performs a simple transformation, like the third grade example shown earlier. Now, rot13 is not a very secure form of encryption, mind you. It is most often used in Usenet postings to obscure information which a reader may not want to see. For example, suppose there is a post with a possibly offensive joke. It may warn the reader, "Some may find this joke offensive; it is rot13-encrypted." Many newsreaders can decode rot13 with the press of a key or click of a button, so it's not hard to decode. But it allows you to pause a second before deciding to read the content of the message. It may also be used in postings which contain "spoilers," or information that may spoil the surprise for someone who may not have seen the movie, TV episode, and so on.

You can get a rot13 encoder/decoder for your computer from just about any major FTP site that you get other software from. Remember, this isn't a secure form of encryption by any means; it just prevents the most casual observer from seeing the information, but little effort is required to decrypt it.

UUEncoding: An Alternative to rot13

Although not commonly thought of as encryption, *uuencoding* can be used to perform a task that is similar to rot13. Uuencoding is normally used to convert binary files into ASCII text, for the purpose of posting to Usenet, or sending as e-mail. But it can be used to obscure text from glancing eyes. As with rot13, it's very easy to decode, and is not secure.

If you already have the facility to uuencode, you may consider using it for light encryption, just not important information. You need to have the file containing the information you want to encrypt already made before uuencoding it. In a UNIX shell, presuming your file-to-be-uuencoded is called **filename1**, you would enter the command:

```
$uuencode filename1 filename1 > filename2
```

The resulting "filename2" will be the uuencoded version of "filename1," and you can then insert that into an e-mail message. If you are using a graphical interface on a Mac or PC, the method of uuencoding varies, but you can find a uuencoder on any major FTP site for your platform, and it will surely have instructions on how to uuencode a file (and how to uudecode, fortunately).

As illustrated in the candid figure that follows, uuencoding is fairly easy to do. Although I once again stress that this is *not* a secure means of encryption, it *is* a convenient way to pass files around without making their contents immediately obvious to someone.

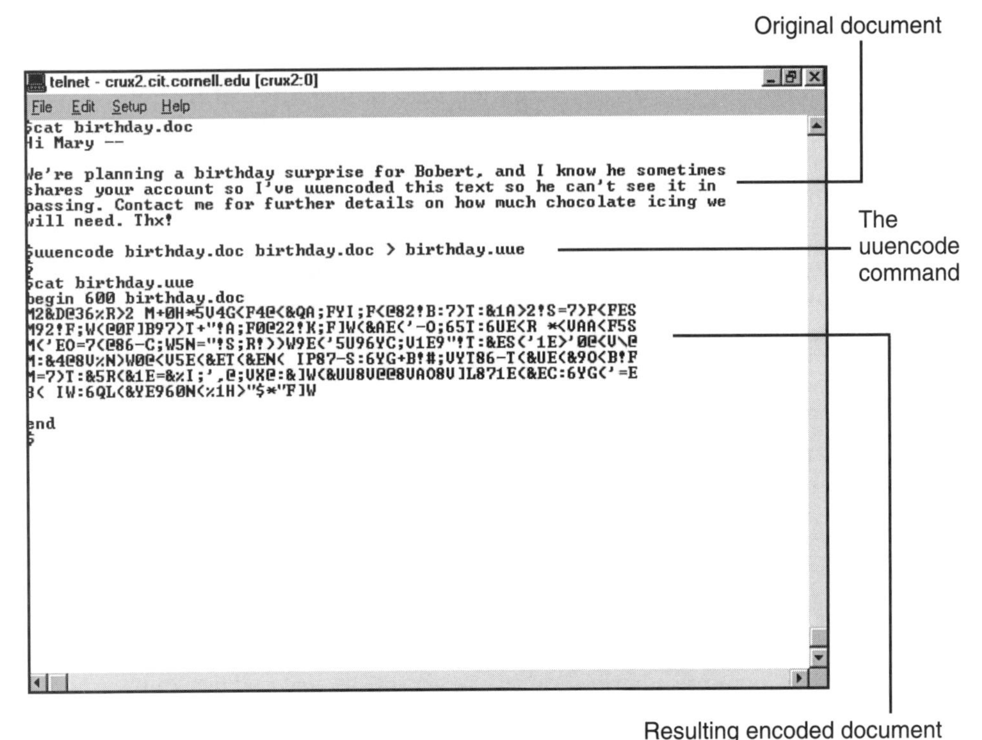

Here's a quick example of uuencoding a short text file. Remember, this is not secure—anyone can decode it easily!

RIPEM and PGP: The Heavy Hitters

There are two major packages that are intended to implement high security public-key encryption systems. One of them is called RIPEM, because it's based on PEM, duh. PEM is alphabet soup for "Privacy Enhanced Mail," and the prefix RI stands for "Riordan's Internet" (that's because Riordan, Mike Riordan in particular, wrote the program, not because it's his Internet). The other package is known as PGP, which stands for "Pretty Good Privacy."

These packages have similarities, but they are not compatible. That is, if you encrypt something with RIPEM you cannot decrypt it with PGP and vice versa. The legal issues surrounding RIPEM are supposedly less muddled than those regarding PGP (which was the specific package I was talking about in the discussion on swirling messy issues in the previous section). However, the reality is that PGP is used on the Internet on a much more widespread scale than RIPEM, and to maximize your ability to walk the encryption walk with the rest of the Internet, PGP is the way to go. Pointers for further information about RIPEM can be found in the back of this book.

The next two chapters will be a detailed course in using PGP to encrypt your files and e-mail. Sorry, RIPEM.

Clipper Chip and Capstone: Future Technology to Ponder

So, what's the deal with the "Clipper Chip," anyway? If you've heard about it, you might be confused as to exactly what it's all about. If you haven't heard about it, you probably should know about it. The Clipper Chip is a product of the United States government, and it is a chip which performs the sort of public-key cryptography described in this chapter. It is intended to be placed into digital telephones (which use ISDN), which are presumed to replace current analog telephones in the next few years. Something called "Capstone" is the sibling to Clipper; it's intended for use in computers and other digital appliances. Both Clipper and Capstone are based on the same encryption algorithm, which is called "Skipjack."

Under the proposed Clipper/Capstone implementation, your data and voice communications would be encrypted and thus kept private from other citizens, thereby affording you a much higher degree of privacy and security than current analog telephones offer. However, to retain their ability to "tap" into suspect communications, the Skipjack system has a back door that allows the government to obtain the necessary keys and "listen in" to any communication that they want. The government's position is that they need to retain the ability to investigate suspect activities, and the Clipper proposal includes a system of hoops involving court orders and two "key escrow agencies" before a government "tap" could take place.

One concern, however, even in the face of the proposed checks and balances, is that abuse can always be expected to occur. But, unlike an abuse of a search warrant, in which the police raid your home without proper orders—probably leaving a mess or other obvious signs of break-in—there is little way to detect if an abusive "raid" has taken place against your communications. The combination of likelihood of abuse and difficulty in detecting such abuse undermines confidence in the court order/escrow system in some people's minds.

In addition to this, there are other concerns. The Skipjack algorithm has been developed by the National Security Agency, in secret status, which prevents any sort of public or independent review of the algorithm. It concerns some that without such independent evaluation, there is some possibility that the algorithm may have weaknesses, which would be "set in stone," as it were, by pressing and distributing chips containing it in many communications products. Another concern is that because countries outside the United States would not be interested in having the Clipper/Capstone in their products, U.S. companies would have to make two forms of each relevant product, one for domestic sale and one for foreign sale, which might drive up production costs and reduce U.S. foreign competitiveness. For more information on Clipper Chip and Capstone, check the "Further Reading" section in the back of this book.

The Least You Need to Know

Encryption is a broad term meaning "some way to hide information," and people have been doing it since before poached eggs were invented.

- Simple forms of encryption involve a secret code that must be shared between parties but that leaves the secret code itself open for interception.
- The public-key system allows parties to encrypt data using publicly available codes. Only a private key held by the receiving party can decrypt the data.
- The public-key system allows for the use of digital signatures, which can be used to authenticate a document as being from a certain individual and to verify that it has not been forged or altered. Pretty cool.
- Even if you're not a criminal, preserving your privacy should be a priority. The desire to keep information secure between yourself and whoever you want to divulge it to doesn't imply shadiness, it implies rationality. Of course, if you are a criminal, it's good for that, too.
- The Clipper Chip is not a low-calorie snack food. It's a proposed device by the U.S. government to protect citizens' privacy from each other, but not from the state.
- For very light encryption, you can use rot13 or uuencoding. It's useful to keep text from being readable upon initial viewing, but it's easily decipherable.
- For heavy encryption, RIPEM is one capable, but not widely used, option. PGP is the de facto standard on the Internet at present, as the next two chapters will torturously prove.

Chapter 8

PGP 101: Encrypting Files

In This Chapter

- Tracking down PGP
- Creating your keys
- Encrypting and decrypting your files
- Safeguarding your keys

Theory is all well and good, but without practical application, what good is it—other than for winning a Nobel Prize? Exactly. So, in this chapter we're going to put the butter to the bread and get into some down n' dirty encryption using the PGP (Pretty Good Protection) program. This is serious stuff—the encryption algorithms we'll be using are extremely secure, and it is considered a virtual impossibility for almost anyone to "break the code." Which means that the weakest link in the security chain is *you*. If you fail to use these techniques properly, you can seriously reduce their effectiveness. Even worse, you might improperly encrypt information and not be able to get it back yourself! So it's important to be awake and alert for these next two chapters. I find that Mountain Dew helps.

Finding PGP for Your System

Before we can encrypt some files, we need the PGP program itself. That's not as simple as it sounds. Actually, the strange legal issues involved are what make the situation a bit deranged (but manageable).

I Fought the Law and the Law Won

The first thing you gots to do is determine what country you are in. (If you aren't sure, that's really a problem, but try asking someone next to you.) The reason it matters is because of the big bad arm of the law. For the United States and Canada, the legal situation regarding PGP differs from what it is in the rest of the world. Admittedly, in everyday personal usage, be-sunglassed agents are not going to break down your door if you use an improper version of PGP. In fact, it's likely that nothing will happen. For your own sake, however, it's best to stay on the happy side of the law, especially since there's no real advantage not to.

Whodunit?
If PGP can't be exported, you ask, then how did there come to be an international version at all? Well, that's because it was exported at one time—illegally—and so now "the cat's out of the bag," as it were. (I'm not sure anyone knows who did it or when it happened. Don't look at me.) Presently the two versions can be thought of as "co-evolving" on either side of the ocean, without continuing to break any more laws. As long as you keep your hands on the version for your side of the ocean, you'll be okay, legally speaking.

Within the U.S. and Canada, there are two official releases of PGP:

- **MIT PGP** is a freely available distribution for individual, non-commercial use. It's the dominant application for use within the United States and Canada (the current version of MIT PGP is 2.6.2, but that may change by the time you read this book). Due to patents on certain portions of the program, MIT PGP cannot be exported outside of the United States or Canada.
- There is a commercial package called **ViaCrypt**, published by ViaCrypt Products and available for many major computer platforms. The cost varies, but it's in the $100-to-$150 range at the time of this writing. ViaCrypt is completely compatible with MIT PGP but is licensed for commercial use (for those who need such).

Outside the U.S. and Canada, there are two "unofficial" packages:

- **PGP 2.6.i** (the "i" stands for "international") is MIT PGP 2.6.2-compatible, but does not use the portion of code that is patented in the U.S. Note that 2.6.i is *not* officially endorsed by the creators of legal PGP, but that's partly because they *can't* endorse it without getting yelled at by the Feds.

- **PGP 2.6.ui**, which is another international version (even more unofficial than the *other* unofficial international version). PGP 2.6.ui is compatible with the old PGP 2.3a, whereas both MIT PGP 2.6.2 and PGP 2.6.i are not. Note that PGP 2.3a is an old, obsolete version of PGP, considered to be in violation of certain patents even within the U.S., and so it is not endorsed for use anymore. That shouldn't be a problem as long as you stick with new releases of PGP. Some people want to retain the ability to decrypt 2.3a, but those are the same people who switch the price sticker from a can of beans to a can of shrimp.

It's not clear that it is necessarily illegal to *use* MIT PGP outside the U.S. or Canada, although it *is* illegal to export it. To avoid that whole situation, just be sure you use the legit international versions for "overseas" communication.

Australopithecus

The old PGP 2.3a can be thought of as the "common ancestor" to the mess that we have today. Because it was thought to be in violation of certain licenses and patents, the effort to re-create a legal version resulted in the branching of the original form into several variations, which we see discussed on these pages. Darwin would be proud.

Even though there are international versions of PGP, encryption is wholly illegal in some countries (such as France—over there you couldn't use *any* of the PGP versions I've just described). This restriction is rare, and it's an exception in most of Western Europe.

Before you tear up these pages in a confused rage, however, let's summarize. *If you live in the United States or Canada, you can legally use*:

- MIT PGP for individual, non-commercial use
- ViaCrypt PGP for commercial use

At the time of this writing, you could contact ViaCrypt Products at:

(800) 536-2664
viacrypt@acm.org
70304.41@compuserve.com
9033 N. 25th Avenue
Suite 7
Phoenix, AZ 85021-2847

If you live outside the United States or Canada (assuming encryption is not illegal in your country), you should most likely stick with PGP 2.6.i for individual, non-commercial use. For commercial use outside of the U.S. and Canada, it depends on the status of the

IDEA Cipher Patent in your country. If that patent holds for software in your country, then you'll need to get an appropriate license—but remember, that's just for commercial use.

Now to Snatch the Booty

Okay, now that you've got your legal status in order, figure out what computer platform you're using. UNIX? Mac? PC? Just like any other program, there are versions of PGP for a variety of platforms, so you do need to know which one is appropriate for your computer.

There's an inherent difficulty in offering specific locations from which to get PGP. Things change on the Internet almost hourly, and although many sites have been relatively stable for many years, I wouldn't be able to guarantee that every single site that carries PGP will have it when you read this book. Even so, I will discuss some major distribution routes that are likely to be stable for an extended period. I doubt this book will still be in print in 2010, so let's give it a shot...

For individual, non-commercial users in the U.S. or Canada (which is probably most of you reading this), we want to grab MIT PGP.

This process involves having you telnet and FTP to another Internet site, so make sure you (and your equipment) are ready and able to perform both of those functions. Usually this just means getting logged into your Internet account through your service provider. (Specifics on using the Telnet and FTP applications are the role of earlier Internet books such as—coincidentally, of course—*The Complete Idiot's Guide to the Internet.*) While this may seem like a strangely convoluted process, its intent is to screen out users who are not legally allowed to obtain MIT PGP. It's possible you might find MIT PGP being made available on another site without this screening process, but that's a no-no.

Step 1: First, there is a license agreement you should read, as part of your contractual obligation when you use PGP. To get the license, use FTP to connect to **net-dist.mit.edu**, and go into the directory **/pub/PGP/**. Here you will find a file called **rsalicen.txt**—which you should get and read, using any text viewer you wish.

Step 2: Telnet to the address **net-dist.mit.edu**. When it asks for a **login: name**, enter **getpgp**. You will be presented with some important legal information and then a questionnaire. First it will ask about your citizenship/resident status in the United States. Then it will ask that you agree not to export the program(s) outside of the United States. After that, it will ask you to agree to the terms in the license you read previously. Finally, you'll have to agree to make only non-commercial use of MIT PGP. (For all of the above, being Canadian is okay, too. The server checks where you're coming from.)

```
% telnet net-dist.mit.edu

Trying 18.72.0.3...

Connected to BITSY.MIT.EDU.

Escape character is '^]'.


ULTRIX V4.2A (Rev. 47) (bitsy)

login: getpgp

This distribution of PGP 2.6.2 incorporates the RSAREF(tm) Cryptographic
Toolkit under license  from RSA  Data Security,  Inc. A copy  of  that
license is in the file /pub/PGP/rsalicen.txt available via anonymous FTP from
net-dist.mit.edu  (note: login  as  anonymous *not*  getpgp).  In accor-
dance with  the terms of that license,  PGP 2.6.2  may be  used for
non-commercial purposes only.

PGP 2.6.2 and RSAREF may be subject to  the export  control  laws of the
United States of America as implemented  by the United States Department of
State Office of Defense Trade Controls.

Users who wish to obtain a copy of PGP 2.6.2 are required to  answer the
following questions:

    Are you a citizen or  national of the United States  or a person who has
been lawfully admitted  for permanent residence  in the United States under
the Immigration and Naturalization Act?

<type "yes" or "no">
```

If you've answered all these questions satisfactorily, you will see the following:

```
To get PGP 2.6.X  use anonymous FTP to net-dist.mit.edu and look  in the
directory:

            /pub/PGP/dist/U.S.-only-XXXX
```

In place of XXXX, you will get some real numbers or letters. *Write* down that whole line, because you need to quit Telnet now. Quit Telnet (try hitting **Ctrl+c**). Run your FTP application, and open a connection to the site **net-dist.mit.edu**. Once there, change into the directory the licensing message told you about (the exact directory changes periodically, which is why you had to take note of what it reported earlier).

When you're in that directory, you will see a number of files available for downloading. There are three basic sets of files—for Mac, PC, or UNIX. There are archives for the Mac and PC with only the necessary programs, and some with the source code (for interested programmers). There is only source code available for UNIX users, because there are so many different specific UNIX variations. For example, the way the directory looks at this writing is:

```
-rw-rw-r--  1 0          0 Mar 25 09:37 .usa-only
-r--r--r--  1 435   504670 Jun 15  1994 MacPGP2.6-68000.sea.hqx
-r--r--r--  1 435   504508 Jun  9  1994 MacPGP2.6.sea.hqx
-r--r--r--  1 435   852665 Jun  9  1994 MacPGP2.6.src.sea.hqx
-r--r--r--  1 435      726 Oct 22 19:48 files.md5
-r--r--r--  1 435   282786 Oct 22 19:39 pgp262.zip
-r--r--r--  1 435   827006 Oct 22 19:02 pgp262s.tar.Z
-r--r--r--  1 435   548053 Oct 22 19:03 pgp262s.tar.gz
-r--r--r--  1 435   658945 Oct 22 19:33 pgp262s.zip
```

Obviously, the files called "MacPGP" are for the Mac. The file "pgp262.zip" is the necessary archive for the PC, and the bottom three are all archives of the PGP source (compressed using different archivers); these are necessary if you want to compile PGP for UNIX.

It's Not Just a Program, It's an Adventure...

At this point, it's worth mentioning that compiling a program for UNIX is not always the easiest thing in the world. (In some cases, it would be easier to build a ship in a bottle using trained termites to hoist the mast.) So, if you have a UNIX shell account and want to use PGP with it, and you are not experienced with compiling anything in UNIX, either contact your system administrator or a knowledgeable friend. For those who do have some experience compiling in UNIX, the PGP distribution isn't too hard to build. There is a documentation file included in the archive that explains what to do, and a wide number of UNIX variations are supported.

Once you've downloaded the archives, you can uncompress them on your computer and install them as per the installation instructions in the archive. Read all the documentation files, at least those pertaining to getting started at first. In the PC and UNIX versions of PGP, you control the program with command-line options—whereas the Macintosh version uses a simple graphical interface.

I'm Not a Locksmith, but I Play One on the Internet

We're going to discuss PGP specifics with the MIT PGP version in mind. (As I said, this is what most of the reading audience will be using.) Other versions may have minor variations on MIT PGP, but they also have documentation. Mac users take note: MIT's MacPGP is exactly the same as the PC and UNIX versions, except it has menu options for executing PGP commands rather than a command line. There is an output window that will display exactly the same information as the example PGP output that appears in this book.

The first thing you need to do when you use PGP is create a pair of keys for yourself. You need a *public key*, with which others can encrypt files meant for you, and you need a *private key* (or "secret" key) so you can decrypt files that were encrypted with your public key.

In the PC and UNIX versions of PGP, you create a key-pair by entering this command:

```
pgp -kg
```

The first thing you will be asked to do is to choose your key size. The bigger the key size, the more secure the key is. The flip side is that bigger keys take longer to generate. (This isn't much of a disadvantage, really, since you only need to generate a key one time.) The prudent course of action is to choose a large key size—1024 bits is considered very secure and is the best choice. Some of the other versions of PGP allow for larger keys, which you may choose to use if you wish, but keep in mind that users with versions of PGP that don't support such large keys may run into problems with your messages.

Next you'll be asked to enter a user ID for your public key. The suggested format, as the PGP program will probably tell you, is your name and your e-mail address in brackets, e.g. **Ron Popeil <rpopeil@pasta.maker.com>**. After that, you are prompted for what PGP calls a *pass phrase* (which is really a password). *Recall Chapter 6. All of it!* Everything in that chapter applies to your PGP pass phrase. A poorly chosen pass phrase can completely undermine the security that PGP encryption offers. So again, I repeat: Chapter 6, Chapter 6, Chapter 6. Read it forwards, upside down, and in the bathroom. Sleep with it (but don't tell anyone). Then enter your chosen pass phrase at the prompt. The procedure will resemble this:

```
% pgp -kg
Pretty Good Privacy(tm) 2.6.2 - Public-key encryption for the masses.
(c) 1990-1994 Philip Zimmermann, Phil's Pretty Good Software. 11 Oct 94
Uses the RSAREF(tm) Toolkit, which is copyright RSA Data Security, Inc.
Distributed by the Massachusetts Institute of Technology.
```

```
Export of this software may be restricted by the U.S. government.
Current time: 1995/04/08 19:38 GMT
Pick your RSA key size:
    1)   512 bits- Low commercial grade, fast but less secure
    2)   768 bits- High commercial grade, medium speed, good security
    3)  1024 bits- "Military" grade, slow, highest security
Choose 1, 2, or 3, or enter desired number of bits: 3
Generating an RSA key with a 1024-bit modulus.

You need a user ID for your public key.  The desired form for this user ID is
your name, followed by your E-mail address enclosed in <angle brackets>, if
you have an E-mail address.
For example:  John Q. Smith <12345.6789@compuserve.com>
Enter a user ID for your public key:
Aaron Weiss <aaron@somewhere.com>

You need a pass phrase to protect your RSA secret key.
Your pass phrase can be any sentence or phrase and may have many
words, spaces, punctuation, or any other printable characters.

Enter pass phrase:
Enter same pass phrase again:
Note that key generation is a lengthy process.

We need to generate 845 random bits.  This is done by measuring the time
intervals between your keystrokes.  Please enter some random text on your
keyboard until you hear the beep:
```

Not only does PGP offer military-grade encryption, it also burns unsightly fat! As you can see at the end of the example, after entering your pass phrase, you'll be asked to type a few hundred random characters. Close your eyes, unbraid your hair, flail with abandon at the keyboard and just feel those fingers getting slimmer—PGP will use the timing and distribution of your keystrokes to generate some random numbers that it needs. After that's done, it will begin to mold your *key-pair*. This could take awhile, especially if your computer is not a speed demon. Practice tossing Fruit Loops onto toothpicks in the meantime.

When it's done, you will have a public and a private key. Each key is stored on a *keyring*. You have two keyrings—a *secret keyring* and a *public keyring*. The secret keyring contains your secret (private) key. You may (in the future) have multiple secret keys; they would all go on this ring, should you find the need to have multiple public keys. Your public ring can contain any public keys of your own, plus the public keys of other people you communicate with. Right now, of course, you only have one key on each ring. The rings will be called "pubring.pgp" and "secring.pgp" by default and will reside in your PGP installation directory—unless you've used advanced commands to store them elsewhere. If you accidentally move the keyrings without re-defining your PGP path (the PGP User's Guide explains how to do that), it will prompt you for their location the next time it tries to use them.

Mac users can do the same as the above by choosing the menu option **Key/ Generate Key**. They'll end up seeing something like the following figure.

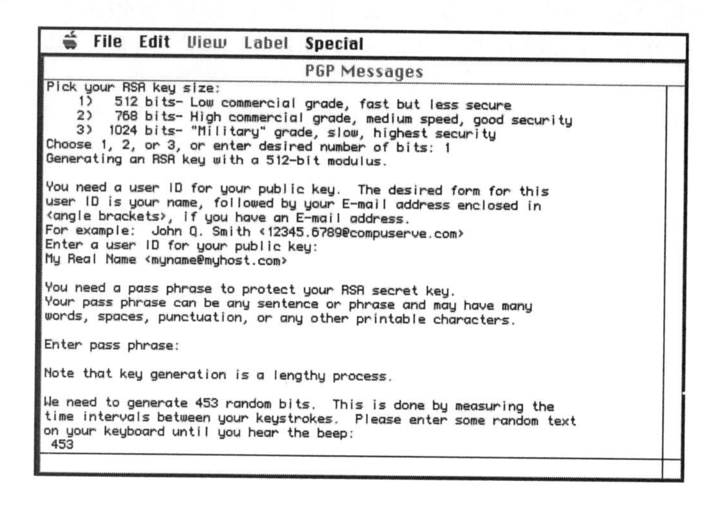

Generating a key with MacPGP. You see, it's exactly the same as PC and UNIX PGP, but with menus.

Clang Clang Clang Goes the Keyring—Key Management

You may want to add other people's keys to your ring, remove someone's key from your ring, extract keys from your ring, or digitally sign keys on your ring. All these changes you make to your original key pair are called *key management*. We're not going to go into every key-management issue (there are entire books on PGP, after all, and we don't want to steal business from them), but I want to tell you about the most important issues you'll run into most frequently.

Assuming you'll want to encrypt data for someone else, you will need their public key. And you'll need to hang their public key on your public keyring. So, first things first—how do you get someone else's public key?

The absolute best, top-of-the-heap, super-duper way to get someone's public key is to *ask him for it directly*. See, there's a big problem that's been a thorn in the side of public-key cryptography: what if a malicious individual manages to steal Joe's public key? Then, he replaces Joe's key with his own, but leaves Joe's username information in the key. An unsuspecting person might then find Joe's key available on some system, download it, and use it to encrypt a file for Joe. But it is the evildoer who would actually be able to decrypt the file, not Joe, because the forged key was unknowingly used. The problem is, if you don't get Joe's public key directly from Joe, how can you be sure that no one has tampered with it?

One way is to get Joe's public key from another trusted source other than Joe. If you trust Paul, and you got Paul's public key directly from Paul, then if Paul says he can give you Joe's public key, you could take it from Paul and ask him to sign Joe's key with his own. You could then verify that Joe's key hasn't been tampered with since trustworthy Paul signed it with his key. Confusing? Believe you me (what does that mean, anyway?), this can quickly become a nauseating spiral of verifying signature upon signature in a world of utter paranoia where nobody leaves the bathroom.

Possible solutions to this involve using *centralized public-key servers*, who would have to be "trusted" as institutions, which could sign the public keys that they disseminate. But even then, they'd have to come up with ways to prevent someone from submitting a pre-tampered key into the public server. For all these reasons, and because it's cold out, it's safest to stick with asking Joe directly for his public key.

So you've asked Joe for his public key, and he sends it to you. Great. Now, again assuming the PC or UNIX versions of PGP, you would enter this command:

```
pgp -ka keyfilename
```

In this case, *keyfilename* would be the actual filename of the public key file that Joe sent to you. PGP will then attempt to add this file to your public keyring—and in doing so, will ask you a few questions to determine what level of trust you want it to apply to the authenticity of this key. If you're not 100 percent positive of the source of the key, answer "no" to the certification question. Doing so will not prevent you from using the key. Assuming the process is successful, your public keyring will now have another public key on it, meaning you can encrypt data for that person (in this case, good ol' Joe).

Peek-A-Boo
You can check to see which keys are on your public keyring by using the **pgp -kv** command.

Mac users can use the menu option **Key/Add Key** to achieve the same results.

Armed with clanging keyrings in hand, now we can go ahead and encrypt some files. I hope you're as excited as I am.

Up One Way—Encrypting

For this example, let's imagine that you have a file called **loveletter.doc**. This file might be an inspired poem to your potential mate, bursting with images of blooming flora and profound cosmic insights into the astrology of romance. Or maybe this is a misleadingly named document that contains the closing details of the Bamberger account. There are two basic uses of PGP that you may want to apply to this file.

1. Encrypt it.

This use of PGP would encrypt the content of the file with the intended recipient's public key (which has to be on your public keyring). The recipient can decrypt the file with his or her secret key. To encrypt a file, use the command:

```
pgp -e file_to_be_encrypted recipient_userid
```

The recipient's user ID must match one of the public keys in your keyring (as you no doubt remember from earlier in this chapter). PGP searches for a *substring match* of the user ID, meaning that if you use the ID "Harry" in the command line just shown, PGP will look for the public key on your ring that contains "Harry" anywhere in the **User id** field. That means either enter the whole user ID or a unique portion of it, just in case you have multiple keys that have some of the same first or last names.

In the case of our amorous (or devious) example, let's say that we want to encrypt the file **loveletter.doc** and send it to Mary B. Wilson:

```
pgp -e loveletter.doc Wilson
```

I could have used "Mary" rather than "Wilson," but I figured that I'm more likely to have multiple users with the name Mary on my public keyring than I would the name "Wilson." Maybe not, but the point is there. After entering the command line above, the resulting encrypted file, called **loveletter.doc.pgp**, would be produced (If you're using a PC, of course, the filenames would not be so long and luxurious; they'd be short, stubby things like **lovltter.pgp**.).

Tea for One

You can encrypt a file for yourself; it doesn't have to be for someone else. After all, you have your own public key on your public keyring, too. You might encrypt a file for yourself if you would like to keep the file somewhere where you don't want anyone to be able to make heads or tails of it even if they manage to see it. In this case, however, you may want to remember to delete the original *plaintext* file after encrypting it. When encrypting the file for someone other than yourself, if you delete the original you won't be able to get it back; you can't decrypt the file made with the other party's public key. That may or may not be important in your circumstances.

2. Sign it.

Here you would use PGP to encrypt a file *and* add your digital signature, so the recipient can not only decrypt the file, but also verify that it was sent by you (and has not been modified since). Digitally signing an encrypted file just adds a little more security and confidence that the file the recipient receives is really from you.

Jargon Attack

In jazzy cryptographic street lingo, **plaintext** refers to the naked, un-encrypted form of data. Usually this "plaintext" is readable with the human eye. **Ciphertext**, on the other hand, refers to encrypted data.

Continuing with the "loveletter.doc" scenario, this time the command would be:

```
pgp -es loveletter.doc Wilson
```

Of course, this command assumes that your secret key is the first (or only) key on your secret keyring. If you have more than one secret key (from having generated multiple public/private key-pairs, for whatever reason), add **-u user_id** to the right end of the command line, replacing *user_id* with the user ID of your desired secret key. That way PGP knows which secret key of yours to sign the file with.

The resulting file will again be called the original filename, but with **.pgp** appended. The recipient of the file can decrypt the contents and verify the authenticity of the sender (you).

As mentioned, both of the above scenarios will produce new files containing encrypted versions of the original file, which may additionally be signed for authenticity or not. You can then transfer these files to the intended recipient—perhaps by copying them onto a floppy or sending them over communications lines, such as dumb terminal uploading/downloading, or FTP over a TCP/IP connection. The one special case is if you want to e-mail an encrypted file to someone, which is another story of its own— a tale that Chapter 9 will tell.

In MIT MacPGP, you can both encrypt and sign your file by selecting the menu option **File/Encrypt/Sign**. You'll be prompted with happy Mac prompts from there.

Pssst...
If you want to check the keys on your private keyring, just use the command

```
pgp -kv secring.pgp
```

(or whatever your private keyring is called, if you named it something else). Of course, these will only be your own keys, not other people's.

Down the Other—Decrypting

Decrypting files is fun and easy. In most cases, all you need to type is this command:

```
pgp filename.pgp
```

Even easier, Mac users can just click on the menu option **File/Open/Decrypt**. Of course, the file has to have been encrypted using your public key—you can't decrypt a file that was encrypted using someone else's public key (otherwise, what would be the point of all this?). PGP will find the public key used to encrypt the file, and it will try to find the complementary secret key on your secret keyring. It will tell you which secret key of yours it wants to use, and it'll ask for the appropriate pass phrase. This prevents someone who may have stolen your secret keyring from decrypting files meant for you unless they also know your pass phrase. Assuming all goes well, you'll end up with a decrypted version of the file, which you can have your way with. If the original encrypted file was signed by the sender, PGP will realize that automatically—and test the signature for authenticity. You'll be told the result of that test.

If a signature authentication fails, it might be a good idea to check with the sender before using the file, because it may well have been tampered with by some intermediate party.

Key Security

You use keys to protect your information from prying fingers, but then you have to guard your keys. It just never ends. Accepting that such is life in our modern, shiny, workaday world, there are some precautions you should take to protect your keyrings.

The rule about your secret keyring is simple: *Nobody should ever have access to it but you.* If anything, that's the cornerstone of your PGP security. It means you have to determine for yourself how close to your person you want to hold your secret keyring. Such a decision is a weighed balance of convenience versus security. If you leave your secret keyring on your Internet service provider's machine (assuming that's where your account is), it is vulnerable to attack from someone who breaks into your ISP. The password to your account and the pass phrase to your secret key are two lines of defense that even an intruder to your ISP would have to break through to make use of your secret keys. If you have well-chosen passwords in both cases, your secret key has a reasonable amount of security residing in your account. But it's far from complete.

Keeping your secret keyring on the computer you physically use is better, taking note of the routes outsiders may have into your computer, such as were flushed out in Chapter 5. Even more secure would be to keep your secret keyring on a floppy disk you carried around with you, as long as you don't risk losing it somewhere. As you can imagine, each of these increased levels of keyring security bring more inconvenience insofar as using the secret keyring goes. If, for example, you use a remote UNIX account and you keep your secret keyring on a floppy, you would have to upload the keyring to your account each time you need to use it—*and* remember to delete it from the account before you log out. If you keep the keyring in your account, then it's always there for you when you need it. Ultimately it's a personal decision based on your security needs. Personally, if I send encrypted e-mail and files mostly to friends, I'd probably keep my secret keyring in my account while making sure I have my account protected in every other way (Chapter 6 and Chapters 13–15). On the other hand, if I worked for Coca-Cola and had the secret formula encrypted in a file, I'd take more severe precautions.

You may also consider making backup copies of your secret keyring and storing them somewhere safe. Consider: If you lose your secret keyring somehow, well, it's a bad, *bad* scene. Even if no one stole it, your public key is rendered useless—and if it's been widely disseminated, you'll have to get word out somehow and propagate a new public key.

As far as your public key itself goes, you do want it to be publicly known. But you don't want it to be tampered with. For one thing, this means to give your public key to those who you want to have it firsthand, so that it goes directly from you to them. Secondly, protect your public and private keyrings in the same way as described in the paragraph above.

PGP is a very complex topic, and there are many more detailed issues which you may choose to learn about. At the least, a thorough reading of the "PGP User's Guide Volume I" will explain everything in this chapter and more. Better yet, it's included in the PGP distribution archive, so there's no excuse *not* to read it!

The Least You Need to Know

Do you want to encrypt your data? Sure, we all do! That's where PGP comes in, by far the most widely used form of encryption-for-the-masses you'll find on the Internet. When used properly, PGP can offer you massively secure encryption, such that it's essentially unbreakable. When used improperly, PGP can offer a false sense of security, leaving you vulnerable.

- If you are in the United States or Canada, you want the MIT version of PGP for individual, non-commercial use. For commercial use in the United States and Canada, you'll need to get ViaCrypt, which is a commercial product.
- Readers in other countries can use the unofficial "PGP international," which is currently available as two different packages—PGP 2.6.i and PGP 2.6ui.
- Create a public and secret key-pair for yourself with the command **pgp -kg**. The result will be two keyrings, one public and one secret, with one key on each at first.
- The safest way to get another person's public key is to ask the person directly for it.
- In an effort to protect your keys and keyrings, choose good pass phrases, take care about where you store the keyring files, don't give anyone your secret key(ring), and keep a backup copy of your public keyring somewhere safe. Don't accept public keys from untrusted sources.

Chapter 9

Intermediate PGP: Encrypting E-mail

In This Chapter

- Coaxing PGP to befriend e-mail
- Including PGP-encrypted e-mail in PINE and Eudora
- Sending and receiving public keys via e-mail securely
- Receiving PGP-mail with a smile

Perhaps the most common usage of PGP is to send and receive encrypted e-mail. The e-mail may consist of encrypted messages or missives, or used as a way to transport other types of files. In any case, encrypted e-mail is the strongest antidote to prying eyes. There are a few ways to combine PGP and e-mail, some quick-and-dirty, others more elegant. We'll look at some of them in this chapter, and learn how to bake a perfect cookie, too.

Marrying PGP and E-mail (and Getting Them to Consummate)

One of the limitations of e-mail is that it can only handle ASCII characters. In short, that basically means the set of printable characters you could type on your keyboard. But some files use "binary" format, which can represent more data than ASCII. Examples of binary files include executable programs, saved word processor documents (unless you

Marcel Marceau Never Had It So Good

There is a new and upcoming form of e-mail which is called *MIME*. If your e-mailer supports adding a *MIME attachment*, you could insert a binary file into your e-mail without the ASCII restrictions outlined. However, the receiving party must also be able to read MIME attachments. If you are sure that both parties can handle MIME, then you could disregard most of the rest of this section and just attach your PGP-encrypted binary files to your e-mail. But many users on many systems still cannot handle MIME, so it shouldn't be assumed.

specifically saved them as ASCII), graphic images, and (not coincidentally) PGP-encrypted files. If you try to insert a binary file into the body of an e-mail message, you'll probably just get a lot of junk, and so will the recipient. It will be unusable. So, the files that were produced when you used the "pgp -e" command in the previous chapter cannot be inserted directly into an e-mail message.

One solution to this problem is to tell PGP to output the encrypted file in ASCII format rather than binary. You can do this by adding an "a" to just about any switch combination on the PGP command line. In other words:

```
pgp -e loveletter.doc Wilson
```

would become

```
pgp -ea loveletter.doc Wilson
```

Rather than resulting in a file called "loveletter.doc.pgp" (as was the result in Chapter 8) you would get **loveletter.doc.asc**. This ASCII file is suitable for inserting directly into the body of an e-mail message or in a Usenet posting. Of course, MS-DOS users should keep in mind that their file names cannot be as long as those I'm using as examples, which UNIX and Windows 95 do allow. Macintosh folk should click on the option **Options/ASCII Output** so that the check mark is on. This will tell subsequent PGP operations to produce ASCII output in the same way as the command-line examples in this chapter.

What is "inserting directly into the body of an e-mail message?" Some e-mail applications give you the option of inserting a file in the place where you would type the message. Additionally, many offer the option to "attach" a file. Our two prototypical e-mail applications in this book will be PINE for UNIX and Eudora for the PC and Mac. Having said that, let's first consider PINE.

PINE offers you two options for inserting a file into an e-mail message. If you are in the message-body-editing area (below the "Message Text" divider on the "Compose Message" screen), hitting **Ctrl+R** should bring up a prompt asking you what file to insert. Once you enter the filename, it will plop right into the message—and look something like the figure that follows.

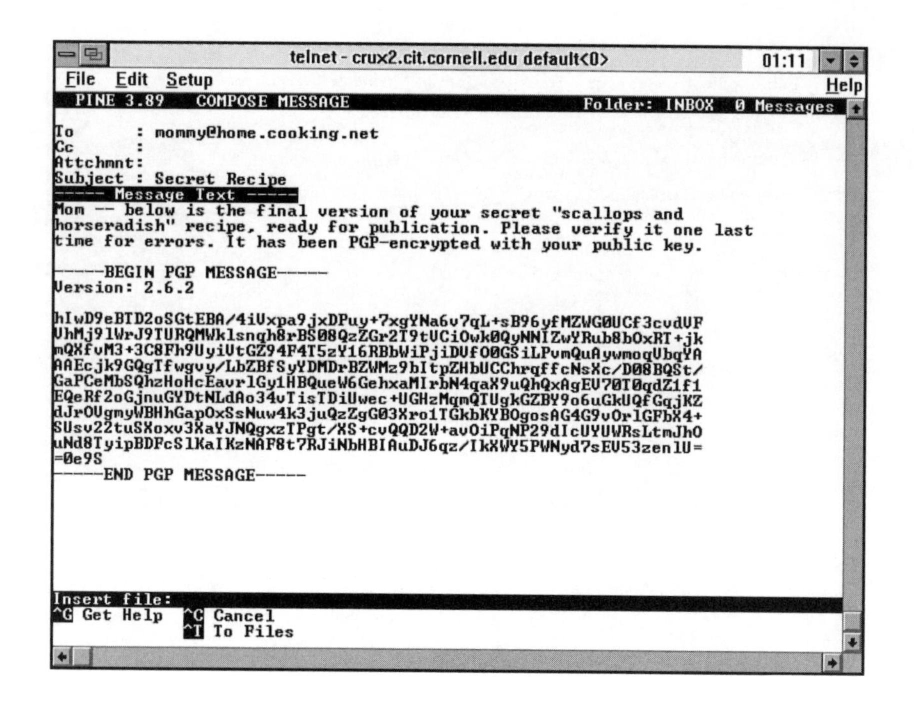

PINE, running in UNIX, with an ASCII PGP-encrypted document inserted into the message body.

Alternatively, at the top of the Compose Message screen there are some header entries, and one is called **Attchmnt:**. If you hit **Ctrl+J**, you'll get a prompt for the filename to attach to your message. Note that if you attach a file, it won't appear in the main body of the message (as in the Ctrl+R example). Rather, the recipient will have to specify that they want to view or save the attachment before they can actually read it.

Eudora users face a similar situation. With Eudora you can attach a file using the **Message/Attach Document** menu option, or **Ctrl+H**. A file dialog box will appear; from it you can choose the file you want to attach (in this case, you want the ".ASC" file that the "pgp -ea" command produced). In Eudora, there is no elegant way to insert a file directly into your message. You could bring up the text file in a window, either with some other text editor (such as Windows Notepad) or with Eudora's own **File/Open Text File** menu option, and then select and copy it to the Clipboard and paste it directly into the message body. This is fine for small files, but for larger ones it's a bit awkward.

Here's a lovely, candid figure of Eudora with a PGP .ASC file attached.

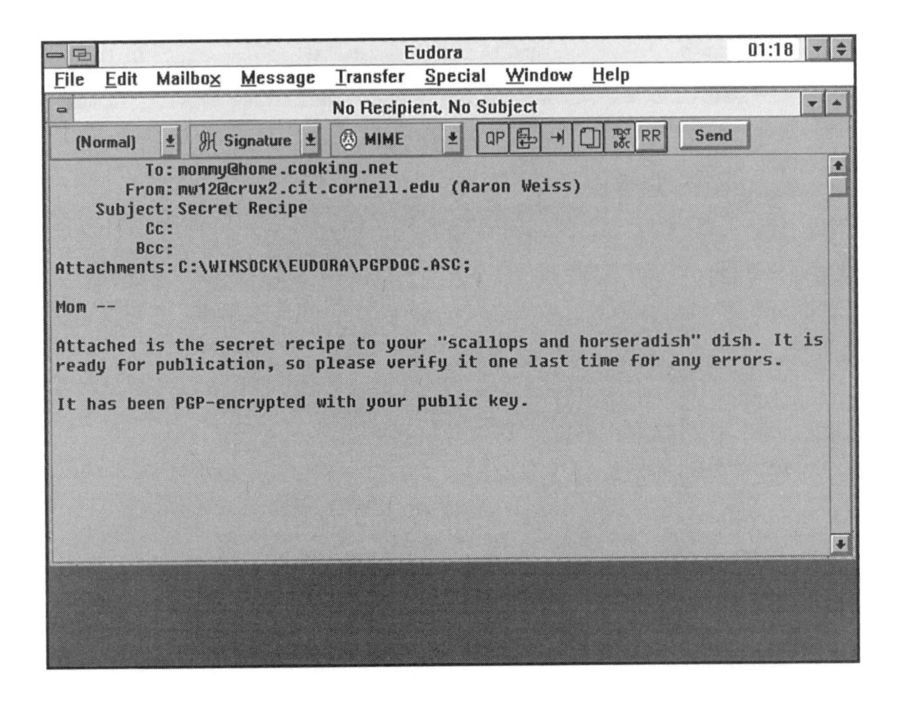

Eudora with a brief note in the message body, and an ASCII PGP-encrypted file listed as an attachment.

It's CLEARly from Me

It's also possible that you don't want to encrypt the content of a message, but you would like some way to prove that it was you who sent the message. Is that what you want? It's always something, isn't it? Gimme, gimme, gimme, that's all I ever hear! Ahem—sorry, a little tense over here. Well, you can create a plaintext document with an ASCII version of your digital signature appended to the end of it, and then include the whole tamale in e-mail.

Using PGP, the command is

```
pgp -sta filename
```

where *filename* is the name of the ASCII file you want to include in an e-mail message. The result is a file named ***filename*.asc**. In this case, "filename.asc" will be the original contents of "filename" with an ASCII version of your digital signature appended to it. Let's take a hard, tangible, visceral example:

You want to send the following message to Mary Wilson (and you've already saved it in the file **noloan**):

```
Dear Ms. Wilson,

I regret to inform you that your loan application has been denied. We simply
could not justify the outlay of your requested funds based upon your earnings
as a juggling tomato street performer. You may have to learn to live in the
woods and speak to animals for survival. I apologize for any inconvenience.

Sincerely,
Mr. Mercy
Neverloan Bank of North America
```

You don't want to encrypt the message, but you do want Mary to be able to verify that it was from you and not from some joker, and that the message hasn't been forged or altered.

Using PGP, enter the command

```
pgp -sta noloan
```

You'll be prompted to enter the pass phrase for your secret key. After that, a file will be created called **noloan.asc**. The file looks like this:

```
-----BEGIN PGP SIGNED MESSAGE-----

Dear Ms. Wilson,

I regret to inform you that your loan application has been denied. We simply
could not justify the outlay of your requested amount based upon your earnings
as a juggling tomato street performer. You may have to learn to live in the
woods and speak to animals for survival. I apologize for any inconvenience.

Sincerely,
Mr. Mercy
Neverloan Bank of North America
```

```
-----BEGIN PGP SIGNATURE-----
Version: 2.6.2

iQCVAwUBL4K9yhbZ40TFh0A1AQEqdQP+P84bSWChX8xG4Z5rKht3VZ00ZQ8ueL77
CjjDwd7jmZJG1n6tzNbXoOAIECPbddISQEtLmwqIBmRXhRHtVbir7DYBUppUOLV2
3xZsA8LwNP3M/L43cfZSfz6SRsSjDyHFzg/SpojuwS2+sS/svir6pnRRFA15HI+0
UI0imPm7JGo=
=fX8K
-----END PGP SIGNATURE-----
```

This file could be plopped into an e-mail message, either directly into the body or as an attachment. The recipient can read the message without decrypting it, and can choose whether or not they wish to verify its origin by checking the signature with their version of PGP. Note, however, that the recipient must have your public key on their public keyring to verify your digital signature. If they don't already have it, you may want to e-mail someone your public key as well.

How Do I Do That? E-mail Someone My Public Key, That Is

Well, the first thing you need to do is extract an ASCII version of your public key from your public keyring. Believe it or don't, there's a command for that, too! Here ye:

```
pgp -kxa your_userid
```

This will spit out a file called ***your_userid*.asc**. In English, now, if the username you gave to your key-pair was "Joe Q. User <joeq@generic.com>," then you might use the command

```
pgp -kxa Joe
```

to extract your public key (assuming "Joe" is unique to that key, otherwise use some other portion of the whole phrase). The file "Joe.asc" will result, and it might go a little something like this ("gimme a beat..."):

```
-----BEGIN PGP PUBLIC KEY BLOCK-----
Version: 2.6.2

mQCNAy+BdJAAAAEEAMh45CBMYJ+Wm6a+jhzrnvPtfj6n1uwhdfWMAwhe+367YF2i
02Kf5/SwthIgs2Y6/p/02Cztf5CfJa30TjvrIcmc0qIUDvb4jUXnteTkzbTBEqFU
bw+UJxWLGySnN4JPz41/yDHPG2K2yz7R3CQSkvw1pfDMy8eivhbZ40TFh0A1AAUR
tAZXZWlzcyA=
=ZAMN
-----END PGP PUBLIC KEY BLOCK-----
```

You may then insert that file into an e-mail message and send it off to someone, and he can add it to his public key ring.

WARNING! There's another security issue at hand, thankfully, since that's the raison d'être ("raisin of the tree" in English) of this tome anyway. What if someone intercepts your e-mail message containing your public key? Remember that you don't necessarily want to hide your public key from dissemination, but you *do* want to protect it from tampering. If someone got hold of your e-mailed public key, he might be able to alter it in such a way that you can't decrypt information encrypted with it, and *he* can. One possible solution to this problem—and I warn you, this is twisted—is to encrypt your public key using the recipient's public key before e-mailing it to them. Recalling the example given earlier, you want to send Mary your public key so she can verify your signature in the previous letter. Assuming you have Mary's public key on your keyring, you can encrypt your ASCII public key with it, like this:

```
pgp -ea Joe.asc Mary -o joemary.asc
```

Normally PGP would call the ASCII output of an encryption ".asc," but you are encrypting a file that already has the extension ".asc"—so we put the **-o** option in the line above, which specifies a different filename for the result file. If we left off the -o, PGP would recognize that Joe.asc already exists, and ask whether we want to overwrite it or enter an alternate filename.

In our example, the result would be a file called "joemary.asc," and it'd resemble this:


```
-----BEGIN PGP MESSAGE-----
Version: 2.6.2

hIwDPT42gZCBxD0BA/48OTyA0taFsUzSbHDMvfIHpBSrqcRZJ5Zwhd7ZQMEM28KN
UNa2Xo5dFAL0J+GcgKJSDrC2jTrI2eLjBuK1WD6BIpGr8CsXp9nwf3ofWh39O6u8
Kj+W8S53tcvmzUMr3b+kfOlaJLQcJfgS8zQqAJuGQdSy8VOhXaPXTLcJsFkU8aYA
AAETS9DG1KS8g1LN1lSXxIGr0TGJ3/5Zowi2UjizboGq6y7hHjLR0AWBT1ZNKkit
Otx9gXBN269ClQcTR81pZp0N6mCR0DOGPkyPaRSDvp/ii4L6apSv+x6kIrkwf606
6oTnRZfz6KaSLuO0YSz5cYVrcv2ZtKJZFyV31kSZBwIT5lbLU00DdcCIUKwBkDYe
zciltrVRdJKnMy7rVpcy4Vv6Fb+1Ipf4+I3p/2iF4jm1v9ds8D+0/nIP1oi5WqIK
QVycm0abR+T4G/AlgYhd7JQxJZufxibtKTyGYWz6aMSZuSc1obvAuA5G8l//Lr/1
u3/Opmzdwn+XGIuvyJDQU5rUFYai/seqdSiglLyAcmht8IwQYG8=
=JBuF
-----END PGP MESSAGE-----
```


When Mary receives this file, she can decrypt it; she'll end up with the ASCII version of Joe's public key, which she can then add to her public keyring (which will be addressed later in this chapter), and verify the loan rejection letter.

The catch-22 in all of this is: What if you don't know Mary's public key? If neither party knows the other's public key, then you have a classic chicken-and-egg situation (it's the egg, by the way, which even a cursory understanding of evolution should make obvious). The only real answer to this problem is that one of you will have to pass on your public key via a means that is as secure as your concern warrants. You could meet in person, you could hide the public key in some other larger text file so it's not obvious to a quick snooper, or you could print it out and send it in the mail. I'm not saying these options are all of equal security, but it depends on your needs. At the *least* secure end, send the first public key in an unencrypted e-mail message. At the other extreme, meet face-to-face and hand over a floppy disk with the keyfile.

Road Test—Sending Some PGP-Mail

We used to sit through an hour and a half of chemistry lectures, where the professor would go on and on about methane, right-handedness, and how benzene can destroy DNA. Those are the three things I remember from two semesters of theorizing and blackboard scribblings. So it might be a good idea to take everything from the first portion of this chapter and *apply* it. That's right—lab! We're going to go through one entire titration, er, I mean *procedure*, from preparing a document to encrypting it and e-mailing it. No safety films, but you can wear goggles if you want.

As in the earlier part of this chapter, we'll look at PINE for UNIX users and Eudora for PC/Mac users. Alternative e-mail applications will have very similar options; and the basic procedure will be the same, even if some menu options may be different.

The scenario: You want to send an e-mail to your supervisor with the details of a product proposal. The message has to be encrypted, because you do not want any leaks. The message has to be digitally signed, so that your supervisor can be certain that it was from you and was not modified in any way by an intercepting party.

First, you open up your document editor and type the message. You can use any application you want to create the document. If the resulting document will not be in ASCII format—for example, if you save it in Microsoft Word 6.0 format—be sure that your supervisor can read a file in that format. It doesn't really matter what format the document is in, as long as the receiving party can read it. In this example, you'll type the message in ASCII form using a simple text editor:

```
Dear Mr. Ogre,

The following is a proposal for a new type of product that I believe will
make our company big, heaping truckloads of money. The product is tentatively
```

```
titled "The Amazing Alchemist." With it, we can convert any inorganic com-
pound into gold. I am very excited about the prospects of this product; I am
sure you are, as well. The inventor suggests that we may even decide not to
market the product, but rather to "re-invest" it and turn our entire facility
into gold. We would have nowhere to sit, but we'd be rich! Filthy rich!

I hope you consider the proposal below, and reply with your usual insight and
ambiguity.

Excitedly but Professionally,
Mort
```

This message is saved to the file "proposal.doc". You already have Mr. Ogre's PGP public key on your public keyring, because he gave each of his employees a floppy disk with the file, and you added it to your keyring using the command **pgp -ka ogre.pgp**.

Next, you want to encrypt the file with Mr. Ogre's public key and sign it based on your secret key:

```
pgp -esa proposal.doc Ogre
```

You will be prompted to enter a pass phrase for your secret key:

```
A secret key is required to make a signature.
You specified no user ID to select your secret key,
so the default user ID and key will be the most recently
added key on your secret keyring.

You need a pass phrase to unlock your RSA secret key.
Key for user ID "Mort"

Enter pass phrase:
```

Here you enter your pass phrase, which you initially chose when creating your key-pair with the command **pgp -kg**.

Assuming you enter your pass phrase correctly, you will then see something like this:

```
Enter pass phrase: Pass phrase is good.
Key for user ID: Mort
1024-bit key, Key ID C5874035, created 1995/04/04
Just a moment....
```

```
Recipients' public key(s) will be used to encrypt.
Key for user ID: Phillip Ogre<phogre@yoyo.com>
1024-bit key, Key ID 6A121AD1, created 1994/01/01
.
Transport armor file: proposal.doc.asc
```

As you can see in the line just above, the output file is called *proposal.doc.asc*. It is an ASCII file that can be transported in e-mail (that's what they mean by "armor"). This file contains both the encrypted message and your digital signature.

Because Mr. Ogre needs to verify your signature, he needs your public key. So you have to package you public key to transport to him, as well. Remember that you don't have to do this if the intended recipient already has your public key.

First you'll have to extract your public key from your public keyring, in an ASCII format:

```
pgp -kxa Mort
```

You'll then be asked for a filename in which to store your ASCII public key. PGP will automatically add ".asc" to the end of whatever filename you tell it. In this example, you told it "mortkey" and so the file mortkey.asc is produced and contains your public key.

Unfortunately, if you e-mailed mortkey.asc to Mr. Ogre in its current form, someone could intercept it and tamper with it. They may prevent you from being able to decrypt messages that Mr. Ogre sends to you based on this public key, or they may even allow themselves to decrypt Mr. Ogre's messages to you. To prevent this catastrophe, you should encrypt your public key with Mr. Ogre's public key before sending it to Mr. Ogre:

```
pgp -ea mortkey.asc Ogre -o mortpgp.asc
```

This will result in a new file, called *mortpgp.asc*, which contains the encrypted version of your public key suitable for decryption by Mr. Ogre. You can, of course, call these files anything you want and manage them as per the level of security that you want. For example, if you are not keeping any keyrings on the same machine that you run PGP on, remember to delete these files after using them.

At this point, you have two files ready for e-mailing: *proposal.doc.asc*, which is the encrypted and signed message, and *mortpgp.asc*, which is an encrypted version of your public key. First, you'll e-mail mortpgp.asc, since Mr. Ogre needs to put your public key on his public keyring before he can verify your signature in proposal.doc.asc.

Using the PINE e-mail program, you'd hit **C** to get to the "Compose Message" screen, and then enter the appropriate information to send an e-mail message to Mr. Ogre. It's up to you whether you want to include your encrypted public key (mortpgp.asc) as an attachment or in the body of the message. For illustration purposes, let's say you include it in the body of the message by hitting **Ctrl-r** when the cursor is in the message editing area (below the `----- Message Text -----` line.) You'll be prompted for a filename. You may have to enter the full path to the file—for example, if mortpgp.asc is in your pgp directory in your UNIX account, you might enter the path **~mort/pgp/mortpgp.asc** (if your username is "mort"). If you can't remember the full path, hitting **Ctrl-t** at the filename prompt will bring you to a screen with all your files and you can move a highlight bar around and find it. Having done all that, you will be staring at a screen that resembles this:

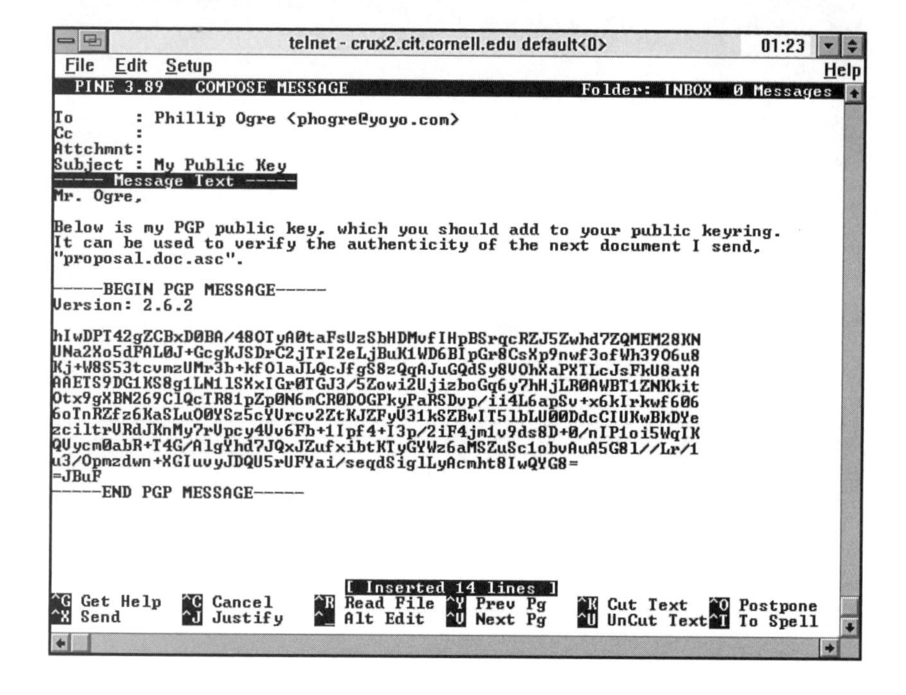

Composing a message in PINE to Mr. Ogre, with a brief note and an ASCII PGP-encrypted version of Mort's PGP public key inserted into the message body.

Send that e-mail off with **Ctrl-x**, and that's that. Your encrypted public key is on its way to Mr. Ogre.

For users of Eudora, the process is conceptually similar. Launch Eudora and begin a new message by choosing the menu option **Message/New Message** or hitting **Ctrl-N.** Address the e-mail to Mr. Ogre. Instead of inserting the message into the body of the message as in the PINE example, you'll use an attachment with Eudora. Do this by choosing the menu option **Message/Attach Document** or by hitting **Ctrl-H**. You can then navigate the file requestor to find the file to attach, in this case, mortpgp.asc. You may want to enter a brief note in the message body just letting Mr. Ogre know what this attachment he's receiving is all about. Such as in this artist's rendering:

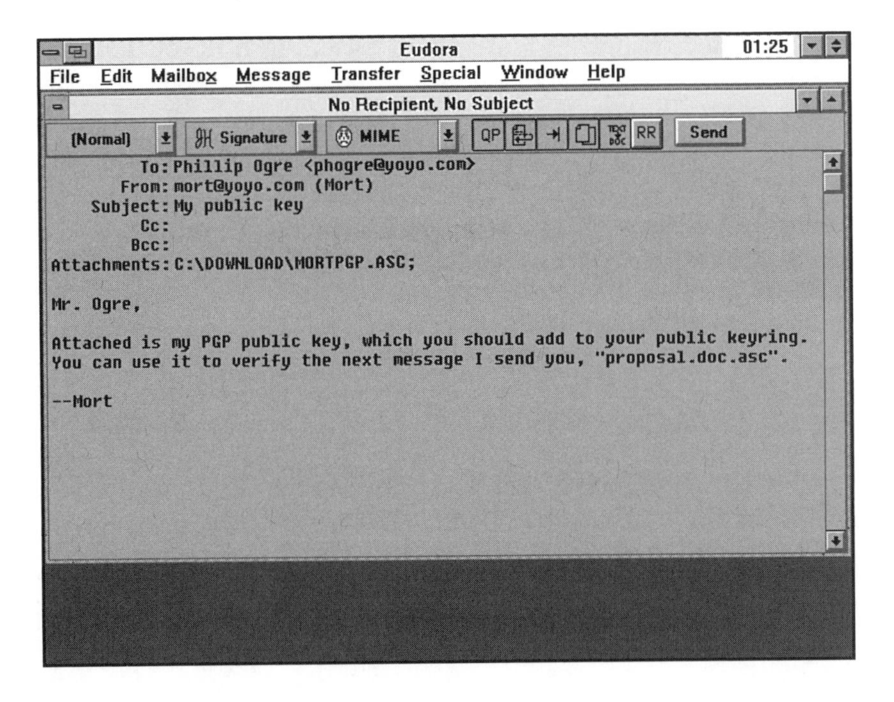

Eudora e-mail composed to Mr. Ogre, with the ASCII PGP-encrypted version of Mort's PGP public key attached, and a brief note in the message body.

Click the **Send** button and Mr. Ogre will receive his lovely package shortly.

The next step, of course, is to send the actual message. If you remember, the file *proposal.doc.asc* contains your proposal, encrypted with Mr. Ogre's public key and digitally signed by you. Not to sound skimpy, but just do the same thing you did before. That is, whether you use PINE or Eudora, open up a new e-mail message, address it to Mr. Ogre, and either insert or attach the file proposal.doc.asc. Users of MS-DOS and Windows (versions earlier than Windows 95) should keep in mind that in your case the file wouldn't have such a long filename, it'd have to be something shorter like propdoc.asc.

Send off that e-mail message, and Mr. Ogre will be receiving his second little gift shortly.

While We're At It—Receiving Some PGP-mail

Remember when Snoopy would play tennis with himself? He'd serve the ball and then run around to the other side of the net to return it. Well, we're going to do the same thing. Now you're Mr. Ogre, receiving the PGP-mail that was just sent to you, by you.

So, there you are sitting at your desk, making rubber-band pagodas, when you hear the "You have new mail" beep (if you don't have such a beep, get one; there's no better feeling in life). The first message, you notice, is from Mort, and it says something about his public key being encrypted with your public key. The first step, then, is to get Mort's public key onto your public keyring.

The message that Mort sent needs to be saved into a file for PGP to work with. In PINE, you would use the "v" key to "View Attachment." Even if Mort didn't send the public key as an attachment, PINE considers the regular body of the e-mail to be attachment one. PINE will ask you which attachment to view, along with a list of attachments. Usually you'll be choosing one or two. Then PINE will ask if you want to view or save the attachment, to which you'll hit "s" for Save and then enter a filename. Voilá. You probably want to delete the e-mail message containing Mort's public key, but not just yet in case the save didn't work for some reason.

If you're a Eudora-head, the situation is only slightly different. If the encrypted file is in the body of the message that you received, just choose the menu option **File/Save As** and save the e-mail into a file. In this case, we'll call that file *mortpgp.asc*. If you have Eudora's configuration (**Special/Configuration**) set to auto-receive attachments *and* if Mort sent the message as an attachment, it will automatically be saved rather than appear in the incoming message window. Either way, we're making believe that you saved Mort's first e-mail as the file *mortpgp.asc*.

Mort's second e-mail has also come in. This one contains the encrypted and signed proposal. So, you want to do the same thing as above—save it into a file. For our example, we'll call it propdoc.asc (keeping it short for poor MS-DOS/Windows users).

Now you've got two files: mortpgp.asc, which is Mort's public key encrypted with your public key, and propdoc.asc, which is Mort's proposal encrypted with your public key and signed by Mort.

Moving into your PGP directory, use this command:

```
pgp -ka mortpgp.asc
```

to add Mort's public key to your public keyring. You'll be prompted to answer some questions determining your level of confidence in the authenticity of Mort's public key. If you are positive that it is Mort's key from Mort, answer yes to the questions; otherwise say no. Saying no will not impair your ability to use the key, but it will affect how much PGP trusts the key for future operations, such as if you received another key that was signed by Mort's key from someone else.

Mort's public key should now be on your keyring. You can check by using the command **pgp -kv**, which will list the keys on your public keyring.

Having done all of this, the last step is simply to decrypt and verify the propdoc.asc file. This is relatively easy:

```
pgp propdoc.asc
```

You'll be prompted to enter your secret key pass phrase, because you need to use your secret key to decrypt this message (since it was encrypted with your public key). Once you've done that, you should see output bearing a remarkable resemblance to:

```
Pass phrase is good.  Just a moment......
File has signature.  Public key is required to check signature. .
Good signature from user "Ogre".
Signature made 1995/04/06 00:30 GMT

Plaintext filename: propdoc
```

Notice in the output above that PGP automatically recognizes that the file has a digital signature. It looks for the public key of the signator, finds it, and reports that the signature is "good." That means that Mort was the originator of the file, as much as you trust Mort as the originator of his public key. And it means that the file was not modified in any way since the signature was applied to it. Lastly, you're told the "plaintext filename" is "propdoc," which just means that the file "propdoc" was produced which contains the original, unencrypted message from Mort containing the Amazing Alchemist proposal. *Trés bien!*

Our lab period is now over for the day. The above should have you sending and receiving PGP-mail and public keys with the ease and grace of a duck sliding across a frozen pond on its head.

The Least You Need to Know

This was a very detailed chapter, don't you know. You should read the whole thing when it comes to something as important as proper encryption, rather than solely relying on a quick summary here at the end. In spite of that and due to contractual obligations, I offer the following encapsulation:

- ASCII-based e-mail is still the standard today, even though it has some limitations in the face of modern communications. For that reason, it's good practice to PGP encrypt files into ASCII format for easy e-mailing.
- **pgp -sta *filename*** will put a digital signature onto *filename* but leave the contents of *filename* unencrypted in the file *filename.asc.*
- **pgp -ea *filename user_id*** can be used to encrypt *filename* for *user_id* using *user_id's* public key, resulting in an ASCII file called *filename.asc* that is suitable for e-mail.
- **pgp -kxa *your_id*** can be used to extract your public key into an ASCII file called *your_id.asc,* which is suitable for e-mail.
- **pgp -ka *keyfile*** adds the public key contained in *keyfile* to your public keyring.
- **pgp *filename.asc*** tells PGP to try to decrypt the contents of *filename* and verify the signature if present, resulting in *filename,* which is exactly the same as the original file before it was encrypted.
- Whenever possible, before sending a public key through e-mail, encrypt it with the intended recipient's public key to prevent any tampering along the way.

Chapter 10

E-mail: The Rest of the Story

In This Chapter

- E-mail—the frequent flier
- Don't be fooled by the forger
- Taking anony-moose e-mail by the antlers
- Peek-a-boo e-mail
- There's safety in storage

In earlier chapters, we've touched on the subject of e-mail from this angle and that. We looked briefly at whether a third party could intercept and/or read e-mail. Most recently, we've been encrypting e-mail as if in some old World War II film (conserve rubber!). Now we'll stop skirting around the issue and take a brutal, hard, antagonistic look at e-mail, with all of the depth and integrity of a prime-time newsmagazine broadcast.

It Gets Around

In a lot of ways, the analogy between the real-world postal service and e-mail is accurate. When you drop off a letter in the mailbox, the mailman (mailPERSON) doesn't take your letter and drive straight to the destination address and stick it in their mailbox. What the mailPERSON does is take it to the nearest post office building. From there it will get sorted, put on a plane or truck, and transported to another predetermined post office—until it reaches the office serving the destination of the addressee (or falls behind a cabinet, not to be found for 30 years). Replace the post offices with computers, replace the postal workers with computer programs, get rid of that cryptic U.S. Eagle logo that took me ten years to figure out what it was, and you've got the basic mechanism of e-mail transport and delivery.

Your e-mail hits a number of different computers along the way to its ultimate destination. There are several possible places along the e-mail pipeline that a nosy person could conceivably intercept your e-mail. First, there's your host computer itself. The administrator of your ISP's host computer—*or* someone who has attained that status illicitly (such as a hacker)—could get hold of your outgoing (or incoming) e-mail. So could the administrator (or illicit imposter thereof) who runs a computer that passes your e-mail along its way. Finally, any of three people could grab at your sent e-mail once it gets where it's going: the person with admin status at the destination computer, the aforementioned imposter admin, *or* someone who has broken into your intended recipient's account. Now, this isn't to say that it happens frequently, even with all those potential snoopers. As with all matters of spying, it's more likely to happen if someone has a particular interest in your communications; the random snoop is rare.

Fortunately, this e-mail vulnerability is very easy to circumvent. Ever hear of Chapter 7? 8? 9, maybe? Exactly—encryption. The security issue just described is one of the major reasons we went into so much detail (in Chapter 9) about e-mail encryption. If your e-mail is properly encrypted, a voyeur could stare at it all day, fondle it, manipulate it, whatever, but he's not going to be able to read it. Furthermore (and this is the real beauty of it), if you use digital signatures along with encryption, even if the interloper chose to mangle it, the receiving party would know it was modified and could simply trash it and ask you for another copy.

The Good, the Bad, and the Forged

Sometimes someone will try to play a trick on you and send some e-mail as if he was someone else. A clever person may disguise the message as if it were from another person you know. A less clever person may, in their own self-perceived burst of wit, forge the e-mail to appear as if it came from some impossible place (like *god@heaven.org*, one of the more popular—and less clever—forges).

At the top of an e-mail message there is a bunch of junk which is properly called a *header*. The header contains all sorts of information about that e-mail message. Many e-mail applications only show you the interesting parts of the header unless you ask to see the whole thing. If you're not really positive that an e-mail message came from the person it claims to be from, it might prove useful to take a look at the full header information. By default, you are presented with the following header information by programs such as PINE or Eudora:

```
Date: Wed, 5 Apr 1995 20:26:05 -0400 (EDT)
From: Richard M. Nixon <rmnix@iamnot.acrook.com>
Subject: Re: Trip to See the Big Ball of String Cancelled
To: scc3@cornell.edu (Steven C Caro)
Cc: cjd2@crux2.cit.cornell.edu (Christian J Doucette), elliotw@netusa.net
(Elliot Weiss)
```

While the above gives you the essentials for reading everyday e-mail, it's not enough to launch an investigation. In the case of the example just given, we're a bit suspicious of this message, because it's unlikely—for more than one reason—that we would receive e-mail from Mr. Nixon. So the inquiry begins: both PINE and Eudora allow you to see the full header if you so desire. In PINE, just hit **h** while reading the message. In Eudora, click on the little box that says **Blah Blah Blah** (which is just to the left of the Subject: line), or select **Show All Headers** within **Special/Switches**. Doing any of these will yield a full header, which, in the case above, would look like:

```
Received: from cornell.edu (cornell.edu [132.236.56.6]) by
postoffice2.mail.cornell.edu (8.6.9/8.6.9) with SMTP id MAA20266 for
<scc3@postoffice2.mail.cornell.edu>; Thu, 6 Apr 1995 12:11:02 -0400
Received: (from daemon@localhost) by cornell.edu (8.6.9/8.6.9) id MAA29751
for scc3@postoffice2.mail.cornell.edu; Thu, 6 Apr 1995 12:11:01 -0400
Received: from crux2.cit.cornell.edu (mw12@CRUX2.CIT.CORNELL.EDU
[128.253.232.64]) by cornell.edu (8.6.9/8.6.9) with SMTP id MAA29727 for
<scc3@cornell.edu>; Thu, 6 Apr 1995 12:10:58 -0400
Received: by crux2.cit.cornell.edu (5.65/2.0)
     id AA10947; Thu, 6 Apr 1995 12:10:37 -0400
Date: Thu, 6 Apr 1995 12:10:35 -0400 (EDT)
X-PH: V4.1@cornell.edu (Cornell Modified)
From: Richard M. Nixon <rmnix@iamnot.acrook.com>
Subject: Re: Trip to see the Big Ball of String Cancelled
To: Steven C Caro <scc3@cornell.edu>
Cc: Christian J Doucette <cjd2@crux2.cit.cornell.edu>,
Elliot Weiss <elliotw@netusa.net>
Message-Id: <Pine.3.89.9504061230.A10896-0100000@crux2.cit.cornell.edu>
Mime-Version: 1.0
Content-Type: TEXT/PLAIN; charset=US-ASCII
```

What a mess, huh? Most of the junk at the top is a description of the message IDs that were assigned to the e-mail and the computers that it was sent from and intended for. It's useful junk, though. All of the above is called the *header*, but we're especially interested in the portion above the "From" line. We can trace the path of the e-mail: the header lines report, in order from top to bottom, the path of the computers that the e-mail traveled through. The topmost line reports the final hop taken to get to the recipient's actual mailbox—in this case, the e-mail recipient is Steven C. Caro (**scc3@cornell.edu**), and his mailbox is **postoffice2.mail.cornell.edu**. As you work your way down the header lines, you can trace the e-mail's journey backward to the originating machine and (possibly) user.

We can summarize much of the above by saying the e-mail was received by **postoffice2.mail.cornell.edu**, which got it from **cornell.edu**, which got it from **crux2.cit.cornell.edu**. Furthermore, you can see that in a couple of places it even notes the username of the person who originated the message: **mw12@crux2.cit.cornell.edu**. Clearly, this does not agree with the username reported in the "From" line. Something smells funny, and it's not lunch. The jig is up—this e-mail was sent by **mw12@crux2.cornell.edu** and not **rmnix@iamnot.acrook.com**.

Many a quick forgery can be traced this way, because most forgers only alter the information that appears in the "From:" line that you normally see.

Two Accounts Are Better Than One

It only makes sense that when you send e-mail or reply to it, the recipient then knows your e-mail address. There are a variety of circumstances under which you may not want others to know your "real" e-mail address, but you still want to communicate with them.

One obvious way to get around this dilemma—related to something we talked about way back in Chapter 2—is anonymous e-mail. That's a good solution for many situations, and the next section will explore it in detail. Sometimes, however, you may not want to be "anonymous"—you just don't want someone to know your private e-mail address. It's sort of like having two phone lines. There's one that the public knows and that you don't answer, but rather just take messages on. Then there's the private line—you select the people who use it to reach you. (I think Batman had something like that.) There are a number of ways to apply such a setup. In essence, it allows you to "screen" your e-mail. If an e-mail comes into your public account and you want to communicate with that person in a serious way, you could reply from your private address, thereby letting them in. Otherwise you could delete the e-mail, or do whatever else you wish with it, without having it clutter up your personal, private e-mail folder.

Perhaps the easiest way to accomplish this screening is to have two Internet accounts. One would be a private account—perhaps on a system that keeps its user list private, doesn't allow incoming finger connections, and doesn't offer e-mail directories.

The other approach is a public account with a name you could disseminate; the name may or may not clue people in to your true identity. Because of the increased complexity (and often, increased cost) of having a two-account setup, this approach isn't for everyone.

If you're not in a position to have two Internet accounts for this purpose, there are other ways to achieve similar results. Some services offer *e-mail forwarding*. You get a stable e-mail address with said service—for example, **aaron@mailme.com**. You inform the service of your true Internet address, and any e-mail sent to "aaron@mailme.com" would be forwarded to the true address. One advantage of this arrangement is that if you change e-mail addresses frequently and need a stable referent so people can reach you, this provides one. Another advantage is that you can choose whether you want to include your true, direct e-mail address in replies to people, or leave only the "mailme.com" address.

Anonymous You

They say there's nowhere to hide, but it's simply not true. At least, on the Internet, you can hide behind anonymous e-mail. Granted, my use of the word "hide" is a bit unfair, because of its connotations. You may want to send e-mail anonymously because of the subject matter, true. Or you may not have a problem with the subject matter, but don't want your true identity revealed. From a privacy and security point of view, using anonymous, encrypted e-mail is about as private and secure as you can get, if that is what you desire.

There is a fair amount of controversy blowing around the area of digital anonymity. Some good newspaper editorials have been written highlighting potential problems with it, and some even better rebuttals have been written arguing for the importance of preserving citizens' right to anonymity. This book will assume, and assert, that the right to anonymity is a good thing, a part and parcel of individual privacy, and as such fundamental to a free society. There are a ton of ways one could abuse anonymity and use it for harm, but the same can be said for chainsaws, ballpoint pens, and sporks. Having said that, let's look at how you can go about using anonymous e-mail services.

On the Internet, anonymous e-mail is sent to and delivered by *anonymous re-mailers*, sometimes called *anonymous servers*. What a re-mailer does is accept an e-mail message from a user, which may contain instructions to the re-mailer and a message intended for another user. The re-mailer interprets any of the instructions it needs to, strips away all information identifying the original sender from the header, and forwards the rest of the message to the destination. In short, you tell the re-mailer, "I want to send the message 'blah blah blah' to user@host" and the re-mailer sends "blah blah blah" to user@host without identifying you in any way. Usually, the recipient can reply to the e-mail, and that reply will go back to the re-mailer (which will remember who you actually were, and forward the reply to you). Identifying information will be stripped from the reply, as well, so the recipient remains anonymous should he choose to reply.

A number of "anonymous re-mailers" have been setup by various individuals. As with everything on the Internet, some of these will come and go, while others may remain stable for longer periods of time. You should try to choose a re-mailer that is considered permanent. A list of currently active re-mailers is available on the Internet and maintained by Raph Levien. You can currently find the list on the World Wide Web at this address:

```
http://www.cs.berkeley.edu/~raph/re-mailer-list.html
```

Otherwise, you can finger this address:

```
re-mailer-list@kiwi.cs.berkeley.edu
```

Finally, a list is periodically posted to the Usenet newsgroup **alt.privacy**. Of course, any of these specific addresses may change over time, but the information will be on the Internet somewhere.

Here are some selected anonymous re-mailers in use at the time of this writing:

```
help@anon.penet.fi
re-mail@vox.xs4all.nl
re-mailer@tower.techwood.org
re-mailer@nately.ucsd.edu
\q@c2.org
```

Sending an e-mail message to any of these—assuming they're still in operation when you read this—should return instructions and further information. Dropping the word **help** into the subject and/or body of your message couldn't hurt, either.

As in Chapter 2, we're going to use the Penet anonymous server for the examples in this book. This server has been around for a long time and is quite established on the Internet.

Anon.penet.fi, Schmanon.penet.fi

Although the **anon.penet.fi** server is well-established and respected on the Internet, a recent incident has worried many. Early in 1995, the Church of Scientology, based in the United States, felt that some private information of theirs had been stolen and distributed on the Internet by someone using anon.penet.fi. They asked the creator and maintainer of Penet, Johan Helsingius, to divulge some information about a user who used anon.penet.fi. Johan, a strong proponent of personal freedom and privacy, denied their request. One of his most fundamental "rules" about his system is that he will not release information about anyone who uses it, thus preserving anonymity wholly and completely.

Unhappy with that response, the Church contacted Interpol and the Finnish authorities, who told Johan that he'd better give them the information. Backed against the wall, Johan had the choice to either reveal the one user's identity or give up his whole computer with its entire database of users. He reluctantly gave the police the identity that they wanted. This is the first case of anonymity on the Internet being violated by an organization or state, and it has jarred many interested Internet users. Whether the event will be an aberration in history or the boding of an unpleasant digital future is still far from clear, but it does raise an issue that all Internet users would be wise to keep their eyes and ears open about.

There are two things you need to set up before sending anonymous e-mail with anon.penet.fi: an *anon id* and a password. Technically, you don't necessarily *need* a password, but for security purposes we're going to make one without looking back.

To request an anon id, send a blank e-mail to the address **ping@anon.penet.fi**. (Note that if you already made a password back in Chapter 2, then you already *have* an anon id and password, and can skip ahead.) After some period of time, which may be as long as several hours or a day, you should get a response that says something like this:

```
From: daemon@anon.penet.fi
To: trey_a@divided.sky.edu
Subject: Reply to anonymous ping.
Your code name is: an75054@anon.penet.fi.
```

Now that you have an anon id, you can go ahead and create a password for yourself. Although we covered this in Chapter 2, we'll go over it again briefly here. For a refresher, see the section in Chapter 2 about posting anonymous Usenet messages.

1. Compose a new e-mail message to **password@anon.penet.fi**.
2. Enter nothing or anything you want in the Subject: line, Penet doesn't care in this case.
3. In the body of the e-mail message, just enter your proposed password, keeping in mind all of the password creation issues beaten into you back around Chapter 6.

   Here's an example e-mail message ready to be sent to Penet creating a password:

```
To      : password@anon.penet.fi
Cc      :
Attchmnt:
Subject :
----- Message Text -----
No]I4=.Pxt
```

Anonymous e-mail to a particular recipient should be addressed to **anon@anon.penet.fi**. The body of your message has to contain instructions to the Penet server, telling it (for example) your password and who the intended recipient of this anonymous e-mail is. Now, when you send instructions to Penet, they must be in a very specific format. Specifically, instructions begin with **X-Anon-** and must occupy the first non-blank lines of the message body. That's a little vague, I know. The example that follows illustrates sending an anonymous message to a user **frankz@surf.sand.org**, with an instruction to the server telling it the password we just established above.

```
To      : anon@anon.penet.fi
Cc      :
Attchmnt:
Subject : You Don't Know Who I Am
----- Message Text -----
X-Anon-Password: No]I4=.Pxt
X-Anon-To: frankz@surf.sand.org

Hi Frank,

This is an anonymous message from me, but you don't know who I am.
```

Assuming that the password is correct for your anon id, Frank will eventually get a message from anon.penet.fi containing the message shown here (*without* the X-Anon directives!). If Frank chooses to reply to the message, his reply will go back to your_anon_id@anon.penet.fi, and Penet will forward it to your true e-mail address.

Sometimes you'll want to communicate with someone who also has an anon id at Penet. For example, let's say you received e-mail from someone whose From: address is listed as **an12055@anon.penet.fi**. In that case, instead of the **X-Anon-To:** line shown in the previous example, use the line

```
X-Anon-To: an12055
```

As is recommended by the creator of Penet, Johan Helsingius, if you plan to send something via the anonymous server that could get you in trouble (such as whistle-blowing, an opinion about your officeplace, or anything else), it's a prudent idea to test your message-sending ability first.

There are three simple ways to send a test message. You could address your test message to **test@anon.penet.fi**, or you could address it to your anon id (in which case you should receive the message that you send). In a similar vein, you could address the message to your real e-mail address and see what the real recipient would see if you were to send the message to someone else for real. Only after you've done a test like this—and verified that you know how to format the anonymous e-mail properly—should you go ahead and write real anonymous e-mail.

The instructions just given are all relevant to anon.penet.fi specifically. Other anonymous re-mailer services probably have their own procedures and command syntax. Some anonymous servers have their own PGP public keys; you can use these to encrypt mail to the server, further enhancing security. You can find a short list of other servers (and pointers to updated lists) earlier in this chapter.

Proper Storage and Handling

A final thought on e-mail security: where, exactly, do you keep it all? Like an exhibitionist sleeping on a park bench, keeping your e-mail in an exposed area where Internet intruders can easily get to it could facilitate a lot of personal information getting into the wrong hands.

If, for example, you have a UNIX shell account, and you keep all your mail folders on that account, then someone who may break into your account—or your ISP's entire computer—has access to all of your e-mail. Of course, this is true for anything you keep on such an account. This is not to say that you shouldn't store any of your e-mail in a UNIX account—rather, just don't store top-secret, for-your-eyes-only e-mail in your UNIX account.

As discussed in Chapters 4 and 5, the type of connection you have to the Internet determines the extent to which outsiders can access your data, depending on where it is. If you use a dumb terminal, then downloading your e-mail from your service provider to your computer is very safe; no one on the outside can get to your computer over a simple dumb terminal connection. On the other hand, if you have a dedicated, static IP connection to the Internet, then your computer may be open 24 hours a day; that makes it not such a safe place to store sensitive data.

For users who use TCP/IP of any type (Ethernet, SLIP/PPP), if you run servers, it's particularly important to make sure they're properly configured. Without proper server setups, you may be allowing people from the outside to poke their noses into places you'd rather not have them when they connect to your computer.

The ultimate point here is: Take note of what computers you use, which ones are the most connected to the outside world, and which ones are least connected. Keep the most sensitive information on the least or not-at-all connected computers, and move less-sensitive information off the connected computers.

The Least You Need to Know

If you've used the Internet, you've used e-mail. If anyone *doesn't* fall into that category, I'd like to meet them. (Actually, no I wouldn't—scratch that.) So it's only sensible to cover some of the major issues related to e-mail and your protection.

- An e-mail message meets several computers on its way to its final resting place. At any of those points, greasy-haired people could potentially intercept your e-mail. An effective way to combat that possibility is to use the PGP-encryption techniques covered extensively in chapters other than this one (8 and 9, if you must know).
- In the interests of protecting both your security and your privacy, you may find occasions where anonymous e-mail is appropriate. There are usually a variety of services on the Internet that can help you send anonymous e-mail.
- If you need to separate incoming e-mail between "public" and "private," there are a couple of ways to have dual e-mail addresses. You could have two separate Internet accounts, or you can use a forwarding service that will accept e-mail at a given address and forward it to you.
- Depending on the sensitivity of your e-mail, you should take due note of where it's stored. Keeping it on a computer that's connected to the Internet 24 hours a day (such as your ISP's) is not a very secure storage place. The less connected the storage computer, the safer.

Digital Illnesses: Viruses

In This Chapter

- What viruses can do for you
- Where viruses come from—and where they don't
- Happy hunting!
- Seek and ye shall disinfect

Apparently, not to be sated with the natural varieties, humans have gone and created infections in the digital realm, too. Computer *viruses* have been a problem for many years, and the Internet has the potential to spread disease like a Roman aqueduct. Exploiting users' fears about viruses is not the answer, but a realistic look at what role the Internet does and *does not* play in virus propagation is. It's closer to an answer, anyway.

Is My Computer Going to Die?

There are some things that a few viruses do, some things that many viruses do, and some things that no viruses can do. First, it's worth looking at the matter of computer platforms again.

In Chapter 5, we talked a little about how different computer platforms faced different security risks insofar as TCP/IP connections to the Internet go. As with TCP/IP, different computer platforms vary in degree of susceptibility to viruses. You might want to know that the heavyweight champion breeding grounds for viruses, by far, are PC "clones," which most often run MS-DOS/Windows. There are over 1,500 known viruses that can infect a PC, although it's important to note than only a fraction of them have gained widespread dissemination. The runner-up virus-prone platform, although quite a bit behind, is the Macintosh, which can be infected by maybe a few dozen potential viruses. Dead last, at the back of the pack, is UNIX, where viruses are basically non-existent (other than experimental ones written for specific research purposes). The other, less-common computer platforms such as the Amiga, Atari ST, and Archimedes fall somewhere in the middle-to-low part of the risk spectrum.

There are several reasons for the differing risks. One is the sheer numbers of computers of a particular type. Having so many PCs around—more of them than there are of all the other computer platforms combined—is obviously a great help in spreading viruses. Other risk factors are more technical, having to do with the way the different platforms manage files, memory, and so forth.

But It's "Octopi," Isn't It?

We may as well get it over with. You've read the chapter title, you've read the intro paragraph, and you're thinking, "Hey, I thought the plural of virus was virii! Were the editors at Que passed out at their desks when this chapter went in for review, or what?"

In the "everything-you-learned-in-school-was-wrong" department, let it be known that the plural of "virus" is in fact "viruses." The reason, so they say, is that "virus" in Latin is a "mass noun"—like "air." For which there is no correct Latinate plural. So there.

If someone insists on saying "virii" around you with the airs of educated dignity, kill their cat (metaphorically speaking, of course) by letting this one out of the bag.

Because a virus is a piece of software, it can only infect the computer platform it was written for. So, if you are a Mac user, a PC virus is not going to be able to harm you (unless you run a PC emulator, in which case it could infect that portion of your system).

Viruses work in several different ways; people who study this sort of thing have broken them down into classes. (None of which I'm going to go into here, because it's boring, and more importantly, because it's not relevant to the question of Internet security per se.) A virus can infect files and spread to other files, yet never cause any damage. It could infect every file that is executed, or opened, on your computer, or it could just hang out and infect a file every so often. It could just lie in wait until a certain condition is met (like a certain date and year) and then leap out and wreak havoc. While a lot of viruses are more of a nuisance than serious threats to your entire system, some can really destroy everything, especially if you're too lazy to keep backups of important programs or data. Corrupting files or boot records beyond repair is one possible problem, especially without backups to restore from. Not all viruses are programmed to cause explicit damage, but their mere act of spreading around your system is likely to cause problems.

The Internet as a Communal Water Fountain

In elementary school, all these little kids stay together for hours on end, day after day, eating dirt and drinking from the same water fountain. Is it any surprise that they're always sick? Not at all, and in some ways, the Internet is like that water fountain, save for the piece of green gum stuck to the drain.

While some illnesses are communicable by the water fountain, some are not. Because a virus is a software program, it has to be *executed* (that is, run) to be able to infect anything.

For this reason, viruses will tend to try to infect other executable programs. Sometimes, however—whether on purpose or not—a virus may infect a *data file* (such as a word processor document or graphic file) you created. The virus generally can't propagate itself further from that file, because it needs to be executed. The process of infecting the data file can damage it, however—possibly beyond repair, which is a real problem if you don't have a backup.

Even though a virus can only infect the specific computer platform it was designed for, other platforms can "carry" or transport the virus. If you use FTP to get a program on the Internet, for example, you may retrieve the file into your UNIX shell account. From there, you might normally download the file from your UNIX account to your PC.

Suppose the program you got has a PC virus in it. Well, it couldn't infect the UNIX system on which you temporarily stored the program. Once you transfer the program (and with it, the virus) to the computer it was meant for, *and then execute that program,* the virus can then infect. To stress that last point again, the mere existence of a virus within a program on your computer cannot spread the infection. Not until you execute the program—and therefore the virus hidden within it—can the infection take place. Once executed, the virus can then begin to spread throughout your system.

Facts, Myth, and the Virus

The fearsome implications of a rampant computer virus have stimulated a lot of rumor and myth-making, especially on the Internet. There have been several instances of people making announcements about a "new" form of virus that is transmitted over the Internet by an unusual means, and probably many people just aren't sure what to believe.

Execute When you *execute* (or run) a program, you tell the computer to begin reading and following the instructions that the program is composed of. Some types of computer files are programs and can be executed. Other sorts of files are not instructions, but some other form of data. For example, a graphic file that contains a picture of a house is not a set of instructions to the computer, it is a set of data representing the picture. Such a file cannot be executed, but it can be read or manipulated by another program (such as an image processing application, in this case), and a program file *can* be executed.

To repeat the main rule of thumb, a file that is not going to be executed by the computer that the virus was programmed for cannot spawn viral infection. An e-mail message, a picture file, a Usenet posting—all of these are data files you can only manipulate by using some other program (a mail reader, a picture viewer, a newsreader). Yet these are all types of files that have been rumored to carry live viruses on the Internet. **They don't. It is not possible.**

To clarify, it is possible that someone could send you a GIF image file and claim that there is a virus in it. It's even possible that you could take this GIF file and run a virus scanner on it, and so detect a virus. Therefore technically, *yes*, there is a virus infecting that GIF file—*but a GIF file is not an executable program.* It is a graphic image. Therefore the virus has no way of spreading out of that file. The GIF file itself may have been damaged by the viral infection, but it cannot spread the virus farther. A GIF *viewer*, on the other hand, is an executable file—were that infected by a virus, it could spread the infection.

Now, if you download an executable program (or an archive that contains executable programs), that's another story. Again, the mere act of downloading an executable program that's infected with a virus will not spread the virus throughout your computer. But if you ever *execute* that program—or if another program on your computer executes it—the virus can then infect your system and begin spreading.

So how many programs on the Internet have viruses on them? 45,843. Actually, I'm just kidding—no one really knows, considering how many new programs are transferred across the Internet (and stored on Internet-based sites) every day. Traditionally, BBSs have been a more troublesome source of viruses than the Internet, but I wouldn't suggest that you let this fact give you a false sense of security. The massive population explosion of Internet users is bound to bring a fair amount of trouble, troubling, and troubled people with it.

When you're finding programs on the Internet, a rule of thumb (albeit far from ideal) is to stick with major distribution channels. For example, the major computer platforms all have a few FTP sites that are the dominant storehouses of software for those computers. Often those sites have a number of "mirrors" that carry the same inventory. Because such sites are the major troughs for users, they tend to have more vigilant administration than smaller, less-well-known FTP sites. Accordingly, those who run the sites may give more attention to scanning for viruses in the files uploaded to that site—and provide quicker removal (and/or notice) of any files on the site that have been found to be infected. It would be wrong to imply that using major FTP sites will wholly eliminate the virus possibility. Even some commercial programs have been shipped from the factory with virus infections; there is no absolutely safe distribution route.

Bulletin Board System (BBS) A BBS is usually a local computer you call with a modem, run by one person or organization as a clearinghouse of information. Although some BBSs offer connections to the Internet, BBSs on the whole are not part of the global network of computers that make up the Internet.

Playing It Safe

What with all these digital infections floating about, there are still some practices and behaviors you can undertake to reduce your risk. (I think we both know that the obvious joke here is just too easy, so I'll just let it rest.)

As mentioned earlier, take note of the source of the computer files that you get. Major FTP sites, although not 100 percent secure, are far less risky sources than some guy on the Internet chat channels who types in all capitals. Even assuming that you've followed all the sage counsel and learned all the techniques in this chapter, and you feel your system is free of a virus ("clean"), BACK IT UP! If there was ever a mantra in computing, it's BACK IT UP. And from now on, in combination with the vigilance techniques in the remainder of this chapter, back up important programs or data as quickly as possible. Usually this means floppy disks, although some people use jumbo tape drives.

If you've got a floppy disk with a backup of a $150 ant-farm design program, and the ant farm data file took two years to perfect, you really don't want to stick that floppy into an infected system. Specifically, you don't want the virus spreading to your floppy, which can not only destroy the files on it but also spread to another computer that you may use the disk in subsequently. Fortunately, that's what *write-protect* notches and tabs on your floppy disks are for. Stay aware of the write-protect status of your floppy disks, and make it a habit to keep them write-protected. Only make a floppy disk writeable when you specifically need to save some data to that disk—and it's a good idea to use only a virus-free computer when saving data to the disk. Once you've saved to the floppy, write-protect it again.

The anatomical details of your floppy disks.

Using floppies in your computer that were given to you by other people (especially folks you don't trust to be very virus-vigilant) can be dangerous. If you *must* do this, the best course of action would be to run a virus scan on every such disk you receive, using programs like the ones described later in this chapter, *before doing anything else* with the floppy. Even before you type **dir** to get a directory of it! Scan it for viruses FIRST.

Above all, remember that there is no single perfect virus-prevention method. Any program or application you get that mentions preventing viruses is only an additional tool and/or weapon, but not the be-all and end-all of what should be your virus vigilance. Believing otherwise can only lead to a false sense of security, which can make you even more vulnerable.

Turn Your RAM and Cough

Just like when you come down with the flu, there are a series of ways you may first notice the malady.

When you start to feel achy and a little fuzzy in the head, you begin to suspect something might be up. On your computer, viral symptoms manifest themselves by way of operational oddities. Inappropriate hard drive access may be a tip-off. For example, if you see or hear your computer accessing its hard drive at times when you didn't tell it to (such as when you're loading or saving a file), that may be a tip. Some drives do access themselves from time to time, though, so that alone is not a 100 percent predictor, but you may notice that it's accessing at unusual times. Another sign is a change in the amount of free space on the hard drive. Some viruses may act in such a way as to reduce your free space—if your hard drive space is diminishing at a rate that doesn't reflect the way you're using it, that may also be a clue.

Any other strange happenings with your computer shouldn't be overlooked. Unusually sluggish operation—even apparent hardware problems—can sometimes be traced back to viruses. For example, there is a virus for the PC that messes with high-density floppy access, making it appear as if the floppy drive is malfunctioning.

Some viruses aren't nearly so subtle as these just mentioned. Some will proudly announce their presence, with animation or musical self-indulgence. Needless to say, if you see a strange message fly across your screen when you boot up the computer, be afraid—be very afraid.

There are other changes to your system that a virus will make, but these aren't so easily detectable by the human senses (unless you have a sixth sense, which can be very useful in a variety of situations). The contents and sizes of files may change due to virus infection. Certain memory locations in your

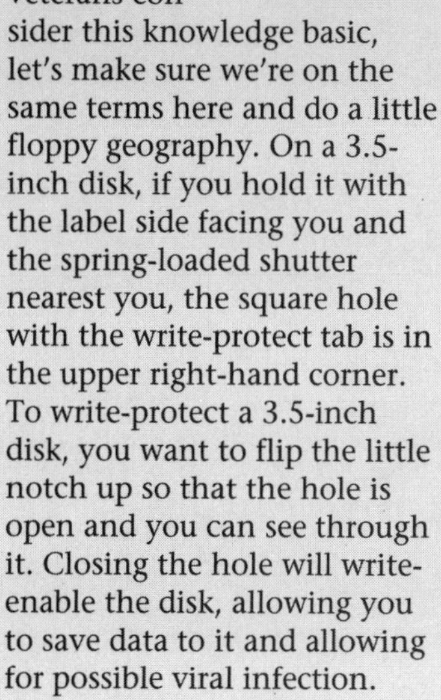

Floppy Basics

Although many computer veterans consider this knowledge basic, let's make sure we're on the same terms here and do a little floppy geography. On a 3.5-inch disk, if you hold it with the label side facing you and the spring-loaded shutter nearest you, the square hole with the write-protect tab is in the upper right-hand corner. To write-protect a 3.5-inch disk, you want to flip the little notch up so that the hole is open and you can see through it. Closing the hole will write-enable the disk, allowing you to save data to it and allowing for possible viral infection.

On a 5 1/4-inch disk, if you still have any of those fossils in use, the situation is reversed. With the label side facing you and the label at the top, the relevant notch is in the upper right-hand corner; *covering* the notch will write-protect the disk, whereas leaving it open will write-enable it.

Caveat Virus: Be warned! No virus utility can work 100 percent of the time—the world of computer viruses is just too complicated and too dynamic. Therefore, the best defense is a combination of ingredients: a vigilant user who practices "safe computing," keeps an eye out for weirdness on the system, and uses virus utilities to scan and prevent.

computer may be altered to provide a "home" for the virus to live in and attack from (note that memory changes only remain in place while the computer is powered on). These aren't changes that the human user is likely to notice, which is why various virus-detection utilities exist.

These so-called *virus scanners* will, appropriately enough, scan your computer's hard disk and RAM memory for *known* viruses. But note the word "known" in that sentence. Every virus has its own characteristics, just as with biological viruses. A virus scanner can only detect the viruses it's been programmed to recognize. The meaning of this is that you should always be sure to use the newest, most up-to-date version of a particular virus scanner program. These programs are updated frequently for this exact reason. If, for some reason, the virus-detection program you are using stops being updated, stop using it and find another. Even if you don't think you have any viruses right now, it's a good idea to stop and pick up a virus scanner and check your system.

We've talked about keeping your eyes out, and safe computing. Now we'll look at using various virus utilities, and top it all off with a beer-'n'-toga party at your house.

F-PROT for PCs

On the PC side of things, one popular and high-quality virus scanner for the PC is called *F-PROT*. F-PROT can be found on any major FTP site with PC software (see the section in the back of the book called, "Some Goodies (Neat Files and Things)" for resource listings). One such FTP archive is **archive.orst.edu**. To get F-PROT, fire up your FTP application and open the connection to **archive.orst.edu**. Once in, change into the **/pub/mirrors/simtel/msdos/virus** directory. There should be a file called **fp-*xxx*** where *xxx* is the current version of F-PROT. Retrieve that file to your PC.

Go Fetch If you are using an FTP application (such as WS_FTP for Windows) over a SLIP/PPP program (such as Trumpet Winsock), just "get" the file. If you are using a UNIX shell account, you'll have to "get" the file to your UNIX account, and then download it from your account to your PC using ZMODEM (the **sz** command in UNIX).

Let's take a quick tour of F-PROT (no flash cameras, please, it scares the monkeys). When you've retrieved the F-PROT archive, unzip the file. You can launch the program by typing **f-prot** at the C:\> prompt. Immediately, F-PROT will scan your computer's memory (RAM) for any viruses that may be hiding in there. Then you'll see the main menu, which should remind you of the figure coming up.

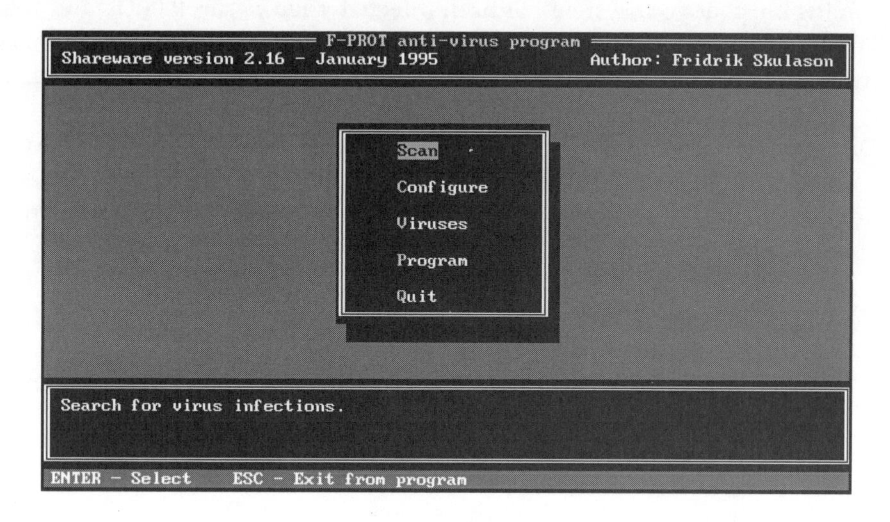

The Main menu of F-PROT. We're choosing "Scan" in our example.

On the main menu, the option we're most concerned with right now is "Scan." It's wise to read the included documentation with F-PROT to learn fully about the program's other features. When you select Scan, you'll be presented with five configurable options: Method, Search, Action, Targets, and Files.

Method is set to **Secure Scan** by default—leave it that way.

Search tells F-PROT where you want to scan. Your three basic options are your entire hard disk, a floppy disk, or a selected directory of your hard disk. If you want to scan your entire system (which we'll assume you do right now), leave it on **hard disk**. You can choose **floppy** to scan floppy disks later. In the future, if you retrieve a new program from the Net, after you unzip it you should run F-PROT *(before even trying out the new program)*, change the **Search** option to **User-Specified**, and then enter the path of the unzipped files. This way F-PROT will run a scan on the new files, just to be sure. This is a preemptive defense, before a potential virus has the chance to spread. We'll wrangle with more dedicated virus-prevention utilities in the next section.

Action determines what F-PROT will do if it finds a nasty little bugger. Leave it on **Report Only** for now, so that it will just tell you about the potential problem. You can then decide what to do about it after seeing the full report.

Targets tells F-PROT where on your system it will scan. By default, the **boot sector**, **files**, and **packed files** options are all checked **yes**, so leave it that way.

Files determines which files on the system F-PROT will scan. For your first scan, be sure to leave the default option (**Standard Executables**) selected. If you do end up finding out that your system has been infected, then re-run F-PROT and select **All Files**. This will hunt down the virus in non-traditional virus hangouts, in case it's really gotten out of hand.

Once you've set up all these measures, select **Begin Scan...** and the hoedown will begin. When it's done, you'll get a report of the results. For now, if F-PROT reports anything funky, just hold tight and we'll look at what your options are in the final section of this chapter.

Disinfectant for the Mac

On the Macintosh, we look briefly at Disinfectant, the very popular virus scanner/ prevention utility. You can find Disinfectant at major Mac FTP sites or its home site, where updates will appear first: **ftp.acns.nwu.edu** in the directory **/pub/disinfectant.** Retrieve the file and install it on your Mac. When you double-click on the **Disinfectant** icon to launch the program, you'll get this screen:

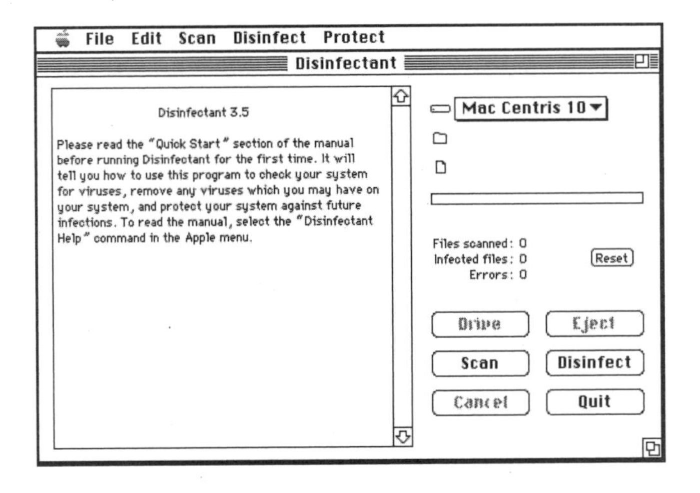

Disinfectant for the Macintosh. Its two basic modes of operation are Scan and Disinfect, as you can see. Very easy to use.

Fortunately, this is quite an easy program to use. It has two basic modes of operation: Scan and Disinfect. Right now we're considering the Scan feature. Like F-PROT for the PC, Disinfectant will scan your system for known viruses. Under the Scan menu there are several choices: File, Folder, Floppies, All disks, Some disks, System file, System folder, and Desktop files. Simply choose whichever you desire to scan. Assuming you've never scanned your current system before, choose **All disks**. In the future, when you get new program archives from the Internet, use Disinfectant's **Scan/Folder** option to check out the new folder *before* executing the program for the first time. Once you've chosen the portion of your system to scan, Disinfectant will begin the search, and report whatever it finds in the output window. If it has turned up something untoward, see the section "Cleaning the Tubes," later in this chapter, for advice.

Virus Prevention the Digital Way

Like the U.S. health-care system, virus scanners don't practice preventive medicine. Rather, they tend to try to find and diagnose existing problems. Attempting to prevent a viral infection in the first place is a good idea, and it can save time and heartburn. What *virus-prevention* utilities do is sit in the background of your computer and watch the goings-on. They might watch memory access, file access, file changes, and so forth. If they think something funky is going down, they'll pop out of the woodwork and give you a holler. One such virus-prevention tool for the PC is **VSHIELD**. As with F-PROT, VSHIELD can also be found at a major PC FTP repository, such as the aforementioned **archive.orst.edu** site, in the same directory path as F-PROT. Its filename should resemble something like **vsh-*xxx*** where *xxx* is the current version number.

Installing and running VSHIELD is easy. Just type **vshield** at the C:\> prompt; it will install itself into memory. It'll lurk there watching for evil. You may want to include VSHIELD in your AUTOEXEC.BAT file so it runs automatically upon boot-up. If, when you execute a program, it initiates a virus that VSHIELD recognizes, the program will be halted; then VSHIELD will pop up and talk to you about the problem.

> **Which Is Which?** If you're not sure which file is the program you're looking for, many FTP sites have a file called something like **00_index.txt** or **index.txt** within each directory path. If you retrieve this file and view it with an ASCII viewer, it will give a brief description of each file within that directory. It's quite helpful.

The scanners and prevention utilities mentioned here aren't the only ones available for the PC, and both have more detailed modes of operation. Reading their respective documentation will be a much more comprehensive lesson than what I've given you here. If you have questions concerning viruses—which scanners and prevention utilities to use, for example, or how to operate them—go over to the folks in the Usenet newsgroup **comp.virus**. They'll be happy to help you out in detail, with the latest information on viruses and virus utilities.

Macintosh users are in luck—the same Disinfectant used to scan for viruses can also work as a prevention utility. The short of it is that you can install Disinfectant as a startup

INIT by choosing the menu item **Protect/Install Protection INIT**. For further information on this matter (and more elaboration on all Disinfectant's features), don't forget to read the documentation—which you can easily get to by selecting **Disinfectant Help** from the **Apple** menu in the upper left corner of the screen. Once installed for startup, Disinfectant will run upon boot-up and sit in the background leering and watching for the little buggery viruses; it'll alert you if it sniffs one.

Again, it's important to remain up-to-date with these sorts of programs due to the ever-changing world of viruses, so try to retrieve new versions of these anti-virus programs from their respective FTP sites on a periodic basis. Every couple of months would be a good timetable to check .

Cleaning the Tubes

Suppose the worst is true—Bob Hope *is* funny. Whoops, I meant, suppose your virus scanner or virus-prevention program reports that you've got a nasty. It's amazing (and convenient) how well the medical model works for this topic: get a second opinion! As it happens, some virus-detection programs can actually confuse other ones. For example, if you are running a virus prevention program that sits in the background (such as VSHIELD), a virus scanner might see that little program wedged into memory and think it may be a virus. So, if you ran a virus scan and found a hit, try another virus scanner. See what it says. It may agree, it may not find it at all, or it may conflict. If you're using new, up-to-date scanners and you get reasonably congruent analyses of your system, you can be more assured that you do, in fact, have a virus before performing surgery.

Actually, in most cases, *surgery* is too severe a word. You probably won't have to reformat your entire hard disk and wipe your system clean to remove the viral infection. Unless of course, you've been getting infected software for months, taking no precautions, and have corrupted everything on your hard drive. *Then* you may have to wipe it all clean. Of course, if that's you, you would have noticed something was awry by now, and be in too much of a panic to have gotten this far into this book. (Unless you're standing in the bookstore flipping through this book, hoping that the clerks don't suspect you of trying to read the entire thing in small portions on each trip back. But they know. I know. We all know.)

If there are only a small number of files that are reported to be infected, and you have properly backed those files up previously, run a virus scan on the backups. Hopefully, you managed to back them up before they were infected. In that case, you can insert the backup floppy (write-protect it!) and restore the files on your hard drive from that. Then re-scan the system to be sure.

If you don't have backups, or there are too many files to back up, or you just don't wanna, the next most popular step is to use a disinfectant program. "Disinfect," in the case of computer viruses, means that the program will try to remove the virus from the infected file, but otherwise leave the file intact. If you've got a clean backup of the file, it's probably safer to delete the infected file and copy the clean one from the backup. But if you have no other way out, try disinfecting.

Recalling the F-PROT example from earlier, we'll continue with this program:

After choosing **Scan** from the main menu in F-PROT, you'll find an option labeled "Action." This defaults to "Report only," and that is what we left it on in the example previously. Well, not anymore. If you click on the **Action** option, six options will appear in addition to "Report only," as seen in this police photo:

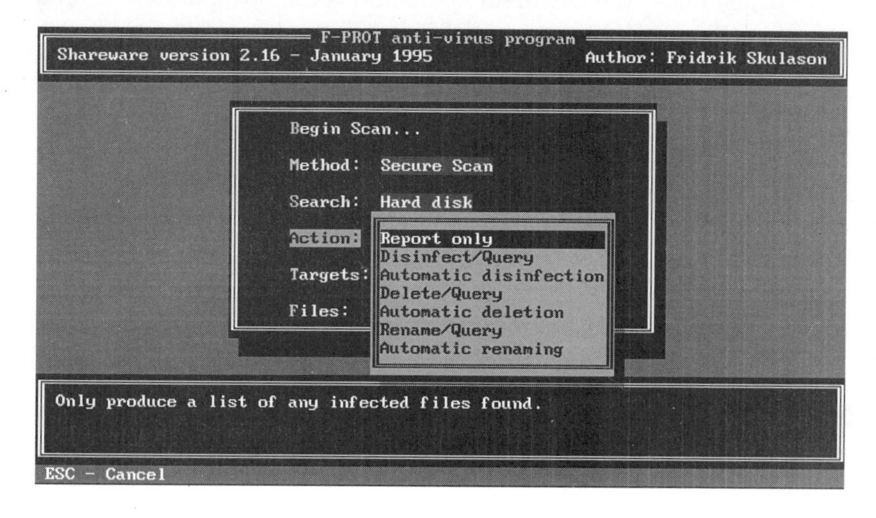

F-PROT once again, this time with the "Action" choice window open. These represent the possible actions F-PROT can take if it finds a virus while scanning your system.

Disinfect/Query will ask you about disinfecting, one by one, each file found to have a virus. Its complementary option, "Automatic disinfection," would bypass asking you to confirm each file. I prefer being queried, because it prevents the computer from just going off unsupervised and doing whatever it wants. There may be a file you'd like to leave alone for the time being, and querying lets you have some say in that matter.

Below these two options, you'll find another pair of query/automatic choices, in this case for deleting the file. If you don't need the file, it's best to delete it—but again, if you haven't any backup and need the file, stick with disinfection. Lastly, there's a pair of choices for renaming the file, in case you want to "hold" the supposedly infected file, perhaps for further examination later, but don't want it to have the same filename as before.

Macintosh people will once again rely on Disinfectant. In fact, the menu options under **Disinfect** are exactly the same as those under **Scan**. The only difference is that after you select the portion of your system to work on, it will first be scanned and then disinfected, rather than merely scanned. Simple enough? So if, when you scanned your system previously, any problems were reported, select the same portion of the system (for example, **All disks**) under the **Disinfect** menu and you'll be hand-held from there. The Mac sure is an easy computer.

In the worst-case scenario—so many files and programs on your computer are infected and/or corrupted that disinfection is infeasible—the system may have to be wiped clean. One hopes that there's a clean, virus-free backup of the system, or at least the vital parts, to restore from. If not, well, there's not a whole lot one can say or do in such a situation, except that Hallmark has a new possible market in our digital age: "Deepest Sympathies on the Loss of Your File System." In any case, if this fate does befall you, it's best to consult an expert on your particular computer platform about how to go about wiping it completely clean and rebuilding.

The Least You Need to Know

Computer viruses are, to put it frankly, a pain in the butt. And sometimes much worse. Unlike biological viruses, there's not even an arguable reason for them to exist—all of this education, prevention, protection, and disinfection is due to the fact that a frighteningly large number of human beings have serious problems. Oh, well, cynical reflections on human nature are better left to cab drivers. We have some viruses to defend ourselves against.

- It's "viruses," not "virii!" Yes it is! Is so.
- Not every computer platform is at equal risk of being infected by viruses. PC clones are the highest-risk machines. Macs are at risk to a much lesser degree. UNIX systems face virtually no virus threat presently. But watch this space.

- Viruses are computer programs, and as such, they must be executed to infect a computer and that computer's files. This means a viable virus can only be carried by an executable program, not a data file.
- As the human operator, you are the first line of defense against viral invasion. Don't take programs from little-known sources. Watch for unusual system activity (such as odd instances of hard drive access, or a reduction in free space on your hard drive). Be disciplined about backing up important programs and data on floppies. Always keep floppies write-protected except for the minimum amount of time it takes to copy files to them.
- Your next defenses are virus scanners, detectors, and disinfectants. Scan your entire system, and once you're convinced it's clean, install a virus-prevention program or virus detector that will run on boot-up and watch for viral launches.

Chapter 12

A Few Words About the World Wide Web

In This Chapter

- The Web's not so bad
- Spies are sparse
- "Form of"—security!
- Learn first, server second
- Your home page, their server

In practice, the *World Wide Web* is something of a catch-all term, encompassing several different types of Internet communications, with varying security issues. The Web has found a great deal of popularity among Internet users, and that's not only because they can drool and click at the same time. Even so, the Web doesn't raise nearly the large number of security issues that are inherent to using the Internet. In this chapter, we'll take a sparrow's-eye view of some security topics the Web does present to the end user (that's you).

Is It Safe?

Relatively safe, yes. In many ways, the World Wide Web is like a newspaper: you, the user, control your reading habits, and you select where and what you would like to read. Rather than flipping pages, you click on *links*—these can lead you to text, pictures, or sounds. Therein lies much of the power of the Web. Not a whole lot of communication goes on between you and the Web server (other than "I want to read this link now"), and the less going out and coming into your computer, the more secure the situation generally is. Of course, some circumstances are exceptions to this, and I'll tell you about those in a tad.

Surfing in the Nude—Can They See Me?

I hinted in the intro paragraph that the Web is a catch-all. One way to explain what I mean is to imagine FTP. When you use FTP on the Internet, you are using a specific *protocol* that defines how to request, send, and receive files across the Internet network. That is why, to make an FTP transfer, you need to use an FTP client connecting to an FTP server. They both "speak" the FTP protocol. Now, imagine Gopher. Gopher is another Internet application, entirely separate from FTP. It has its own protocol for transferring information between the server and the client (in this case, a Gopher server and a Gopher client).

Protocol
Defines the form that communication will take between two parties. In the server/client situation, the protocol defines what sort of things the client can say to the server and how the server should respond. That is why servers and clients have to "speak" according to the same protocol to achieve some end (otherwise they'd be called "governments").

The World Wide Web brought with it a new protocol, more modern and slick than the older FTP and Gopher protocols. The new protocol is called *HTTP* and stands for *Hypertext Transport Protocol*, which is a lot of fun to say rapidly after a highball or two. The *feature célèbre* of HTTP is *hypertext*, or the ability to link documents to each other by select words, phrases, pictures, or sounds. That's what makes the Web what it is—you surf the Web by clicking on text or images, and by doing so, you're using hypertext. In this way, every conceivable piece of data in the world—whether it's text, video, sound, or whatever—can be linked together through hypermedia. The possibilities quickly boggle the mind, and often cause pains in your head where there shouldn't be any.

Just like with FTP and Gopher, you need a client with which to access the World Wide Web. The first widely used client was called "Mosaic," and has since become synonymous with the Web today. People call Web clients *browsers* because you use them to "browse" the Web. Mosaic is one popular Web browser; Netscape is another. Still others are MacWeb, WinWeb, Lynx, and Cello. As with any bunch of competing programs, each one has its pros and cons, and which one you use is ultimately a personal decision. They all do essentially the same thing in essentially the same way.

To Clarify...
Hypertext is one form of hypermedia, just like a mango is one form of fruit. Linked images, video, audio, and so forth all constitute the whole of "hypermedia." This is not the same thing as popular press coverage of the Internet, which can also be called "hypermedia" but for a totally different reason.

One of the great advantages of Web browsers is that in practice "the World Wide Web" is a catch-all for several different protocols, not only HTTP. Having said that, I should remind you of the security issues that arose with other types of client/server situations. That is, remember how an FTP server can determine where you are connecting from? And what files you transfer (Chapter 5)? Well, if you use the FTP protocol over the Web, the same is true. After all, your Web browser is behaving just like an FTP client. With a few exceptions, any information passed between your Web browser (the client) and a server is just as "in the clear" and "sniffable" as any of the client/server issues explored in Chapter 5.

Browser Magic

When you click on a *hypertext link*, it is possible that the document attached to that link is not being offered by an HTTP server. There's a reason. Before the Web was born, there were thousands upon thousands of files already being offered by other information servers, such as FTP and Gopher—so Web browsers are able to "speak" multiple protocols (rather than only HTTP). If the link you select connects to a Gopher server, then your Web browser will "speak Gopher." If the link leads to an FTP server, the Web browser will "speak FTP." All of this is *transparent* (that is, hardly noticeable) to you, the user—you don't have to concern yourself one way or the other about the protocol being used.

Recall the opening couple of chapters in this book and the issues of spying, snooping, and the like. A good question is, "Can someone spy on my Web surfing?" For most users in most circumstances, the practical answer is, "No, not really." Most of the Web browsers listed earlier are graphical—you use the mouse and click on icons and windows and so forth. Using one of those means that you have to be using some sort of TCP/IP connection to the Internet (SLIP/PPP or Ethernet). That being the case, there's no easy way for someone to catch a glimpse of what sites you connect to with your Web browser. It's possible that someone could sniff you, but it's unlikely someone would do that for random voyeuristic kicks—they'd have to be motivated by some burning desire to track you down personally.

I Can See Clearly Now "In the clear" means that plaintext is sent over the network, as opposed to ciphertext. If someone is sniffing (or in some other way intercepting the data coming out of your machine), he can steal anything that is transmitted "in the clear," such as a password or credit card number. This is why it's so important to use encryption on *both* the client and server end, so that any intercepted data is useless to a spy. Unfortunately, this type of encryption is not commonly available on the Web yet.

Remember, a dumb terminal can only display text. If you are using a dumb terminal to access a UNIX shell account, you are probably using a text-based Web browser, most likely the one called "Lynx." Also remember that another user logged onto the same UNIX system as you can check what you are doing with the "w" command. But if you launch Lynx by typing **lynx** at the UNIX prompt, all a potential spy will see output from the "w" command is "lynx." Of course, if you type **lynx http://www.*place*.com** at the command line, the "w" command will report that whole thing. So if you don't want people to see where you're connecting to, don't enter the Web address on the command line. Just run Lynx first, and once you're in Lynx, then connect to a Web site using the **G** key (for "Goto").

Your Web browser is merely one Internet application among many, similar to the way that your word processor is one type of application among many on your computer (spreadsheets, desktop publishing, image processing). Because it's the "Ginsu knife" of Net applications and performs so many Internet activities (even e-mail and Usenet news in some cases), it's easy to forget that your Web browser is *not* the "main control panel" of your Internet account. That is, security issues between you and your ISP (such as your password, your finger information, and so forth) don't fall under the jurisdiction of your Web browser—be it Mosaic,

Netscape, or any of their peers. This means that you do not use your Web browser to change your account password, alter your finger information, or other such account-management activities.

Viruses? I Thought Those Were Only in Chapter 11

When you use a graphical browser over a TCP/IP connection (such as Mosaic or Netscape), you are transferring the document from the remote server to your computer; your browser then views the document. In the majority of cases, though, the file you receive from the Web server is a data file, not an executable program. For example, the content of a Web page is a data file, which your Web browser (an executable program) displays for you. If you click on a link to an image or sound, the appropriate data file is transmitted to your computer. Your Web browser then has to view or play that file. Most Web browsers don't know how to view graphics or play sounds by themselves, so they use "helper" programs that take on such tasks. Often, you have to tell your particular Web browser which helper applications to use in such cases when you first install it. But again, these data files are not possible sources of viral contamination.

Sometimes, however, you will retrieve an executable program via the Web. Usually this will be in the form of an archive (such as a .ZIP file for the PC or a .SIT or .SEA file for the Mac). In essence, this is the same thing as FTPing a file. Therefore the same concerns from Chapter 11 exist in this case. You're retrieving a program from a foreign source, and it may or may not have a virus. So follow the same precautions as were outlined in Chapter 11, especially this one: use a virus scanner on the unpacked archive before executing the program for the first time.

Filling Out the Forms

Clicking on hypertext links is cool, but it's not the only thing you can do on a Web page. Many Web pages nowadays have something called "forms." *Forms* are places in the page where you can fill in information of your own accord. This may include choosing an option out of several, or entering text into a fill-in box. The following figure shows a typical usage of forms.

Form On the World Wide Web, a *form* is an entry blank where you fill in some requested information. Come to think of it, a form is basically the same thing in real life. Imagine that.

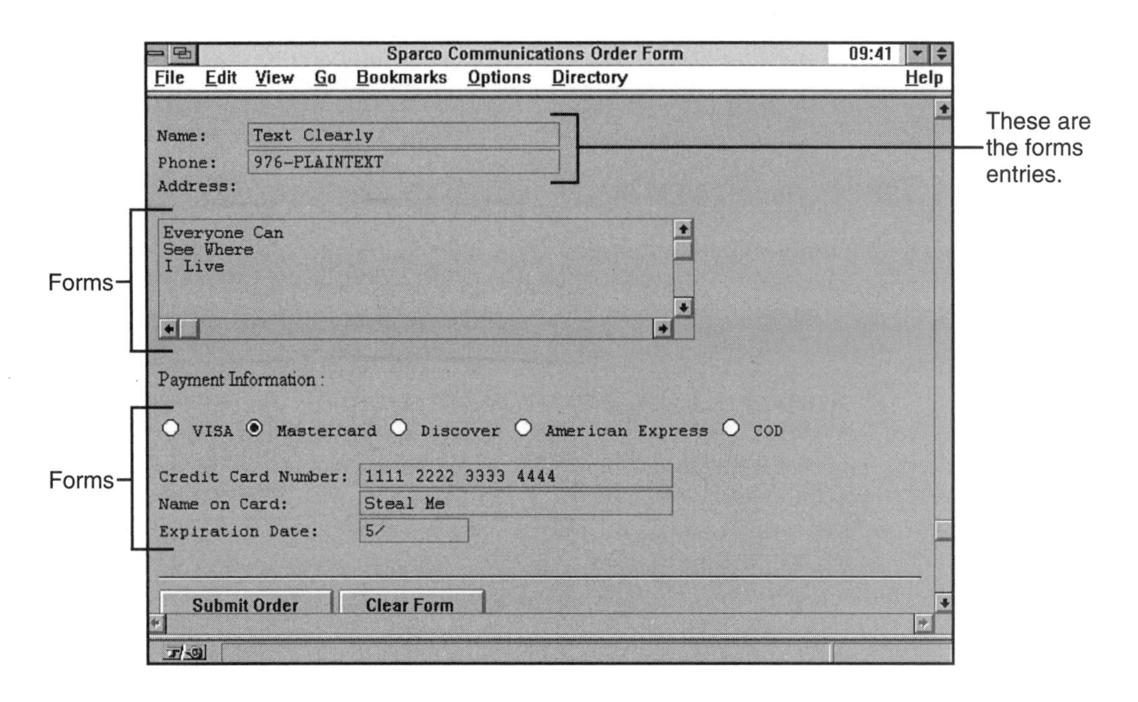

The information you enter in these forms will probably be transmitted "in the clear" across the Internet, unless this site has been specially designed otherwise.

Forms can be used for a wide array of possibilities. A page might ask you to enter a user ID and password, if that page is restricted to certain users. Some pages offer the opportunity to order a product, as in computer parts, compact discs, horse food, and so on. These pages may ask you to fill in your name, address, and possibly credit card information. It's important to recognize that this information will most probably be transmitted over the Internet *in the clear*. That means no encryption is used, and someone could possibly intercept the information (more on credit cards and Net purchasing in Chapter 17).

If you've read this far into this book, you realize that some form of encryption between Web browsers and Web servers is probably a good idea. Unfortunately, this is not yet implemented in a widespread manner on the Internet. Some Web browsers (such as Netscape) offer the option of popping up a little window and reminding you when you're about to transmit insecure information across the Internet. This provides you with the chance to think, "Hmm, maybe I don't want to risk that," and find an alternate, more secure route for the communication. Furthermore, there are advances being made in secure send and receive protocols being used between Web browsers and servers, which the newest generation of Web browsers are beginning to implement.

On the other hand, most Web forms request information that spies aren't likely to find all that interesting. It's the form that requests personal information—such as addresses or credit card numbers (as in the previous example)—that should flick the little light bulb over your head. In those cases, you may want to think twice or see if you can find out if any security measures have been implemented on that server. Until these types of precautions can be assumed, major financial activity across the Internet will be limited until extremely secure, transparent communications are implemented on the World Wide Web.

All in all, just keep in mind that what you enter in forms can possibly be intercepted by someone who really wanted to, but most forms involve relatively innocent information.

Server Security

While the user (client) side of a Web relationship doesn't face many major security issues, the Web server has a little more to worry about.

As we discussed in Chapter 5, running a server opens up an entire route of incoming communications into your computer. For that reason, it's vital to have the server configured properly so that it allows the sort of access you want to provide others—and prevents anything else. There are different servers for each computer platform; they offer varying degrees of capabilities and security.

Not to pass the buck, but I'm going to pass the buck. The plain truth is that if you are a new Internet user (and you probably are if you're reading this book), it's not likely you're going to be setting up servers of any sort. If you are, you probably shouldn't be. Imagine, for example, that this book were titled *The Complete Idiot's Guide to Protecting Yourself in a Restaurant* (a bestseller, no doubt). I might offer advice ranging from the typical nutritional compositions of popular dishes, to tipping, to dealing with bad service. The point being, *owning and running* a restaurant is very different from *patronizing* one. It carries with it a whole host of concerns that only someone with business experience, culinary experience, or celebrity should try. Those without said qualifications risk serving poorly prepared food and/or running a bad business. Similarly, running information servers in any serious capacity requires at least an above-average understanding of the Internet to reduce the possible risks to yourself. In no way am I trying to discourage you from running your own Web server. The Internet is composed entirely of the contributions that its users make to it. What I *am* saying is that this book is for the new and/or casual Internet user. If you're reading this book, and if it's teaching you anything, you shouldn't be running a server... yet.

Servers Versus Pages

Now, having justified my way out of a few extra paragraphs, I should highlight the difference between having your own Web *server* and your own Web *page*. Many users have the opportunity to put up their own "page," often called a *home page*. You can use this to provide information to the rest of the world on any topics you might have interest in. Some service providers offer users "Web space" for such pages, and other providers sell "Web space" for such things. If you have such a page, understand the way it is different from the section above. The server is the computer that accepts incoming requests for data and sends out that data. A Web page is just a set of data files. If your service provider offers you "Web space," that means you're being allowed to make some of your own data files available on their Web server. It's their computer that is serving the information in response to requests from outsiders, not yours. Even a new Internet user can have their own Web page if his service provider allows for it, and that is not the same as having one's own server. The risks are definitely not the same—your computer isn't involved in any way.

Page A document you view with your Web browser. If you have your own Web pages available for others to browse, then the "first" page of your set is your "home page."

If your service provider helps you create or design your Web page, still keep a few things in mind. Any information you provide in the page is available to the rest of the world, so (just as with your finger information) use your own discretion. All in all, you don't put yourself at much direct risk by having your own Web page on someone else's server. For the sake of the integrity of your page, one would hope that your service provider's Web server is well-secured itself.

The Least You Need to Know

Another shorter chapter, and once again, for good reason. The World Wide Web is a popular thing on the Internet, but it's not a terribly great source of insecurity. There are just a few things to keep in mind while surfing your day away.

- It's not feasible for someone to spy on your Web surfing habits with the ease and comprehensiveness of something like the "last" command in UNIX. Web servers can track that you connected to them, but outsiders aren't so likely unless they're really hunting for you specifically.

- Don't forget about your virus vigilance! If you transfer any executable programs over the Web, remember to virus-scan after installing them but before running them.
- When entering information into forms, take note of what you're writing. This information will most likely be transmitted "in the clear" across the Internet, so you may want to find a more secure method for very sensitive personal data, such as credit card numbers.
- Servers are a can of worms better suited for the more experienced Internet users. Web servers can be a very rewarding service to run, but aren't for the new user. If running your own server interests you, read other books beyond this introductory one (but preferably by the same publisher, as we'll make more money that way).
- If you have your own Web page residing on someone else's server instead of your own computer, that's not too risky. Just stay aware of what information you choose to give out on your Web page so that it doesn't come back to haunt you like a boomerang in a stiff breeze.

Part 3
A Beast Named UNIX

Without this part devoted to UNIX use, there's no way this book could have adequately covered all the security issues out there. (As well, it would have been much shorter.) The novice UNIX-shell user faces a daunting task. Not only is there a steep learning curve, but there are more security issues in UNIX than there are raccoons in my dumpster.

What's worse is that some people actually get stuck ***administering*** *UNIX machines, and a paycheck is supposed to make up for that. Although most of their time will be spent in therapy, UNIX admins will have to use what little time they left to attend to security concerns. There's a chapter for them, too, but I can't guarantee it will be as effective as an antidepressant.*

As time elapsed, his house collapsed:

Chapter 13

It's Mine!—File Ownership and Permissions

In This Chapter

- Account for rent: your home directory
- Read strange UNIX notations in 10 minutes or less
- Letting people touch your files (and saying "No!")
- You are what you own

Until now, you may have been getting the impression that this book has a slight UNIX bias. Well, you ain't seen nothin' yet! UNIX is not a pretty thing to most people. However, it is a powerful thing, and it's very well-suited to the Internet (not entirely unrelated to the fact that the two were virtually developed hand-in-hand). Many users don't have a great deal of choice one way or the other about it, anyway. Many providers, especially educational institutions, provide Internet access by way of UNIX shells only. In some ways, using UNIX is like car maintenance: there are potentially a thousand little things to learn about, but understanding a few major concepts should keep you humming happily most of the time.

If you don't use UNIX at all, if you've never seen it, or if you refuse to go near it, then these next four chapters are basically superfluous reading. You might skim them for the good jokes, but the material is otherwise fairly inapplicable to other sorts of Internet access. On the other hand, if you use UNIX at all, even with a minimal level of understanding, this section is mandatory reading.

This first chapter of the UNIX blitz deals with one of the biggest routes of insecurity (and one of the easiest to secure): file and directory ownership and permissions. Don't worry about what those mean just yet, you'll find out in a few short sentences.

Renting Space on a UNIX Box

To make sure that we're on an even playing ground, let's explore what this UNIX thing is all about and what exactly your UNIX account is in the first place. UNIX is an operating system, very much like MS-DOS and System 7 are operating systems. All of them serve to work with your hardware to manage every conceivable computer-related task: gaining disk access, managing files, running programs, sending video to a monitor, and so forth. Furthermore, they are largely responsible for the interface through which you communicate with the computer. Some operating systems have very simple, user-friendly interfaces, such as System 7 on the Mac. Others have more cryptic interfaces, such as the MS-DOS prompt or a UNIX shell command line.

Three's a Crowd A *multiuser filesystem* allows many people to share one computer—with appropriate division of resources and security measures so they don't stomp all over each other's work. Common personal computer systems are not designed for such a situation, as they assume you will be the only user of the system.

One notable aspect of UNIX that separates it from MS-DOS or System 7 is that it supports a *multiuser filesystem*. That means the operating system is constructed to permit many users to share space on one machine—and *that* means implementing user accounts and passwords, and dividing up the computer's resources (memory, hard drive space, CPU time) among the many users. "Personal" computer systems such as the Macintosh and PC are not built with multiuser environments in mind, and hence do not have this extra level of complexity and security built in. This is one reason why UNIX is so natural an operating system for the Internet —it allows one computer to serve as the connection point for a large number of users who share its communicative abilities.

When you sign up for a UNIX account, the system administrator and/or service provider has to make a number of changes to his UNIX machine to allow you in. He has to create a password entry for you, of course, and set up the machine to handle e-mail that may come in for you. Most importantly, he needs to set aside an area on the system for your account. In a general sense, this area is some hard drive space that only you can access. This hard drive space is used to store any of the files in your account (such as configuration files), and it is where anything you save in your account resides, such as e-mail or files you've retrieved by FTP or Gopher. The more you store in your account, the more of your ISP's hard drive space it takes up, which is why there are usually limits on how much you're allowed to store in your account at one time. Beyond that quota, you are often charged extra—presumably to help the ISP buy more hard drive space (or more pizza).

In specific terms, your area is created as a subdirectory on your ISP's computer. Just as you may have a subdirectory on your own computer for *documents*, your ISP has a subdirectory for *your_username*. And, so that nobody else can look into your subdirectory and at your files, passwords are implemented to regulate access to your subdirectory. Of course, your ISP can look at any of the files in your subdirectory because it's his computer—he's not restricted by the password protection. If you don't trust that your ISP is keeping his nose to himself or you have evidence that he's not, you have reason to sever your business relationship. However, your password is not the only safeguard regulating access to your subdirectory. Your password mostly regulates outsiders from gaining access to your account and the UNIX machine that your account is on. But you share the UNIX machine with a number of other people already; those people have other opportunities to sneak over to your subdirectory unless you take further precautions.

It's Bad to Share

Remember that your UNIX account is made up of files and directories. By definition, you have at least one directory: the subdirectory within your ISP's computer where your account resides. That is your *home directory*. For example, your home directory might be called **/home/bob** if your username were **bob**. You can usually find out where your home directory is (and so can other people) by fingering yourself, as in **finger bob**. As we discussed back in Chapter 2, a shortcut for referring to your home directory in UNIX is the tilde (~). So, **~bob** means "the home directory of bob," which may be **/home/bob**, for instance.

Within your home directory, you probably have at least a couple of subdirectories. There's probably one called **Mail** and maybe one called **News**. There may be other subdirectories that you've made yourself using the **mkdir *dir_name*** command.

Here, for example, is a typical UNIX account directory, which you can get for your own account with the command **ls -l *~username/***:

```
total 601
drwx------   2 aaron         512 Feb 17 08:14 Dox
drwx------   2 aaron         512 Feb 16 18:33 Mail
drwx------   2 aaron         512 Feb 17 08:14 Misc
drwx------   2 aaron         512 Feb 16 18:33 News
```

```
drwx------  2 aaron        512 Mar  1 20:47 bin
drwx------  2 aaron        512 Mar 12 18:33 ftp
-rw-------  1 aaron     169753 Mar 20 18:09 proposal.doc.asc
-rw-------  1 aaron      54235 Mar 20 18:10 secretdata
-rw----r--  1 aaron     209302 Mar 20 18:14 mydog.gif
```

As you can see, this account has a number of subdirectories for documents, e-mail, FTPed files, saved articles from Usenet news, and miscellany. Furthermore, there are three data files in this home directory: a PGP-encrypted document from Chapter 9, some secret data, and a picture of Barney the Perpetually Overweight Beagle. Because UNIX is a shared multiuser filesystem, it has to have some way to determine whose file is whose. And that's what *ownership* is. In addition, UNIX has to have a way to know who can access a particular file or directory, whether or not they own it. That's what *permissions* are.

Each of the directories and files is owned by someone, and each has permissions determining which users may access a file or directory. The reason it is so vital to make sure your files and directory have the proper permissions is to prevent an unauthorized user on the same UNIX system from accessing them. Even if you have an amazing, unbreakable, super-duper password, if you have a directory with permissions set to allow anyone access, someone else on the same UNIX machine can have at it.

You cannot change ownership of a file or directory yourself; only the system administrator can do that. But that's okay—you don't need to change ownership to prevent unwanted access; that's what permissions are for. You should, however, use your knowledge of ownership to verify that nothing untoward is happening in your account (which I'll explain in the third section of this chapter).

UNIX Hieroglyphics—Making Sense of Permission Bits

The adrenaline is pumping, the sweat beginning to break. You want to know how to identify permissions, and you want it now! Okay, okay, your wish is my food money.

Let's take an excerpt from the output we saw previously:

These are the permissions.

```
drwx------  2 aaron        512 Feb 17 08:14 Dox
```

The above is a directory, called **Dox**. As you can see, there are 10 placemarkers at the left-hand side of the output. The first placemarker tells you whether this entry is a file or a directory. If it has a "d," as this examples does, the entry is a directory. If left as a dash mark (-), then the entry is a file. There are a few advanced types of files that may have something other than a plain dash in the first placeholder, such as an "l" or "c". You're not likely to encounter many of those in your UNIX account. Basically, it'll be a "d" or a dash.

Now, moving to the right of the first placemarker, notice that there are nine remaining places. Actually, there are three sets of three places each. "What??" you bemoan. Don't spit at me, hang on. Remember that we're talking about permissions right now. There are three actions that a user could conceivably take with a file: reading, writing, and executing. That is, given a particular file, you could read that file. For example, if you view the contents of a text file with the UNIX command **more *filename***, you're reading *filename*. Secondly, you could write the file, which means you can edit and save it, or delete it. Lastly, you could execute the file (if it contains a set of instructions that UNIX can understand).

Remember when I said that the rightmost nine places shown previously were three sets of three places each? Each set contains three places: readable, writable, and executable. Enabling or disabling each of those three places allows or disallows that respective action to be taken on the file. Action by who, though? In other words, *you* may want to allow *yourself* the ability to read a file, but not anyone else. Hence, there has to be a way to distinguish between different classes of people for whom these permissions apply. No need to fret, though, they've got this all figured out. That's why there are three sets of places. There are three classes of people that each set of permissions apply to: user (you, the owner), user-group (I'll explain this later), and "other" (i.e., "everyone"). Let's take yet another look at the previous excerpt, with a little visual manipulation to better illustrate these concepts:

d	rwx	---	---
Directory or file	Permissions for user (you)	Permissions for group	Permissions for other (everyone)

The "group" refers to a set of users that can be defined and that may access the file—like a secret club, sort of. As a mere user of the system, rather than its administrator, groups are out of your ballpark, so in our examples we're going to treat group privileges as something you don't want to allow. In summary, you can determine what *you're* allowed to do with a file (or directory), what a select few can do, and what anyone can do.

Using proper UNIX terminology, it should be pointed out that what we've been calling a "placemarker" is called a *bit*. And a dash (-) is called *off*, while a letter means *on*. So, in the excerpt here, we would use standard UNIX grammar and say that "the first four bits are on," and "the last six bits are off." To be even cooler, we might say for the above that "the other-readable bit is off," or, more generally, "all of the 'other' bits are off." Feels good, don't it? Works great at parties, too.

In most cases, you'll want to give yourself full permissions to a file. After all, it's your account and your file. However, if a file is very important and even if you have a backup, you might choose to remove write permissions even from yourself, so you don't accidentally delete it.

The biggest security issue in this chapter concerns the permissions that you allow for the third set: "other." In colloquial UNIX lingo, this group is often called "world" because it makes more sense than "other." Anyone on the same UNIX machine as your account is considered "world." Therefore, if a particular file or directory is "world-readable" (read permissions in the third set are enabled), then anyone with an account on the same system as you can read that file. Your account password is completely irrelevant to this situation. Now, you may *want* to have a file world-readable. Or, you may want to have a file world-executable. For example, you may have written a program for UNIX that other people would like to use. You could make that program file world-executable so others can run it, but can't delete it or otherwise change it as long as its world-writable permission remains disabled. Of course, if you're inviting people to use a file that is in your account, it's that much more important that every other file and directory have proper permissions so that they can't go snooping around elsewhere.

When you have a file that has world permissions disabled, if someone other than you tries to access that file he'll get the message "permission denied." (You 1, Him 0.) If you have a directory with world permissions disabled, then another user cannot even find out what files are within that directory. He'll get the same "permission denied" error.

Let's look at one more example from the "ls -l" output earlier in this chapter:

```
-rw----r--  1 aaron      209302 Mar 20 18:14 mydog.gif
```

Shortcut The command **ls -l** will output the contents of the entire directory. If you merely want to check the permissions on a single file, you can specify that file on the commandline, as in **ls -l** ***filename***.

You can tell the above is a file, because the first bit is off. The user has permission to read and write the file, but can't execute it. However, since this file is a GIF graphic image as opposed to a computer program, it can't be executed anyway, so that doesn't matter. The only other "on" bit is number eight, the world-readable bit. This means that anyone can read this file; most likely they'd download it and load it into a GIF image viewer. The user above (me) has decided to allow others read-access to this file, so that anyone can see the extreme cuteness of my dog.

In general, you should prevent anyone from having any access to your directories or files. Don't take the attitude "I'll just secure the files I need to be secure." Rather, take the attitude "I'll only unsecure the files that I want unsecured." I think I read that in a fortune cookie somewhere. Secure everything unless absolutely necessary. Specifically, this means that you should enable whichever permissions for yourself that you want and disable all permissions for user-group and other ("world").

Lastly, remember that your entire UNIX account is a subdirectory within your ISP's computer. That subdirectory also has its own permissions. Even if everything within your account is properly protected, if your home directory is not, then someone could at least see what files and directories you have—even if they can't access any of the files. It's best to block all access to your home directory so someone can't even peek in and be tempted. You can check the status of your home directory with the command **ls -ld ~*username***. You will see something like this:

```
%ls -ld ~aaron
drwx------ 12 aaron         1024 Apr 11 15:09 /home/aaron
```

As you can see, only the user permissions are enabled. That means that no one but me can even look into my home directory. However, say, for example, the above command yielded this:

```
drwx---rw- 12 aaron         1024 Apr 11 15:09 /home/aaron
```

That would be a bad thing. As you see, the user (me) has full permissions, but "other" (everyone) has read and write permissions. That could potentially be a major problem. Not only could anyone see what's in my account (because read permissions are on), he could write to my account, allowing the possibility of inserting an evil program that can compromise me or the entire ISP computer further (Chapter 15).

So, if you check out the permissions of your home directory and find that other users have wide-open access to your files, read the next section immediately and learn how to change those permissions and plug up that gaping hole!

Watch That Link

Due to a strange convolution in UNIX, there is a twist that, if it affects you, could invalidate the output of the above command and show you misleading permissions output. Some ISPs "link" your home directory to a different place than it would normally be. In these cases, the convention ***~username*** refers to the link, which then refers to the actual location of your home directory. Normally, this shouldn't concern you, and using ***~username*** as I have in this book will not be affected. However, when you execute the command **ls -ld ~*username*** on a linked home directory, you may be shown different permissions than those you really want to know. They could be misleading, as they may not match the actual permissions you're looking for.

How do you find out if you have a linked home directory? Well, first let's consider what you would see if you *do not* have a linked home directory. The command **ls -ld** ***~username*** might produce output like this:

```
drwxr-x--x 18 aaron         4096 Apr 12 18:44 /home/aaron
```

Now, you might not see **/home** necessarily; it could be **/user** or **/u** or anything your ISP makes it. However, if you had a linked home directory, the above **ls -ld** ***~username*** command would produce output like this:

```
lrwxrwxrwx  1 root 11 Apr 22  1994 /home/aaron -> /true/dir/aaron
```

There are two ways to identify whether a directory is linked. Number one is the first bit at the leftmost end of the line is an "l", not a "d" or a dash. That means "link." Second, you see the right arrow (->) on the right side of the line. That means just what it looks like; the directory **/home/aaron** is actually at **/real/dir/aaron**. If you encounter a situation like this when checking the permissions on your home directory, then the directory listed after the right arrow is your actual home directory. You will have to specify that directory explicitly rather than use the ***~username*** convention. So, if you've read the above and find out that you do indeed have a linked home directory, you can check its true permissions using the command **ls -ld** ***/true/dir/aaron*** (inserting what you are told as your real home directory in place of */true/dir/aaron)*.

On behalf of UNIX people, I apologize for all that mess. I hope most of you won't have linked home directories. Linking is useful for ISPs so they don't have to rearrange everything on their computer frequently, but it can also result in potholes like this one. It's like city planning that way.

Taking Control of Your Life... or Your Permissions, Anyway

Having been scared witless by all of the previous material, you might like to be able to do something about it. Well, you can't. Just kidding—whoa, that was too funny—in fact, you can do plenty about it. The magical command that you want to memorize is called **chmod**. That's probably short for "change mode," but who knows with UNIX; it could just as easily stand for "cheese makes odorous diapers."

The chmod command is your key to changing and managing permissions. And, believe it or don't, it's relatively easy to use. Here's the basic template for the command, which I'll explain:

chmod (*class*) (+ *or* -) (*permission*) *filename*

In the model, (*class*) is one of user (u), user-group (g), or other (o). The plus or minus means to enable (+) or disable (-) the permission. And lastly, the permission is read (r), write (w), and/or executable (x). Let's jump right into the shallow end and look at a quick example:

```
chmod u+r testfile
```

The above would enable (+) the read permission (r) for the user (u) on the file "testfile." Remember, the "user" means you in this example, assuming it's your UNIX account. If we started with a file "testfile" with all permissions disabled, we would have seen the following in the "ls -l testfile" output:

```
---------- 12 owner        1024 Apr 11 15:09 testfile
```

After executing the above chmod command, another "ls -l testfile" would yield the following:

```
-r-------- 12 owner        1024 Apr 11 15:09 testfile
```

Now you could read the file called testfile. "Read" basically means anything that involves accessing—but not changing—the contents of the file. That includes reading with a text viewer, copying to another file, or downloading. That doesn't include deleting, modifying, or renaming testfile, as those are all writing activities. However, we can enable the user's permission to write to testfile like this:

```
%chmod u+w testfile
%ls -l testfile
-rw------- 12 owner        1024 Apr 11 15:09 testfile
```

Now, imagine that you had a very important file called secrets.doc. After reading this chapter, you want to check the permissions on this file. So you enter this command:

```
%ls -l secrets.doc
```

To your utter horror, you see the output

```
-rwx---rwx 12 username        1024 Jul 15 16:09 secrets.doc
```

This is bad, because world permissions are all enabled. Anyone could read this file. Technically, that's not exactly true, because it's possible that you have this file inside a subdirectory that has world-readable permission disabled (more on that later). But that's not a chance worth taking. What's worse is that because world-writable permissions are enabled too, someone could possibly delete this file.

So, without stopping to fix a hair, let's correct the above problem using the chmod command:

```
chmod o-rwx secrets.doc
```

Whoa! What is that? Well, if you look closely, you'll see that it's basically like what we've been doing so far, we just combined permissions. In essence, we said "for the class other (o), please disable (-) the permissions for read (r), write (w), and execute (x)." You can combine any permissions in one command, so we could have used **chmod o-rw secrets.doc** to disable only the read and write permissions. Having done the above, we now verify that it worked with this command:

```
%ls -l secrets.doc
-rwx------ 12 username        1024 Jul 15 16:09 secrets.doc
```

Yay! It worked, and now this file is safe and secured for your eyes only.

It would be a good idea to change the permissions on everything in your account so that user-group and other permissions are all disabled. You can then alter later any particular files you want others to access. To change everything in one fell-swoop, try the command:

```
chmod -R og-rwx ~username/*
```

This will remove all permissions from "other" and "user-group" for every file in your account, including all subdirectories and their contents. Note the combination of parameters, which lets us do everything at once, in the above line. The "-R" tells chmod to be recursive; that is, dip into every subdirectory and work its magic there, too. Now everything in your account will be secured such that only you have any permissions enabled.

The Permissions Pecking Order

File permissions work in something of a hierarchical order. That is, if your home directory has world-writeable permission disabled, then nobody can write to anything inside your home directory, regardless of the permissions of specific files or subdirectories. Likewise, if your home directory has world-readable permission disabled, nobody can read anything inside your account regardless of the permissions of the files inside. In short, any file is subject to the permissions of the higher level directories above it. Here's a little diagram:

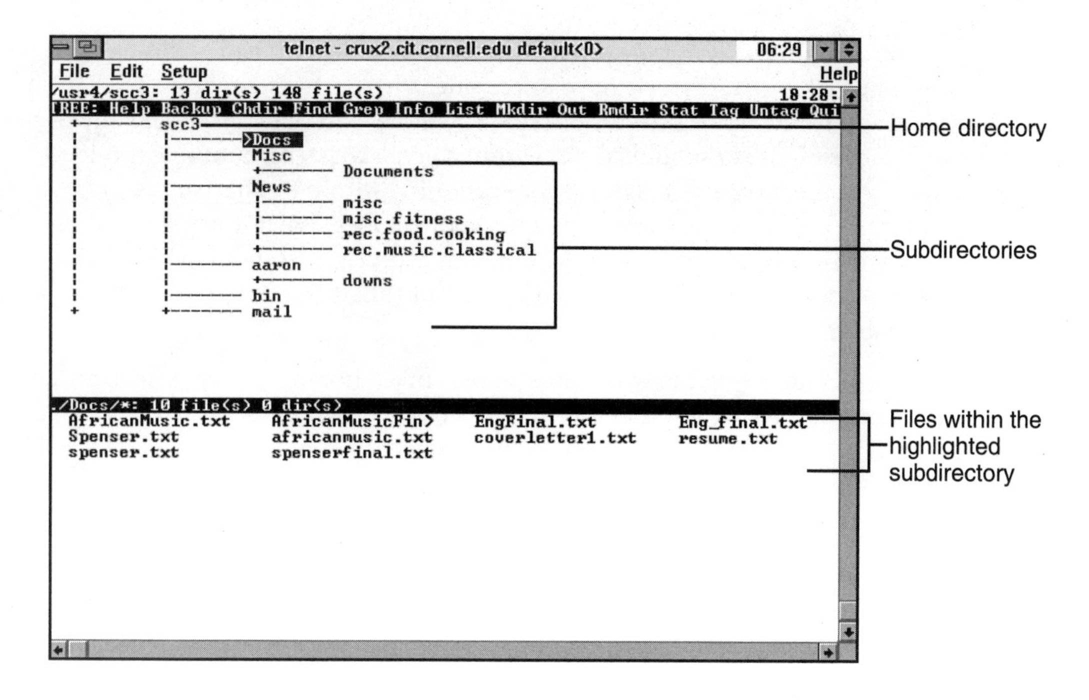

This picture shows a "tree" of directory hierarchies within a single UNIX account.

The topmost directory in this tree diagram is **scc3**, as you can see in the figure. That is the username of this account. This is the home directory—what we've been calling **~scc3** in this book. Within the home directory are several levels of subdirectories. The first level is **Docs**, **Misc**, **News**, **aaron**, **bin**, and **mail**. Within some of those subdirectories are yet more subdirectories. At the bottom of the picture are some of the files that reside in the highlighted subdirectory **Docs**. The permissions on those files are subject to the permissions of the directories above them, the topmost directory taking top precedence.

For example, let's imagine that the file resume.txt within the Docs subdirectory has all world permissions enabled. Without taking anything else into consideration, that would mean that anyone could read or modify resume.txt. But, what if the Docs directory had world-writable permission disabled? In that case, someone cannot modify the file resume.txt because the permissions of the directory that it resides in (Docs) take precedence.

But, what if both resume.txt and the Docs subdirectory had world-writable permission enabled? In that case, we have to consider the *next* higher-up directory; in this case that would be the home directory, ~scc3. Therefore, without considering any of the permissions of files or subdirectories within a given UNIX account, the top-level home directory is the ultimate gatekeeper for everything within it. This isn't to say you should neglect the permissions of your files and subdirectories. What it means is that *in addition* to properly protecting everything within your account, you should protect your home directory itself. If you recall, I warned you about this at the end of the previous section in this chapter.

If you didn't read the whole spiel about linked home directories, go back and read that. Assuming you've got that down, here's how you should set the permissions to your home directory. You want all permissions enabled for you (user) and all disabled for group and other. Like this:

```
chmod u+rwx ~username
chmod g-rwx ~username
chmod o-rwx ~username
```

If you have a linked home directory, the above will still work in modifying its permissions. You only have to deal with that linked and "real directory" stuff for checking the permissions, not setting them. It's a crazy world, what can I say?

Verify that the above worked by running this command:

```
%ls -ld ~username
```

The ouput should be:

```
drwx------ 18 username         4096 Apr 12 18:44 /home/username
```

Very good. Linked home directory users: Remember to read the earlier information on verifying your permissions.

Who Owns What

Way, way back at the outset of this chapter I threw around the term *ownership* with reckless, wanton abandon. You may have noticed by now that a username keeps popping up in the "ls" output. Look:

```
-rw----r--  1 aaron      209302 Mar 20 18:14 mydog.gif
```

See, there it is, just to the right of the permissions section: **aaron**. This is the *owner field*. In short, it means that the user **aaron** owns this file. With few exceptions, you're going to be "owner" of every file and subdirectory within your UNIX account. Like I said earlier, you cannot change who owns a file, and there's no real reason that you'd want to. But the owner field does provide you with some information on who created a file. Specifically, if you notice any files in your account that you don't own, and some other username owns them, that should raise a warning flag. It doesn't necessarily mean a security breach has occurred. You may allow someone to copy a file from his home directory on the same UNIX system into your own. They may set the world permissions so you can use the file, but he may remain owner of it. That's okay.

Also, you may notice a few files owned by **root**. Root is your system administrator. It's probably okay if there are a few files owned by root, but there shouldn't be a whole lot. That's a vague explanation, but it's a potentially messy situation. If someone is illicitly posing as root, ownerships would be misleading. An intelligent hacker posing as root probably won't leave such obvious tracks as erroneous ownerships.

But if a file or files begin to appear that you don't own and you don't know how they got there, notify your system administrator. It could mean that someone else's account on the system has been breached. Were your own account breached, files the intruder created would be owned by your username, so those wouldn't stand out (and hence, ownership is not so helpful in diagnosing break-ins of your own account).

When doing a thorough check of your subdirectories and files for ownership and permissions, don't forget about hidden "dot files." We made a few of these back in Chapter 2 for a plan, project, and signature. Use **ls -la** to see *all* files in a directory. Normally, you omit the "a" because it often produces very long output that you don't need to see, but when hunting for insecurities, you don't want to leave any corner untouched.

The Least You Need to Know

Like Disney World, UNIX is filled with all kinds of colorful little surprises, and if you forget about them they can sneak up from behind and kick you. One of these is file permissions and ownership, which determine who can do what with files within your UNIX account.

- The output of the **ls -l** command will show the permissions in order of user, group, and other. The output of ls -l will also include the owner of a file or directory. Usually this will be you, but if you notice owners that you haven't pre-approved, be suspicious and notify your system administrator.
- There are three classes of people that the permissions apply to: the user (you), a user-group (which we'll ignore), and other (everyone).

- There are three types of permissions each of these classes can get: read, write, and execute.
- You can modify permissions using the UNIX command **chmod**. You must tell chmod which class of person you want to modify the permissions for, whether you want to enable or disable the permissions (using a plus or minus sign), and which permissions to act upon. For example, **chmod o-rw** will disable read and write permissions for "other."
- Except for special circumstances, all of your files and directories should have all permissions for user-group and other disabled. Use the command **chmod -R og-rwx *~username*/*** to properly set all of the permissions on everything within your account.
- Don't forget to protect your home directory itself: **chmod og-rwx *~username***.

Chapter 14

Rlogin Is Evil

In This Chapter

- The UNIX hop—moving between accounts
- Proper hopping
- Protect yourself if you do
- Protect yourself if you don't

In a strange way, "rlogin" is like sex education. There are two possible schools of thought on the matter, assuming that I believe rlogin to be an inappropriate behavior: If I educate you about it, in doing so I also make you aware of its existence, risking that you might then try it. On the other hand, if I say nothing about it, then maybe you'll never find out in the first place. But, ever the pragmatist, I know you're going to find out about it anyway, and I'd rather you hear about rlogin from me than out on the streets.

Why It's Fun and Bad

In the short run, *rlogin* can be used to make your life a little easier in some cases. The word means "remote login," and it's essentially a way of getting from one UNIX account to another, like leapfrog. Rlogin can help you only if you have more than one UNIX account, or one UNIX account shared on more than one machine. While this may not be likely if you're a home Internet user, if you're at an educational institution (and many Internet users are), there's a higher chance that you match one of these criteria. Many schools and departments have multiple UNIX machines for multiple purposes, and you may have an account on one or more of them. Yet other schools have single UNIX accounts that are shared across several machines. That is, you've only got one username and password, but there may be five different machines you can connect to with it. A service provider would do this to distribute the load of users so that there aren't 500 people sharing one computer simultaneously, causing it to perform calculations more slowly than Forrest Gump.

Of course, you may not have anything to do with an educational institution whatsoever and still have multiple UNIX accounts. Some people have a for-pay account they can dial up using a local number, but perhaps that account doesn't offer everything they need. They may then have another account elsewhere, to which they telnet from the local account. However you do it, if you log in to multiple UNIX machines, this chapter applies to you.

Let's say that one of your accounts is on a system named "AccountOne." You have another account on a system named "AccountTwo." These accounts may share your username and password, or they may be entirely separate systems where you have different usernames and passwords on each. Either way, you might want to connect to AccountTwo from AccountOne. One way to do this (and the way you've probably been doing it if you don't yet know what rlogin is) is to use Telnet. Very simply, you probably type **telnet AccountTwo** from the UNIX prompt of AccountOne; you log in from there and go on your merry way. After doing this a number of times, a lot of users get impatient with having to re-log in to the second account. Searching for a shortcut, they inevitably discover "rlogin," most likely by hearing about it from someone else. What rlogin allows you to do, when configured properly, is connect from AccountOne to AccountTwo without having to enter a username—and, more significantly, without having to enter a password. Let me repeat that: rlogin allows you to connect from one UNIX account or machine to another *without* having to enter a password.

Now, in light of the big stink I made in Chapter 6 about passwords and how they are your strongest line of defense, can save your life, heal the sick, and so on, you may be wondering why in the world such a feature as rlogin would exist. I can really only fall back on an historical answer: when UNIX was first developed, they weren't thinking of globally connected environments; they were thinking of five physicists sharing a network with no security concerns because everyone else was out disco-ing to "The Dancing Queen." (And you thought ABBA had no significant impact on the course of computing history.) It may seem that this whole issue of people wanting to take a shortcut and use rlogin rather than Telnet is trivial, and it would be if nobody did it. The problem is, lots of people do it, because we humans are inherently lazy. Why do you think they call it "KFC" now? Everyone just got tired of saying "Let's go to Kentucky Fried Chicken." And so it is with rlogin.

We've established why, like ABBA, rlogin is fun. But why is it bad? If that analogy alone doesn't answer the question, here's an "actual explanation." In order for AccountTwo to allow you to gain entry from AccountOne, it has to "trust" who you are. Not just anyone could rlogin to your account on AccountTwo. So you have to create, in your AccountTwo home directory, a special file that tells AccountTwo what incoming rlogin connections are allowed in. In other words, you have to tell AccountTwo, "If you get an rlogin connection from AccountOne, let them in." AccountTwo will reject anyone other than those whom you specify explicitly. Actually, it won't reject them as such, it will simply prompt them for a password, just as if they were trying to log in to your account through Telnet. Assuming you have a quality password, they'll be thwarted.

Obviously, then, there is some security built into rlogin. But not enough, really—if some devious mind manages either to fool AccountTwo into thinking he is an allowed connection, or alters your configuration file to allow other connections, then he'll have free entry into your account without having ever had to worry about your password. As you can imagine, a "backdoor" such as this can serve to totally undermine the best password in the world—by circumventing it entirely. This is why rlogin is bad. It serves no other purpose than as a shortcut, and a shortcut that opens you up to a major vulnerability—circumventing your password. What good is that? None, which is why you simply shouldn't use rlogin at all.

If I left it at that, though, this would be just another abstinence speech, and those never work (besides, it would be too short a chapter). So we'll look at the details involved in rlogin, information that (I hope) you'll use responsibly. More importantly, this knowledge will also help you defend against others who might try to use rlogin against you. At this point I must ask the little girls to assemble in the auditorium, and the little boys should go to the gymnasium.

The .rhosts File Exposed!

There has to be some way of informing AccountTwo of which rlogin requests it should allow in without prompting for a password. This is exactly what the .rhosts file is for.

If you recall the .signature, .plan, and .project files from earlier in this book, you may have gathered that UNIX has a predilection for configuration files that begin with a period. It's wacky that way. If you have not played with rlogin in the past, you probably do not have a .rhosts file in your UNIX account(s) (although you might have an empty one that was created with your account's birth). Even so, it's a good idea to check. Although we've been using the example of rlogin from AccountOne to AccountTwo, one could move in either direction. For that reason, we want to consider a .rhosts file in every UNIX account you have. First, let's check to see if you have such a file already. Do this by logging in to each UNIX account you have (use Telnet if connecting from one UNIX account to another), and enter the command

```
ls -la ~username/
```

Don't leave off that trailing backslash. You'll see a directory output like this:

```
total 992
drwx—x—x 12 aaron       1024 Apr 13 11:40 .
drwxrwxr-x435 bin       7680 Apr 12 20:14 ..
-rw———   1 aaron           0 Feb 16 18:35 .addressbook
-rw———   1 aaron        1257 Feb 16 18:35 .addressbook.lu
-rw———   1 aaron        1328 Feb 18 18:06 .article.save
-rw———   1 aaron        7151 Feb 17 08:35 .cshrc
-rw———   1 aaron           0 Feb 16 18:32 .gopherrc
-rwx———  1 aaron         103 Feb 17 15:04 .hushlogin
-rw———   1 aaron           8 Feb 16 16:36 .ircrc
-rw———   1 aaron         302 Mar 17 09:35 .login
-rw———   1 aaron         300 Apr  4 11:05 .ncrecent
-rw———   1 aaron         623 Feb 17 08:15 .netrc
-rw———   1 aaron      152967 Apr  8 10:36 .newsrc
drwx———  2 aaron         512 Feb 18 09:45 .nn
-rw———   1 aaron       13352 Feb 18 11:05 .picorc
-rw———   1 aaron        5457 Apr 11 15:09 .pinerc
-rw——r—  1 aaron          72 Oct  1  1994 .plan
-rw——r—  1 aaron          12 Feb 16 21:12 .project
-rw———   1 root            0 Feb 16 16:37 .rhosts
-rw———   1 aaron           0 Feb 16 16:36 .startup
drwx———  4 aaron         512 Apr  8 10:36 .tin
drwx———  2 aaron         512 Feb 17 08:14 Dox
drwx———  2 aaron         512 Feb 16 18:33 Mail
drwx———  2 aaron         512 Feb 17 08:14 Misc
drwx———  2 aaron         512 Feb 16 18:33 News
```

```
drwx———   2 aaron          512 Mar  1 20:47 bin
drwx———   2 aaron          512 Mar 12 18:33 ftp
drwx———   2 aaron          512 Apr 11 15:09 mail
```

As you can see, there are a whole lot of dot files. If you've been using your UNIX account for awhile, you may have a lot of these, too. Often, other programs that you use—such as newsreaders, e-mail programs, Gopher, and so forth—will create their own configuration files. Notice that there is a .rhosts file in the directory shown here—although, as you can see (just to the left of the date stamp), its size is 0; there's nothing in it. Nonetheless, it's still not so hot to let that file even exist.

For now, however, we're going to assume that you *do* have a .rhosts file and *are* going to use it. What's in the .rhosts file is rather simple. It contains an entry for every machine from which you might try to connect to AccountTwo; continuing with our example, you want to tell AccountTwo to allow AccountOne to connect to it. To do this, you merely enter the name of AccountOne in AccountTwo's .rhosts file. If AccountOne is actually "accountone.joe.college.edu" (as opposed to just "AccountOne" as we've been calling it for clarity's sake), you would enter "accountone.joe.college.edu" in AccountTwo's .rhosts file. I realize this can be a little convoluted to explain. Let's take another look at it:

You are logged in to AccountTwo. You used "ls -la ~username/" to get a directory listing of your home directory. You would like to rlogin from AccountOne to this account, AccountTwo. So, you edit the file .rhosts with your favorite text editor. In this case, we'll use emacs:

```
%emacs ~username/.rhosts
```

If there is no .rhosts file in existence, you'll get a blank screen; when you save, .rhosts will be created. If you've already got an existing .rhosts file, the text editor will open it and you can modify it. Assuming (for now) that the .rhosts file is empty, on the first line you would enter:

```
accountone.joe.college.edu
```

That's it. If you save this file and exit the text editor, the .rhosts file will be created, and it's now configured to allow entry to AccountTwo from AccountOne without prompting you to log in. As you can see, it's quite easy to configure the .rhosts file—and that should scare you a little bit.

What if, for example, an intruder were to break into your account and edit your .rhosts file himself? He could conceivably alter it in such a way as to allow himself into your account in the future without needing to use your password. Therefore, he only needs to break your password once, intrude, and modify your .rhosts file. Then, even if you changed your password to something better, it wouldn't matter; he's already allowed himself in. To be fair, it should be noted that said intruder could create a new .rhosts file in your home directory from scratch—so not having one doesn't ensure your security by any means. If you know that you have no .rhosts file, however, and one day you notice one when you're looking at your home directory with "ls -la," that's a sign of trouble. If you have one already and an intruder modifies it, it won't be as obvious to you (you could look at the date stamp, but that's a hard fact to remember very well).

UNIX Runneth Over

It's not as strange as it sounds to have three, four, or five UNIX machines. At my alma mater, technically we had only one UNIX account. That is, we had one username and one password. But there were five different UNIX machines we could use at any time. We didn't actually have five different UNIX accounts—or five different home directories; each of the five UNIX machines accessed one home directory. But because they were five different physical computers, one had to telnet (or rlogin) to get from one to another. Because of this setup, at any time one could invariably find several users rlogin-ing (is that a word?) all over the place, from machine 2 to 4, from 4 to 3, from 3 to 1, and so forth. Such a mess is as ripe as a week-old banana for something rotten to happen.

There's one other piece of information you could include in your .rhosts entry, making rlogin that much more flexible—and that much more dangerous. Suppose you didn't have the same username on AccountOne and AccountTwo. What we've done so far with the .rhosts file will only let you in without a password if your username is the same for both accounts. But let's say that on AccountOne your username is "bobsmith" and on AccountTwo your username is "roberts." If you had the one-line .rhosts file shown here in your AccountTwo home directory, and tried to rlogin from AccountOne to AccountTwo, you'd be denied, or at least asked for a password. Because the rlogin program would think to itself, "Well he wants to get onto AccountTwo, does he? Let's see, his username on AccountTwo is roberts, and his .rhosts file says he's allowed in from AccountOne. So, roberts from accountone.joe.college.edu may enter. Uh-oh, AccountOne tells me that roberts is not his username over there. I can't let him in, then. I'll have to ask him for a password."

The way around this problem is to include the username of AccountOne to the right of the machine name of AccountOne in the .rhosts entry. If you recall from earlier, your current .rhosts file on AccountTwo looks like this:

```
accountone.joe.college.edu
```

But since you have a different username on each account, we'd have to modify this .rhosts entry to look like this:

```
accountone.joe.college.edu bobsmith
```

With the arrangement shown here, AccountTwo would allow bobsmith to rlogin from AccountOne. Here we see another possible security hole: What if a hacker managed to fool AccountTwo in thinking that he was bobsmith, and that his machine was AccountOne? It can happen!

I've shown you the essence of the .rhosts file here. A more complex version of the file would merely contain more entries, allowing more connections from more machines. As you might guess, that only makes the potential risk greater. It's like hiding an extra house key for yourself under your "Welcome" mat. And then hiding another one in your floodlamp. And another under the back porch. And so on...

What You Don't Include in .rhosts

If you aren't yet convinced that UNIX is full of land mines, check this one out:

```
+ +
```

Looks pretty innocent, doesn't it? Almost like two eyes, if we just added a nose beneath it. But to rlogin, it means "wildcard." If your .rhosts file contains "+ +" as an entry, that means *anyone* from *anywhere* can rlogin into that account without a password. Sweet, huh? Sweet if you're a criminal—but scary as a talking mouse if you're just trying to be a law-abiding UNIX user. Sure, you can protect yourself insofar as you *don't* include "+ +" in your .rhosts file. But remember from earlier how an intruder could modify your .rhosts file to allow himself in at some future time? In fact, if he's really knowledgeable he could stick "+ +" in your .rhosts file—which will allow him (and anyone else who tries) to walk right into your account without so much as a blink from your UNIX system.

There are two basic morals to this lesson. One, of course, is that you shouldn't put "+ +" in your .rhosts file. The second is that if you are scanning your account for signs of break-in and find that your .rhosts file magically contains a "+ +" that you never put in it, *fix it immediately!* You can fix your .rhosts file in one of two ways. Either edit the file and remove the offending wildcard, or—better yet—delete the .rhosts file altogether. (The magic word that makes it disappear is **rm ~username/.rhosts**.) It really is a can of worms best left closed.

If You Insist...

In the end, your Internet security and behavior is your business. If you want to take certain security risks, that's entirely your right. We all choose to take security risks every day; that's an inherent part of life. I risk my wallet by walking outside. I risk my car radio by parking in a parking lot and going into the store. There are varying degrees of precaution you might take to protect your car as it sits in the parking lot. Some people have loud, sensitive alarms. Some people merely lock the door. Some people leave the door open, and the keys in the ignition. Using rlogin and keeping a .rhosts file is probably about equivalent to leaving your keys in the ignition, but leaving the doors locked (assuming you've got a second set of keys). An intruder would have to break in first, but once in, he could drive away with your stuff.

The Follies of Youth

In my early, naive student days, I came up with an interesting and horrific solution to a situation. When I dialed in to my university account with my modem, I was assigned a machine name that varied according to whichever university modem answered my call. Once logged on to that machine, I was able to telnet or rlogin to my UNIX account on a different computer. Because I wanted to use rlogin, I tried to set up a .rhosts file for myself. The problem was, how would I know what machine to include in my .rhosts file, since I could be "coming from" any of a number of different machines? Specifically, the university had 96 modems at that time, and each one would assign me a different machine name. I had no way of knowing which of those 96 modems would answer my modem call. So, I figured I'd be clever and cover all the possibilities. I created a .rhosts file with the names of all possible 96 machines I could connect to my UNIX account from. It worked like a charm—no matter which modem answered my call, I could login to my UNIX account without having to enter a username or password. Not only did I make my life so much more convenient, but many a possible hacker would have been quite pleased, too. After all, he had 96 possible options to masquerade as me for my .rhosts to allow him in. That is a hacker's buffet, and were one hungry, my UNIX account would have been the main course.

So, if you do elect to use rlogin and keep a .rhosts file, at least *try* to keep it secure. Keeping your account secure from rlogin abuse rests upon how well you've protected your account in several other ways. For instance, if half the living population knows that you've got an account at *name@come.intrude.me*, it might not be so wise to have a .rhosts file on that account. But if you have a relatively "secret" account that is not well-publicized (in that you don't send e-mail from it to random people and you don't post to Usenet from it), rlogin can be used with a reasonable degree of safety. Be sure that you only put very trusted machines in your .rhosts file. If there is a machine in your local area network that you feel is quite vulnerable to break-in (or has a history of such problems), don't include it as a trusted source for rlogins. Who knows who could have gotten into that machine and begun masquerading as someone else? Most importantly, never, never, *never* include "+ +" in your .rhosts file. Just say no.

As well, don't include too many machines in your .rhosts file. The more you include, the greater the risk—there's that many more machines someone could break into and masquerade from.

...And in the end (to mangle *Abbey Road*), the security you have is equal to the security you keep. If you don't have a .rhosts file, the sudden appearance of one (as shown by "ls -la ~username/") would definitely not be a good thing. After all, if *you* didn't create the .rhosts, *who* did? If you *do* have a .rhosts file, don't overlook the possibility that an intruder may have modified it, compromising your account's security in the future. You can look at your .rhosts file with the command **cat ~*username*/.rhosts**.

The Least You Need to Know

One of the strongest arguments for telling the new UNIX user about rlogin is that alerting you to it empowers you to recognize if someone is using its capabilities against you. Hopefully this chapter has done that, and not inspired you to take unnecessary security risks.

- Rlogin is a UNIX command that allows a user to move between UNIX accounts with a minimum of security.
- Using it can also allow someone else to move into your UNIX account with a minimum of security.
- Don't use it.
- If you do use it, make sure that your .rhosts file is properly created, as explained within the chapter. Never include the wildcard "+ +" in your .rhosts file.
- If a .rhosts file appears in your home directory, or your existing .rhosts file's contents are modified, delete the file immediately and notify your system administrator of the event.

Chapter 15

Don't Take Programs from Strangers

In This Chapter

- Poison candy
- It melts in your account, not in your hands
- Tricks of the trade, Trojan style
- Neighborhood crime watch

While UNIX systems and accounts aren't particularly vulnerable to computer viruses, that doesn't mean they are free from the scourge of human troublemaking. Computer viruses like those we discussed in Chapter 11 are but one type of digital mischief. In some ways, programs meant to terrorize UNIX users can be even more damaging than viruses. A virus often spreads easily within the system it resides on, and of course it can be propagated by passing infected executables to other computers, such as by disk or network. But because most computers that make up the Internet are UNIX-based, mischievous programs can actually spread *themselves* from computer to computer. Humans, no doubt, aid in that spread—sometimes knowingly, sometimes not. This chapter is bound to be somewhat depressing, because I cannot offer much concrete security advice, such as "do this and that and you'll be safe." Hey, that's life—it's not so much different from the real world that way. If someone is determined to shoot you, he probably can. But there are some guidelines you can follow to minimize your exposure to risk (for example: don't go into post offices in suburban America).

Why Not?

The major theme of this chapter is be cautious when choosing sites from which to download programs. We talked about this with regard to viruses already (Chapter 11). But imagine the following scenario (house lights dim... a large bramble drifts slowly across the stage... writer exits stage left...). You've been communicating with someone over e-mail, whom you met by responding to a posting he made to Usenet. At one point in the e-mail exchange, he recommends that you could accomplish some task more easily if you used Program X. Thrilled at the prospect, you accept his offer of Program X, which he sends to you. Okay, that's the scenario setup. I know, it sounds like a "Partnership for a Drug-Free America" advertisement, but this happens all the time on the Internet. As you probably suspect, I'm heading somewhere dark with this. In short, Program X could be anything. I'm not even implying that your e-mail friend was intentionally trying to trick you.

E-mail is only one way in which you could come in contact with someone who offers you a program. A lot of Internet users quickly discover the addictive pleasures of Internet Relay Chat, a.k.a. *IRC*. This is where you can join in a CB-style discussion on various channels with loosely-defined "topics." Thousands of people from all over the world can be found on IRC at any one time, and most of them are just learning how to type. There are ways to transmit files through IRC, and a lot of people use that capability to exchange files. If dangerous programs were athlete's foot, then IRC would be an enormous locker room. So you'd best wear socks—meaning, don't take programs from people on IRC unless you know them personally or are confident in your ability to check the programs for viruses before running them.

Now, I may have said in the introduction to this book that my intent is not to incite paranoia (I may *not* have said that—who knows? At this point I haven't written the introduction yet). It's true; the message here is not "on the Internet, trust no one." It's closer to "understand what can and cannot happen, and use your head." (Or maybe it's "food, folks, and fun," I forget.) Just about any program that is very useful will be available via a more trustworthy distribution route than some guy on IRC. Don't forget about Usenet, either. People sometimes post executable programs on Usenet, inviting others to grab it. Again, these programs are almost always available at major (or at least minor) FTP distribution sites for your computer platform. Grabbing them off of IRC or Usenet is mostly an attempt at a shortcut, and we had a harsh lesson in shortcuts in Chapter 14.

Now for one of those depressing moments. As I said in Chapter 11, even major distribution routes cannot offer a guarantee strong enough to justify dropping your guard. You do what you can (it's an underlying theme throughout this book). Perhaps you may even catch athlete's foot with socks on, but it's certainly less likely than if you bent over and licked the floor (which, of course, would cause athlete's tongue).

A Clever Disguise

Until now, I've been rather coy about what the other nasties are out there besides viruses. Hopefully you found that very attractive, as that was my intent. Probably the biggest other class of very dangerous pranks are known as *Trojan horses*. That's because they are, well, Trojan horses.

The Classics Never Die

Several thousand years ago, the Greeks had this supermodel beauty queen named Helen. Due to some hairy circumstances, she ended up leaving Greece and hanging out with the Trojans. The Greeks were not pleased with this (perhaps everyone else in their population was an eyesore), so they launched a war to retrieve Helen. Sailing to the city of Troy, which, coincidentally enough, is where the Trojans lived, the Greeks tried to take their claim. Unfortunately, after nine years, the effort was still not progressing well.

It was time to dip into their bag of ancient Greek tricks and pull out the ace card. As the story goes, they built a big wooden horse and presented it to Troy. The Trojans took it, not realizing that the clever Greeks had hidden all sorts of troops inside the horse. Once accepted inside the city, the Greeks popped out of the horse and were led to triumph. Several proverbs later, we now use this story to explain the effects of computer programs that do very much the same thing. While there is some consensus that the Trojan war did take place, the question of whether the horse trick is a myth or fact remains open for glorious scholarly debate. And to think, people told me that a liberal arts education was of no use.

The basic psychology of a Trojan-horse program goes something like this:

1. Advertise Yourself as a Useful or Cool Program
2. Convince Someone to Run You
3. Run
4. Either Look Like You're Doing What the User Expected or Appear to Do Nothing At All
5. In Reality, Do Something Really Terrible
6. Laugh

In truth, step 5 is a bit flexible, as the program doesn't necessarily have to do something "terrible" to be classified as a Trojan horse. The key is that it does something other than its stated purpose without the user's permission or knowledge. Many of these doings *are* terrible, otherwise we wouldn't be concerned about them.

Let's take a closer look at that first step—advertising oneself in a misleading way. By definition, the Trojan horse program has to convince you to believe it's something other than what it truly is. In practice, this isn't the job of the program itself, but rather a function of the distribution source. That's one big reason why the source of your programs is so important. Random, unknown individuals are especially useful distribution sources for the Trojan, because both malicious *and* ignorant people can help spread them.

Confounded Confusing Words

There is another meaning of the word "source" in this domain, and it's worth noting. The set of instructions to the computer which make up a program is also called *source*, or more accurately, *source code*. A programmer writes source code, and then sends it through an interpreter that turns the source code (which often resembles English, sort of) into the little ones and zeros that computers find so tasty. A trained individual can look at source code and figure out what a program would do if it were run. In the realm of Trojan horses, the instructions that comprise the Trojan horse are within the instructions for the rest of the infected program. An experienced programmer, then, is the only one who can reliably find a Trojan horse before it strikes—by analyzing the source code before executing the program. That's why, when I said, "the source of your programs is so important," it was kind of like a pun. (Benny Hill, watch out.)

There are two popular façades that Trojan horse distributors put up, and one especially sneaky trick. Some Trojans will live inside programs that are advertised to do something that is merely "cool." One example of this was the Turkey Trojan horse of several years back. The façade was that if you ran this program, it would draw a neat picture of a turkey on your screen. What it actually did was spread itself into the network, and damage some files in your account. The "cool" façade should be a relatively poor one because it's intuitively easier to spot. That is, if someone offers you, or makes available, a program through a risky distribution source that is said to do nothing but be "cool," that's a sure sign to be wary. New users, especially, are prone to try out something for the cool-ness factor without realizing the potential dangers lurking within.

The second, and probably most common, form of façade is the "I'm useful" visage. In these cases, said program is actually claimed to do something of use. What that use is can be very wide-ranging; the Trojan horse can claim to be a new file manager, for example, or an improved version of an already-existing command. In some cases, the "improved" version of the command merely contains a Trojan, which few would consider much of an improvement. It is possible the Trojan-ized program even does what it claims to do, which is very clever; the user, upon seeing the program behave as expected, may be even less suspicious that a Trojan lies within. As you can imagine, these sorts of "I'm useful" façades are harder to spot, because you haven't a confident way of distinguishing truly useful programs from Trojans.

The especially sneaky Trojan is the "hack." Here's the idea: Suppose that I'm a malicious person with a grudge against the world. I want to launch a Trojan, and I want it to spread as far and wide as possible. Being an especially clever nogoodnik, I eschew both the "cool" and "I'm useful" façades. Rather, I look for a program that is already very popular. A program that many more people can be expected to retrieve. I grab a copy of that program, and I create a Trojan which I then "hack" into it—sort of like grafting a new limb onto a tree. Then, I find a distribution source that carries the uninfected program and replace it with my newly "hacked" version. There's no need to convince people to get the program, because I've already picked a popular one. If I'm a good hacker, I may even be able to get my hacked program onto a major distribution source in place of the original. Otherwise, I can pursue other distribution routes. After all, people may be less suspicious if they say "Hey, I'm looking for Program X" and I can wave my hand and answer, "Yep, got it right here. Here you go... ." I'm probably not going to win the Mother Theresa award anytime soon for doing something like this, but it sure will be effective.

You may be wondering how exactly these Trojan horses differ from viruses, and why I'm talking about them now (and not in Chapter 11). One question at a time, please. The biggest difference between the two sinister beasties is that the virus' main goal is to spread itself anywhere possible. So the virus' program code is oriented toward finding places to hide (or reside) in the computer system, from which it can infect more files and media. The Trojan horse does not generally spread itself. That's the role of the distribution routes, the façades, and so forth. Once executed, the Trojan horse usually tries to accomplish some particular task. A virus may or may not do something specific to your computer other than try to spread itself. Much of the virus' harm comes by the mere act of spreading, although some will do other things (such as target specific files for destruction) as a bonus. A Trojan may spread itself over a network, but not merely for the sake of spreading per se; in those cases, doing so is related to its particular goal.

While Trojan horses can and do exist on any computer system, they tend to be most common on UNIX platforms, whereas viruses are most common on personal computers, especially PC clones.

The Greeks Knew What They Were Doing

Of course, the "effectiveness" (in a bad sense) of the methods of dissemination we've discussed ultimately rests on what the Trojan actually does. If I simply wrote a Trojan horse that printed "Hi there, I am a Trojan horse of course of course" on the user's screen, it may spread far and wide, but it doesn't really do anything. From the evildoer's perspective, there's little use in that.

So, the question is, what kind of malice can a Trojan horse engender? Since we're talking about Internet security in this book, consider this example:

You've retrieved the program "better_telnet," which you've heard is a much-improved Telnet client, way ahead of the one your UNIX account uses by default. You install "better_telnet" and you run it. All seems fine. Maybe the program does have some nice improvements over the old Telnet. Maybe you don't notice anything different at all, and figure, "Hmm, I guess I can't tell the difference." Either way, you use the program to telnet into an account.

You Miss Marples out there have already guessed it—Trojan horse! That's right, while you're typing away connecting to sites with "better_telnet," every keystroke you type is being recorded without your knowledge. That includes your username and password, if you telnet into another account. Good ol' "better_telnet" is watching everything you do and writing it all down. It may take this information and store it in a file someplace you're not likely to find it. Then whoever gave you the Trojan program might come by and get the resulting file, and have a nice little reading by the fireside of everything you did. Or the Trojan may even be programmed to e-mail the results back to an address. Imagine that—the Trojan's author just has to sit back in his chair and watch the e-mail come flowing in from users all over the place, with detailed records of everything they typed.

This is not a good thing. And this example is actually a very simple taste of what a Trojan horse might do. In an operating system as complex and powerful as UNIX, a well-written Trojan horse can be extremely sneaky and can achieve a lot of illicit goals. If someone wants to break into your ISP's computer, he could help his cause using a good Trojan. All he has to do is get one user of that ISP to take his Trojan program and run it. Then the Trojan can gather information about the ISP's computer that only someone with an account on it could find out, and send that information back to the Trojan's author. If you recall Chapter 5's section on firewalls, this is a perfect example of how one type of firewall can be beaten.

Imagine a firewall that only allows e-mail in and out of the local network. The bright hacker writes a Trojan, which will gather information he needs from inside the local network. Then he manages to get into an e-mail conversation with someone who works inside that network, and eventually smooths her into accepting this program he's offering, which he sends via e-mail. The user takes the program inside the network, runs it, and voilà! Trojan gallops free, collects the information it needs (which can be over any length of time), and e-mails the results back to its master's lair.

This whole scenario is just *one* possible Trojan behavior. Suppose a less subtle Trojan writer just decides to be blatantly aggressive. His Trojan doesn't quietly hide in the background when you execute the program it's hiding in. Instead, it goes all out and deletes every file you have. Oh, sure, you'll find out about the Trojan pretty quickly, once your files are gone! (As if you needed yet another argument for making backups of important files.)

As a new or inexperienced Internet user, you may be wondering how in the world you could defend against any of this. It all seems so advanced and so subtle; the unfortunate truth is that it is. There are intelligent people and there are terrorists, and there are intelligent terrorists. As in the "real world," though, not every second person is a terrorist. Nor every third person, or fourth, or fifth. Compared to the sheer number of programs that are written, distributed, and run by new and veteran Internet users all over the world, every day, the number of Trojan horses is quite small.

Airlines face the same problem. A terrorist bomb receives all the news coverage, whereas the other 9,000 flights that day—and the 500,000 since the last terrorist bombing—get no press. Similarly, you'll see reports of Trojan horses become big news on the Internet. And well they should be—like a terrorist bombing, they're important news. If you're worried about terrorist bombings, there is a limited amount you can do to protect yourself. You can avoid airlines that fly between high-risk nations. You can look out for strange bags left alone in the airport. Airports themselves use metal detectors to try to screen bombs out, and you might frequent only those airports with high security. But (cynical as this sounds from a young person) if a terrorist is well-trained, intelligent, and determined, he can probably get a bomb onto your plane. So it is, too, with Trojan horses. Fortunately, Trojans on the Internet aren't life-and-death issues, but they can still cause massive amounts of damage in the right circumstances.

Take a Byte Out of Crime (Ugghhh)

Twisted as it sounds, there is one potential advantage to receiving a Trojan horse (or a virus, for that matter) from a major distribution source: other people got it, too. Now, I don't mean that in a "if-I'm-going-down-everyone-else-is-coming-with-me" sort of way. Rather, I mean that if you don't immediately notice the Trojan horse, it's likely that someone else will. Granted, if you've already been damaged or compromised by the Trojan, a lot of good it does you if someone else finds out about the Trojan. Malicious programs take advantage of the Internet's light-speed communications to propagate as widely as possible. But we can use the same technology to fight back. Word of found Trojan horses (or viruses) can be spread via the Internet as quickly, if not quicker, than the diabolical code itself.

One of the best sources of information regarding newly found evils is Usenet. Several newsgroups on Usenet may entertain discussion of this topic: **alt.security**, **comp.security.misc**, **comp.security.unix**, and **comp.virus**. Certainly, if you've recently acquired a program that raises your suspicions—perhaps because it didn't appear to do what it claimed to do, or something else in your account seems funky—ask in one of these newsgroups for advice. If the program has been discovered to contain a Trojan in the past, people will know. Furthermore—and in the "giving back" department—if you've been lucky enough to encounter a new Trojan, acquiring others' help can determine whether there is truly a new Trojan, and word can be passed around the Net.

Seek and Ye Shan't Find Don't trust a virus scanner to find Trojan horses. The two are very different things. For one thing, a Trojan horse is often a modified version of a program that affects its operation, which is not something a scanner can analyze. That's as opposed to a virus, which is often a known series of instructions that appends itself to a known place in an existing program. Besides that, remember that most Trojans live in UNIX programs, where most viruses and therefore virus scanners are on the PC and other home computers.

It's unlikely you'll ever be able to confidently determine who the creator of a Trojan is. Remember, even if you got an infected or hacked program from someone on IRC or on Usenet, the distributor may not be the creator. He or she may not have even known that the program had a Trojan. In fact, he or she may have been struck by it without even knowing.

This raises another issue: you don't want to help spread Trojan horse programs around! It's a great thing to be enthusiastic about contributing to the Internet and helping others out. If you are on IRC or Usenet, you may find someone asking for a particular program. The urge to help them out may be strong, and in general, I encourage it ("helping others" is always such a risky political position to take, after all). For the sake of everyone, though, don't spread any program you have unless you are sure it's safe. As I said earlier, most programs *are* safe, but you never know—especially when it comes to strange little UNIX utilities.

Keep your eyes and ears open regarding every new program you get. If you keep an eye on your account for any strange happenings (unusual files appearing, especially slow response consistently after running a certain program)—you'll probably at least sniff a scent if a Trojan has sent something askew.

The Least You Need to Know

Digital terrorism has one of its strongest weapons in Trojan horses and similar "false front" programs. Designed cleverly, they can elude even the most experienced user. The best defenses are—dipping deep into my sack of clichés—good offenses.

- ➤ Trick programs are often distributed to unsuspecting users from non-major distribution sources. Be wary of programs offered on IRC or Usenet.
- ➤ Trojans can elude firewalls if sent via a route that a firewall does not safeguard against. Note especially e-mail, and be very suspicious about accepting programs e-mailed to you by others.
- ➤ A good Trojan can seriously compromise your security, from stealing your password by watching your keystrokes, to damaging your files, to stealing passwords from your ISP's entire computer.
- ➤ Because a Trojan can often be difficult to spot, even in action, perfectly well-intentioned users might contribute to its spread. Don't be one of them—if you have programs to offer others (especially in wide-distribution systems such as Usenet), don't offer them unless you're confident they're safe.
- ➤ When in doubt, consult with those in the know. The Usenet newsgroups **comp.virus** and **comp.security.misc** are good places to learn more and find out about known or possible Trojans. Do the hokey pokey and shake it all about.

Chapter 16

So You're a Sysadmin—An Introduction

In This Chapter

- The perils of UNIX
- Keeping your users in line
- Fun with file systems (exporting and mounting)
- Ouch, right in the sendmail
- Setting up shop, or anonymous FTP
- How to be a better sysadmin

In a perfect world, Twinkies wouldn't be defenses, I'd have more hair with fuller body, and UNIX systems would only be administered by those with years of networking experience. Unfortunately—sometimes due to lack of resources, lack of understanding, or lack of sympathy—people who are better qualified elsewhere are put in charge of UNIX systems. It's not that there's anything inherently difficult about understanding UNIX for a reasonably intelligent person. Rather, it's that the learning curve is steep and the risks can be high. Imagine a steamship, recently acquired by MegaCorp, with no one to captain it. For whatever reason, MegaCorp can't get an experienced captain, and so they assign the best and brightest head of sales to the task. Well, Mr. Head of Sales might be the greatest salesman the world has seen, but pirates on the high seas will get word that he's trying to captain this ship, and they won't be long in paying a visit. This does happen in the real world, at least as far as UNIX is concerned. While this may not apply to very many readers, some may find themselves (now or in the future) in the unenviable position of having a UNIX system under their jurisdiction.

Some organizations underestimate the complexity of UNIX and the possible security compromises that come with it. This chapter is intended as a brief introduction to the issues involved in system administration, and it covers some of the bigger possible security holes. (To the experienced user, this chapter will seem more akin to teaching someone to close windows and lock doors than it is to installing alarm systems and motion detectors.)

A Brief Debriefing

Ideally, system administration should be a full-time position, so that one individual can dedicate his or her time to the task. In some organizations with especially sensitive needs, full-time positions are dedicated to security experts alone. (Those organizations know who they are, and probably aren't reading this book.)

A system administrator, heretofore referred to as a *sysadmin* because it's easier to type repeatedly (and because that's what people call it), has a variety of concerns. Often this person must communicate with the users of the UNIX system, helping them with difficulties and making system modifications when necessary. Hard drives fill up, e-mail folders overflow, users forget passwords, and so on, and on, and on. Often those are the easy problems. Sometimes the sysadmin has to custom-write programs to handle certain situations peculiar to the system. On top of all that, sysadmins have to worry about security holes and security breaches. With such heavy silicon on their shoulders, it's no wonder their hair looks the way it does.

There are several philosophical "ways in" to your UNIX machine; these form the broad backbone from which most specific security issues hang. All of this assumes that your UNIX machine is networked, and in the case of this book, networked to the Internet. The only 100 percent sure way of protecting anyone from gaining unauthorized access to your UNIX system is to unplug it from the network altogether. And the only sure way of protecting *anyone* from getting to the computer, whether by network or in person, is to unplug it from the wall and throw it off a bridge. Since you're not going to do that (unless it's a department-owned computer, in which case it's fun), you're not going to be 100 percent secure. But that's okay, if there's any theme that's been waved around throughout this book, it's that one. The most popular, and potentially easiest, way that outsiders will break into your UNIX system is through user accounts.

Those Darn Passwords Again

User accounts make easy targets, because they are routes of pre-authorized access into your system. In many ways, the security of an individual user's account is the responsibility of that user—that's been the focus of most of this book. Like a "friendly Gestapo," however, you as sysadmin can check up on your users' security habits. Most notably, their passwords. As much as it is in a user's self-interest to have a quality password, it's in the sysadmin's interest that *all* users have quality passwords. If a hacker can break into any one user's account on your system, his ability to compromise your entire system is greatly enhanced if the passwords aren't up to snuff.

As sysadmin, you have "root" privileges. That means you can log in with the username **root**, enter the root password, and have total access to the system. The "jewel in the crown," as it were, for a hacker is to get your root password. Deduction number one from this logic is that the quality of root's password is of ***UTMOST*** importance. After all, if a hacker manages to log in as "root," the entire system is his. Users' individual passwords immediately become irrelevant.

The most common way a hacker will try to obtain root's password is by a two-step process. There is a file on your UNIX system that contains all the passwords for everyone on the system, including root. In most systems, this file is located in the path **/etc/passwd**. (Some systems have more advanced passwording techniques, and the situation may be different there, but that is an advanced topic.) The garden-variety UNIX system will have an "/etc/passwd" file. One of the unfortunate realities of this file is that it has to be world-readable (see Chapter 13). Therefore, step one for a hacker is to get into the account of a user on the system.

There are a variety of ways a hacker can try to get into a user's account. One of them, and one of the simplest, is to exploit a poor password or a revealed password. You, as a sysadmin, can't really prevent a user from blabbing his password to other people, but you can prevent a poor password from being chosen or from lasting very long. A popular tool of hacker and sysadmin alike is a program called "Crack." Crack is essentially a logic routine; based on entries of a supplied dictionary file, it attempts to crack passwords. At first, this may seem terrible, and it's true that it can be used terribly. As sysadmin, however, you too can run Crack. If it succeeds in cracking any user's passwords, you know that a hacker could do the same. That's a solid reason to send the user an e-mail saying, "Your password is insecure. Please change it." If you really want to get harsh, you can disable a user's account—and then, when the user calls you to ask what happened, you can say, "You had a terrible password. I must spank you." Some sysadmins run Crack periodically to check up on their users. There's also a special version of Crack that can tie in to the password-creation program, so that a user's password can be checked immediately when he changes or creates it, and disallow poor passwords on the spot. More information on finding Crack can be found in the "Further Reading" section in the back of this book.

Now, in the two-step process I'm describing, the hacker couldn't use Crack on a given user's account; using Crack requires having the "/etc/passwd" file, and acquiring that file is the goal of this process. But if a user had an easy-to-guess password (or one that has passed around through word of mouth), a hacker may get into that user's account. And don't think the underground doesn't pass around and trade revealed passwords—they do. Once inside a user's account, the hacker can retrieve the "/etc/passwd" file from the system, and then use his own computer to run Crack on it, trying to break root's password.

This is the ultimate reason that root's password should be of extremely high quality. That way, the "/etc/passwd" file won't be of much help in cracking root. Now for the bad news: there are ways into a user's account other than password-guessing; there are ways to grab the "/etc/passwd" file without breaking into a user's account; and there are ways to compromise your entire system without ever knowing root's password. Quit now while you have the chance! Stick someone else with this hideous job. Ah, but, like Sisyphus, you persevere.

The rest of the issues in this chapter cover various routes through which a hacker might accomplish any of the aforementioned atrocities. But be warned—I'm only covering the real biggies. This is a chapter that could easily be a book, and in fact, it is—several books, many of which a well-stocked bookstore probably carries.

The Trouble with finger

We looked at some of the personal risks of the finger command many pages ago. As a sysadmin, you'll find finger no more heartwarming. If a hacker is going to work on drilling into a user's account, he's got to know some usernames on your system first. Finger makes this a very easy task. Often, using the finger command without specifying a user (and using only your hostname) results in a list of all users currently logged on. Look:

```
%finger @your.system.edu
[your.system.edu]
Login       Name                TTY Idle    When             Office
gem2        Chicken Lady         p0  22: Mon 13:20   315b CCC
cwg7        Dan Husk            *p1   14 Fri 01:12
```

```
dqt13    Gavin                 p4        Sat 13:30
chm5     Darrill               pe   20: Thu 23:41
kth3     Kathy                 q2      6 Sat 13:44   655 E&TC
cth3     Cathy                 q3        Sat 01:02
jl16     Mr. Peterson          q5        Sat 12:26
```

Well, our hacker's got a nice little list of usernames now. Another way to get usernames from some systems is to **finger 0@*your.system***, which may result in a list of all users on that system. (Note that it's a zero, not a letter "O," before the @.) Using either technique, he gets it. Once the hacker has a username, recall that the output of a typical finger command does specify a user:

```
%finger dqt13@your.system.edu
Login name: dqt13                         In real life: Gavin
Directory: /home/dqt13                    Shell: /usr/local/bin/tcsh
On since Apr 15 13:56:25 on ttyq4 from DIALUP-0522
Project:
Plan: How much do you think my head weighs?
```

From the above, not only can he find out everything we talked about in Chapter 2, but he can also nab the user's home directory. (That can be valuable information, especially for a special reason we'll look at in the next section on mounting file systems.)

As a sysadmin, your best defense against finger is to disallow it. You can allow outgoing finger requests (the "finger client"), so that your users can finger other systems, but you can prevent incoming finger requests (the "finger server") so nobody can finger your system. Whether or not you want to do this really depends on your particular situation. Many users may want others to be able to finger them, so there's the issue of democracy to consider. Furthermore, if your system is well secured in other ways, then the information that finger provides may not help a hacker much. The finger client is called **finger**; the finger server is usually named **fingerd**. Therefore, if you just kill (or don't launch) the "fingerd" process, the finger server will be disabled; outsiders will not be able to finger your system.

Sur-Mounting Your Guard—A Look at Mounting File Systems

One of the great benefits of networked computing is that you can share information between systems. Actually, that's more than a benefit, it's the whole purpose of networking. *Mounting* is one way to share information (files) between computers. A *file system* basically means a section of your storage space, such as a hard drive, hard drive partition, or subdirectory. When you "export a file system," you allow another computer to share one of your file systems, and possibly vice versa. The person on another computer can "mount your file system," meaning they can access your exported area as if it were their own.

The potential problem with mounted file systems is that they can offer yet another route into your UNIX machine. When mounting file systems, you have control over what specific computers may mount your file system, and which of your file systems can be mounted. The process is similar to rlogin in that respect (with its corresponding .rhosts file); there is a file named **/etc/exports** on your UNIX machine that regulates who can mount and what they can mount. Here is a sample "/etc/exports" file:

```
# exports       This file describes which parts of the local file
#               system are available for mounting
# Version:      @(#)/etc/exports        2.00    04/30/93
#
/home           machine2.mydomain.edu
/usr/public -o
/usr            machine2.mydomain.edu machine3.mydomain.edu
# End of exports.
```

Okay, let's make some sense of this. Any lines with a # at the beginning are comments, not commands. The first actual line begins with "/home." The brief structure of each of these entries is

```
file system to export — options — allowed hosts
```

So, in the first line, we are exporting **/home**. Please note that you must explicitly define any file system or directory to export—that is, exporting /home does *not* allow the listed hosts to mount subdirectories within /home. Therefore, the first line allows the computer named **machine2.mydomain.edu** to mount the **/home** directory on your computer (but not subdirectories within /home).

In the second actual (non-comment) line, we offer the directory **/usr/public** for export. Note that no machines are listed in this entry. That means "everyone" by default—that is, anyone can mount this directory. In this example, we've made believe that you keep files available for public use in **/usr/public**, which is why you allow everyone and anyone to mount it. Note that there's an important option (**-o**) in the second line. That means the mount is "read-only." So, while anyone can mount your

"/usr/public" directory, they can only read it, not write to it. If you omit the "-o," as we did in the first and third entries, then the exported file system or directory is *both* read- and write-enabled.

Moving to the third, and final, line, we see that **/usr** is available for export. There is no "-o"—so it is being exported as readable and writeable. Lastly, two machines are listed that may mount it, each separated by a space. This is essentially the same idea as in line one, except we're allowing multiple machines to mount this exported directory.

The result of all this is that someone logged in to **machine2.*mydomain*.edu** may mount your **/home** and/or **/usr** directories, while someone logged in to **machine3.*mydomain*.edu** may only mount your **/usr** directory. Anyone logged in to any machine can mount your **/usr/public** directory, but it'll be read-only.

One possible vulnerability this can lead to is that if you export an important directory or file system to another host, someone who breaks into that host could then gain access to your exported file system. By definition, then, exporting to other machines increases your vulnerability; you are, to a degree, adopting *their* vulnerabilities. Exporting does have its uses, however (and sometimes its necessities), so the key is to be sure you export the least risky directories on your machine—to other machines that you trust to be secure themselves.

Now, the *big* problem with everything we've just said is that you might export a sensitive directory to "everyone." This is one of those things that can just fall through the cracks, especially when sysadmin tasks are given over to someone without this type of detailed knowledge (perhaps because he has better things to do). Unless you check, you may be sitting there with a UNIX machine whose "/etc/exports" file is allowing anyone and his brother to mount your important directories. When person or persons unknown mount a directory—especially if he has write-access to it—he can do anything he wants in it (such as replace your programs with Trojans). Even with read-only access, a user who mounts your **/etc** directory (if you've exported it) could snag your "passwd" file and let Crack work on it.

The safest thing to do is check your **/etc/exports** file right now, using the command **more /etc/exports**. If you see anything that looks awry (like directories being exported to the world), investigate further. It's highly advisable that you read the full manual that covers exporting—which you can enjoy by entering the command **man exports**. It's not even that long.

Sendmail: The Wild Child

There's no one who doesn't enjoy a good e-mail message. In fact, the Internet came about largely because the concept of e-mail caught on. The Net's purpose was initially to share research, but it rapidly became apparent that even wire-spectacled academics were writing, "Hi Bob, how are little Bobby and Jan?" So virtually every UNIX system connected to the Internet can send and receive e-mail. One of the culprits responsible for this state of affairs is a program called "sendmail." Aptly named, that's pretty much what it does. What you might not know is that people from outside your computer can talk to your sendmail. It's a very affable program and always enjoys chatting with people, but it can also be gullible, and outsiders can influence your sendmail to behave badly. One can initiate a conversation with your sendmail by telnetting to your UNIX machine at port 25. Here's how it's done, and a sample conversation follows (the bolded words are what I said, the non-bolded are sendmail's responses):

```
% telnet yourmachine.edu 25
Trying 128.128.128.128...
Connected to YOURMACHINE.EDU.
Escape character is '^]'.
220 yourmachine.edu.XXX.com Sendmail 5.51/5.17 ready at Sat, 15 Apr 95
15:46:57 EDT
help
214-Commands:
214-     HELO     MAIL     RCPT     DATA     RSET
214-     NOOP     QUIT     HELP     VRFY     EXPN
214-For more info use "HELP <topic>."
214-To report bugs in the implementation contact eric@Berkeley.ARPA
214-or eric@UCB-ARPA.ARPA.
214-For local information contact postmaster at this site.
214 End of HELP info
expn harryb
250 Harry Baker <harryb>
expn root
250 Admin <root>
mail from: hacker
250 hacker... Sender ok
rcpt to: harryb
250 harryb... Recipient ok
data
354 Enter mail, end with ."" on a line by itself
```

```
Hello there harryb. I can send mail to you now or do other sneaky things.
.
250 Ok
quit
```

The exact purpose of everything I did here is not important for our discussion; what I wanted to illustrate is that through a conversation with "your" sendmail, I was able to find out (or confirm) the identity of a user and convince your sendmail to send a message to that user from a fake name ("hacker"). The serious problem isn't that I could have sent "harryb" a fake message. No, the problem is that some versions of the sendmail program—versions that were distributed with UNIX machines from various vendors for several years—have bugs that I could have exploited in this little exchange of pleasantries, and used to do some real crafty things.

What things? Well, one sendmail bug would have allowed me to create a .rhosts file and stick it into harryb's account. Think about that for a moment! Using another trick, I could have told harryb's account to get the "/etc/passwd" file from your system and send it back to me. I'm not going to elaborate on how these tricks are done, because it's not necessary, and the solution can be had without my revealing these very dangerous holes in specific details. The philosophy behind the solution is the important part, and that philosophy is this: *make sure you have a recent version of sendmail!*

If and when you get involved with security issues like these, become familiar with an organization known as the Computer Emergency Response Team, or "CERT" for short ("with Retsin!"). They have a Gopher and an FTP site at **info.cert.org** and a World Wide Web page at **http://info.cert.org**. (Although I've been hesitant to offer too many specific addresses that would become obsolete in this book, with names that logical, they've got to last!) There you will find all the latest (and in the archives, the oldest) information on UNIX security issues—and on bugs like the sendmail ones I've referred to. You'll also find instructions on how to fix the bugs; if you require new versions of a program, like sendmail, they'll tell you how to get it.

Many bugs, especially in well-known UNIX programs, have fixes, patches, or replacements available, and CERT is the best way to keep informed of these things. The sendmail example just given is both a real story and a parable; other common UNIX programs have been found to have similar security holes. Again, CERT is one way to inform yourself and stay informed.

What's a CERT?

CERT stands for "Computer Emergency Response Team." This organization was created to educate the Internet community about security issues and to advise and aid them in dealing with security breaches old and new. Born in 1988 out of the infamous Internet Worm incident (in which a program that propagated itself across the Internet was launched and spread so far that it caused the entire network to come to a halt), CERT maintains a 24-hour hotline, as well as file archives and mailing lists. It helps anyone deal with any security issue at any time. It's run out of Carnegie Mellon University and can be reached by e-mail at **cert@cert.org**.

Anonymous FTP Caveats

Quite a number of UNIX machines offer what is known as *anonymous FTP*. If you've ever used FTP at all, then you're probably familiar with anonymous FTP. FTP, as we've discussed, is a protocol for transferring files between computers. This capability has lead to the creation and growth of "FTP sites," which are computers that make available large libraries of files for Internet users to transfer for their own use. To help keep these repositories available to the general Internet public, they don't prompt you for an individually-assigned username and password when you log in. Rather, you log in with the username **anonymous**; often you can enter your e-mail address as your password. From there, you can move around the directories made available to you and retrieve files. In some cases, you can put files you already have onto the FTP site for others to use.

By the Way...
To follow the procedures here, you must be currently logged in to your UNIX machine as user "root." You can do this by either logging in to your UNIX machine from scratch with the username **root** and root's password, or by typing **su** at the UNIX prompt and then entering the root password. Now—back to the show... .

Good as this all is—and it's very good, since much of the Internet's success has been related to anonymous FTP—from the UNIX sysadmin's point of view, allowing incoming FTP connections from the general public is yet another route into the poor little UNIX machine. Configured improperly, an anonymous FTP server could allow users more freedom inside your machine than you want them to have. There are several basic steps to securing your anonymous FTP server. If you already have anonymous FTP available, you might check to make sure the following safeguards are in place. Take heed, as well, if you're about to set up a site.

There is probably a "user" on your system named **ftp**. That's okay, but you want to be sure nobody from the outside can log in *as* user "ftp" and start snooping from there. The way to plug this hole is to place an asterisk (*) in the password field of the ftp's entry in the "/etc/passwd" file. For example, if you look at your "/etc/passwd" file, one of the lines may look something like this:

```
ftp:gf43kjklfjdi0:3001:3001:Anonymous FTP:/pub/ftp:/bin/noshell
```

The major key in the above is the second "field," **gf43kjklfjdi0**, just to the right of the **ftp** at the beginning of the line. That is the *password field*. In the example, it's a bunch of gobbledygook, which is actually the ciphertext of a true password. You want it to be an asterisk. There's one exception: if your system uses something called *shadow passwords*, then the situation is different—and more complicated. It would be best to find out from someone who knows whether your system uses shadow passwords (if it's a "garden variety" UNIX, it probably doesn't). If it does, the password fields of the entries in "/etc/passwd" wouldn't contain the gobbledygook that is ciphertext, but something that simply "marks a place" and doesn't look encrypted. Assuming that you don't use shadow passwords, you'd want the line shown here to look more like this:

```
ftp:*:3001:3001:Anonymous FTP:/pub/ftp:/bin/noshell
```

There's a decent chance that the above is already correct on your UNIX system, in which case you're one step ahead already.

The second big issue regarding anonymous FTP is having proper ownership and permissions on the files and directories that make up the space in your machine where anonymous FTP users will be allowed. First, ftp's home directory (**/pub/ftp** in our example) should be owned by root. You can verify this by entering the command **ls -ld ~ftp** and checking that root is listed as owner. If it is not, make root the owner with the command **chown root ~ftp**. Having done that, it's important that ftp's home directory not be writeable to anyone other than root (ftp's owner, in this case). You can check the permissions on ~ftp with **ls -l ~ftp**, and if any permissions allow write access, fix it with **chmod 555 ~ftp**.

In finishing off the instructions for securing your anonymous FTP, we'll be making copies of some of your important system files within ftp's home directory and protecting them from abuse or spying. It may take one or more times reading over this section to get it all the way through—read it as often as necessary, or until your sanity becomes perilously slippery. Readers who aren't UNIX sysadmins should avert their eyes!

Users need to be able to retrieve directory listings from your FTP site, which means they need access to the "ls" command. But you don't want them to have access to your "real" ls command, because that's located somewhere they shouldn't be. So we're going to create a copy of your "ls" command that anonymous users can use safely:

1. Start by creating a "bin" directory within ftp's home directory, like this:
   mkdir ~ftp/bin.
2. Now copy your "ls" command into this new bin directory:
   cp /bin/ls ~ftp/bin/ls.
3. That done, the **~ftp/bin** directory must also be owned by root, so
   chown root ~ftp/bin.
   Oh, and it shouldn't have any write access:
   chmod 555 ~ftp/bin.
4. You then protect the new "ls" command itself this way:
   chmod 111 ~ftp/bin/ls.
5. Now you need an "etc" directory within ~ftp, too. The fun never ends:
   mkdir ~ftp/etc.
   Just to be sure, **chown root ~ftp/etc** and then **chmod 555 ~ftp/etc**.
6. Now you want to make copies of your **/etc/passwd** and **/etc/group** files and put them into this new directory:
   cp /etc/passwd ~ftp/etc/passwd and **cp /etc/group ~ftp/etc/group**.

   This next part is very important. As you can see, there is now a copy of your **/etc/passwd** file in your **~ftp/etc** directory. You don't want anyone grabbing this copy and running Crack on it with all your account entries in it.
7. Fire up a text editor and delete every entry in "/ftp/etc/passwd" except for the "ftp" entry. Remember, you want to make these modifications to your **~ftp/etc/passwd** file, *not* your "/etc/passwd" file!
8. Protect these two files in **~ftp/etc** this way:
   chmod 444 ~ftp/etc/*.
   We're almost done!

   Lastly, since this is an anonymous FTP site, you need a directory for the public to use. We'll call this "pub" since that's the traditional name for it.
9. Make a "pub" directory: **mkdir ~ftp/pub**. Root should own this directory, too:
   chown root ~ftp/pub.
   But we want this directory to be world-readable and world-writeable, so that people can actually use it to exchange files:
   chmod 777 ~ftp/pub.

The one possible downside to the last step we just did is that you may not want users uploading just anything to your FTP site for others to download. That is, you may be happy to offer files for the public to retrieve, but you want to screen files that the public puts onto your site before you let the rest of the public at them (for viruses, content, copyright violation, etc.). In that case, you don't want the "~ftp/pub" directory to be world-writeable, only world-readable. So do a couple of quick procedures:

1. Issue the command **chmod 644 ~ftp/pub**.
2. Within this directory, create another directory that the public can upload files into, but they can't retrieve files from—that is, world-writeable but not world-readable. For example, try **mkdir ~ftp/pub/incoming. chown root ~ftp/pub/incoming. chmod 733 ~ftp/pub/incoming**.

Now you'll have a subdirectory "incoming" within **~ftp/pub** that the public can put files into, but can't retrieve files from. You can then review the files for approval before copying them into **~ftp/pub**, where anyone can then retrieve them.

Well, congratulations for making it this far! If this has been your first time through, go back and read this entire section again. If not, collect $200 (the weekly pay raise you deserve for having this job) and go on to the end of this chapter.

But Wait, There's More!

In the hopes of sounding redundant, these last several sections are just a little sample of UNIX "sysadminning" issues in the area of security. People make their careers out of this topic, but that doesn't mean you have to. A reasonably secure UNIX machine can be attained with the information I've provided in this chapter. (Obviously, if you work for the CIA, "reasonably" isn't good enough, but they've got their own people for that sort of thing, with fake names and government houses.)

The reason I highlighted these UNIX situations in such gory detail is simple: improperly configured, they are some of the biggest, most glaring openings that a smiling hacker will just swagger right through. I've hesitated to do too much scare-mongering in this book, but if your UNIX system has such gaping openings as exporting important file systems to everyone (or improperly secured anonymous FTP), it won't be long before an attacker strikes.

You may have heard recently about a new UNIX program called "SATAN." It's gotten some press in the big media, though it's largely misunderstood. The purpose of SATAN is basically to provide a suite of tools for the UNIX sysadmin to find security holes in his system. Some have expressed concern that unscrupulous people might use SATAN to find holes in other people's systems. They're probably right, but then, won't unscrupulous people always do that? Although it serves to make checking your system easier, it's still not a program for the inexperienced user. Without some knowledge about the holes that SATAN tracks down in the first place, a hacker-wannabe is going to be hard-pressed to make use of the program's findings. Using SATAN might make it easy for a true hacker, but that's always been a central irony in computer security: the protectors and the hackers use the same tools to combat each other. It's basically a matter of who gets to whose system first with the tools, and that's the way it will always be.

If security is truly a top priority on your system, then it's best handled by someone experienced and dedicated to that role. If security is not of the utmost priority, but you want to be reasonable, then periodic readings of CERT advisories (which can be found at their sites listed earlier, or in the Usenet newsgroup **comp.security.announce**)—along with a willingness to learn about UNIX—should serve you well against the dime-a-dozen hacker.

Further, it never hurts to have security-minded users on a UNIX system. Educating your user base about such issues as passwords, Trojans, and so forth can help avoid headaches in the future—as will watching for troublesome users. If you find, for example, that a user is using an inordinate amount of disk space, it's worth an inquiry. It's certainly possible that he's working on a legitimate project, and if you touch base with the person, you can work it out. But it's also possible that somebody's using your machine as a trading post for files you may not want to be involved in trading; the shady trader could be an actual user on your system, or an outsider using a cracked account. Watching out for such things, even though the break-in has already occurred, you can still stave off further damage.

Oh, and lastly, if you've found yourself in the role of part-time UNIX sysadmin, the best advice is probably to take lots of lunch breaks! Chew slowly.

The Least You Need to Know

UNIX sysadminning is hardly a job for those who value sanity. Nonetheless, some find themselves in the sysadmin's shoes anyway. Assuming you're not at a top-security organization where missiles are assembled and colas are formulated, some moderate awareness can keep your UNIX machine in relative safety from everyday hackers.

- The behaviors of your users can contribute to the (in)security of your machine. If they create poor passwords or spread their passwords around, others have an easy way in. You can use the program Crack to seek out user accounts with easy-to-break passwords.
- Exporting file systems can be a very useful way to share information between machines. Done improperly, however, it can allow outsiders to walk right onto your system. Learn the proper use of the "/etc/exports" file, both from this chapter and the **man exports** command.

- You need sendmail to handle e-mail for your system, but older versions of sendmail (for different UNIX versions) present holes that hackers can exploit. The best course of action is to stay on top of new versions of sendmail. Check out CERT (**http://info.cert.org** on the World Wide Web) information for specifics on these and related issues.
- Using anonymous FTP is like allowing people into your house to borrow stuff. It's a great service to the community, but you have to be sure the hallway and bedroom doors are locked, so to speak. Doing so requires proper ownership and permissions on relevant files and directories. The exact procedure is too complicated to summarize here, but the full details reside within this chapter.
- Educate your users to help stem the tide of security problems, and watch out for abuses of your machine. The earlier you catch the abuse, the more you can prevent further damage. Be especially alert for unusual login behaviors and/or excessive usage of your disk space; these are only two of the possible warning signs.
- Eating lunch is often a good solution to these problems—not so much for the UNIX machine, but for your head. So eat a lot of lunch, and stay alert and aware. The UNIX sysadmin is like a town sheriff, except you don't get a star or a gun. If you're lucky, you get a really big monitor.

Part 4
The Good Society

For better or worse, the Internet is not a wholly self-inclusive structure. The outside world still has an impact on the Net. People rip each other off, exchange very exciting and/or evil pictures, stomp all over copyright, and scream at one another. We all can't just get along, and this part is about many of those times when we don't.

There are a number of interesting areas where pre-existing social institutions clash with the Internet, and we'll smell some of that swirling around these chapters. There's not as much concrete tutorial material as earlier in the book, but rather "rules to live by." Or something like that. Be good to each other, as a TV judge used to say.

…And he was left with a pile of rubble.

Chapter 17

Yay, Capitalism!

In This Chapter

- You better shop around
- Cutting the deal
- One for me, one for you (the Grand Exchange)
- The Great Credit Debate

To the chagrin of some old-guard types, commerce on the Internet has boomed within the past couple of years. The not-so-free market system has smelled a bounty in them thar phone lines, and I'm not only talking about the phone companies. Before many commercial vendors took up Net presence, there was plenty of trickle-sideways going on the old-fashioned way—from person to person. Now, both the used (second-hand) market and new markets are exploding on the Internet. Although there are great things to be had in Net commerce, several words of caution are in order so that you get what you pay for, you get paid for what you give, and nobody else butts in-between.

From Whom the Price Tolls

There are two basic classes of *vendors* on the Internet: commercial entities (which practice business and sales in much the same way they do in the "real" world) and private individuals (as in a giant classifieds section). It's tempting and intuitive to think that dealing with commercial enterprises is necessarily safer than with private individuals, but Net reality hasn't proven this either true or false.

Remember that on the Internet, there is no official governing body. This also means there is no law enforcement and no Better Business Bureau. Getting ripped off can be a real hassle, because traditional bureaucratic institutions such as the "real" Better Business Bureau may have difficulty understanding your circumstances on the Internet. Even so, there's a theme I'll repeat several times (okay, maybe only a couple of times) in this chapter: thousands of Internet transactions take place daily, most of them successful and with both parties happy. That, too, is like the real world, minus the screaming babies.

Commercial vendors are, of course, much more likely to be selling new, unused products. The range of such vendors on the Internet varies widely; it can include:

- Well-known mail-order firms who have an established presence outside the Net
- Well-known Internet-only-based firms
- Fly-by-night operations trying to skim the Net for quick riches

When searching for a commercial dealer on the Internet, you'll want to do your best to determine their trustworthiness. One way to do this is to ask other netizens for opinions on Vendor X. Those in search of computer products, for example, might check in on the Usenet newsgroup **misc.forsale.computers.discussion**. In other circumstances, you might just hang out in newsgroups related to the product you're searching for. Often you can find people there who have had either good or bad experiences with certain vendors, and people who've had extremes of one or the other are quick to share their stories. A sometimes-sound predictor of a dealer's integrity is their adherence to *netiquette*. Netiquette basically refers to the general set of social customs that have been established on the Internet, largely by the people who've been on the Internet for a long time. For the most part, rules of netiquette are rather congruent with those of the real world.

For a couple of historical reasons, however, customs relating to business practice on the Internet are a little strange. Briefly, until recently, the Internet was not allowed to be used for commercial endeavors, and this was largely due to the sources of funding that were supporting it. That's all changed, but many beliefs have not. One of these mores was that commercial advertising should not be "forced" upon others, such as in Usenet newsgroups. Since the change of funding for the Internet, and subsequent "legalization" of commercial activity, there has been a good deal of controversy about advertising on the Internet. There is a good reason, aside from funding sources, to frown upon random, blanket, inappropriate advertising on Usenet. That is, newsgroups are meant to focus on a particular topic, and if any company just randomly spewed their ads into any newsgroup they wanted, the clutter would undermine this positive aspect of Usenet. Furthermore, even within a topic, too much advertising will drown out any discussion, and the newsgroup will rapidly become vacant of real content, like television.

Having said that, I'll point out that businesses who consider themselves good netizens—and understand the Internet—will avoid making pigs of themselves. There are very many (and very successful) ways to advertise one's business on the Internet, and those who care about doing Net-positive business will learn about these. From the consumer's point of view, it's probably best to avoid businesses who seem to blatantly ignore Internet customs and practices. This is partly ideological, and partly practical—if said business cares so little about the community they are advertising to that they don't bother to learn Net customs (or consciously ignore them), their products and/or transactions may not be worth trusting.

Lastly, when you're trying to evaluate potential commercial dealers, there are—to borrow a term from hockey—the "intangibles" to consider. When you do encounter a business on the Internet (be it in an appropriate Usenet newsgroup or on the World Wide Web), the way they present themselves can serve as a useful impression. Do they seem professional? Are they forthright in their return policies, payment, technical support availability, and contact methods? All of these variables combine to give you an overall picture of the company—to which you may respond by thinking, "I'm impressed, they really know what they're doing," or "Do they think I'm an idiot?" We do the same thing in the real world, really. When you drive down a highway looking for a place to buy furniture, you consider a number of impression factors: if the store looks all right, you may go in, see how the business is run, how the salespeople are, and so forth. On the Internet, it's only reasonable to expect that you'd do the same thing, with minor changes in the digital domain.

Peer Shopping

Second-hand sales are a massively popular endeavor on the Internet. For good reason—lots of people have good stuff to sell for low prices. If you're looking to unload a computer, stereo, or collection of rare coins, what better market to advertise to then the entire country—or world? With the right price, making a sale on the Internet is virtually guaranteed.

Unfortunately, just as in kindergarten, some people can ruin it for everyone else. "Ruin" is too strong a word, I admit, but it's worth looking out for the bad apples before sinking your teeth into a Net deal. If you do find something you want for sale, consider a few things about the offer: Does it seem truthful? Does the poster seem to know what he's doing? Does it lack important information? Here's an example of a posting you might see that offers a product for sale by an individual:

```
From rec.music.marketplace Tue Jan 17 14:33:26 1995
From: reba@butcher.net (Reba Bagittagit)
Newsgroups: rec.audio.marketplace
Subject: *** Stereo forsale ***
Date: 14 Jan 1995 19:10:07 -0500


Anyone want to buy my stereo?
```

This isn't a particularly good post, but you'll find some posts like this on Usenet. Were you shopping for a used stereo, you'd be wise to avoid this poster. Not necessarily because she's trying to rip you off—in fact, a con-artist would have a much slicker post than that—but she doesn't really know what she's doing. In addition, you can't get a sense of what this person is about, because she wrote so little.

You continue browsing, and come across this posting:

```
From rec.music.marketplace Tue Jan 17 14:33:26 1995
From: Oreo@provider.net (Mmmm...Cookies)
Newsgroups: rec.audio.marketplace
Subject: FS: Sony AXG-5070 Receiver $220
Date: 14 Jan 1995 19:10:07 -0500


Greetings -

I'm interested in selling my Sony receiver because I just purchased a more
powerful one for a larger house. This receiver has served me very well for
about 1.5 years, when I bought it new. It has no operational problems, al-
though there is some discoloration on the left side of the case because my
cat once spilled some coffee on it :-).

I'm interested in getting $220 for this unit, plus you pay for shipping. I
have the original box and manual, and the FM antenna that came with it. Here
are the specs as listed in the manual:
```

```
Sony AXG-5070
blah blah blah

If you're interested, let me know and we can discuss the transaction.
Thanks,
Greg
Phone (555) 555-5555 or e-mail to oreo@provider.net
```

Now, this is much more impressive. Greg is forthcoming in all the relevant details about the product, including the flaw. In reality, you will find some posts like the "bad" one, some posts like this "good" one, and many in-between. Therefore it's a good idea to ask the selling party some questions about the product. Initiating a mini e-mail conversation about the product can give you a better idea of the sincerity and honesty of the person. Some people ask for—and offer—references to other netizens who've dealt with them; if you like that idea, pursue it. Personally, I don't get that deep for most purchases. Of course, the more money at stake, the more precautions you want to take.

Agree to Agree—Common Terms

When dealing with either a commercial vendor or a private individual, you want to have a solid understanding of the payment terms. Not only does an explicit explanation of the terms assure that each party is on the same wavelength, but because e-mail conversations can be saved, there's a solid record of the agreement (so save your e-mail conversations until the deal is history).

When dealing with businesses, you're probably going to be limited to the terms that they offer. Hopefully, a good business will offer several options to suit your needs. Putting purchases on credit card is often the safest form of payment, because if there are any problems your credit card company can come to your defense. Note that this is aside from the issue of how you communicate your credit card information, which gets its own section later in this chapter.

You can make up any payment arrangement you want with another individual, as long as it doesn't involve infants. Some people even engage in trades rather than financial transactions, if each party has something the other wants. Combinations of trades and money are not uncommon either. As with commercial dealers, each side in this agreement wants to have a clear understanding of the terms. Never assume anything, and don't make implications. Tell the other party flat-out what terms you're willing to offer, and make sure they agree outright. If they push hard for a certain term of payment without giving you any good reason, be suspicious. It's very important to have good records, so be sure to save every e-mail exchange. That includes the e-mail messages you send. Some Internet accounts are set up by default to save copies of the e-mail that you send (often called "sent mail"), others will not. One simple way to preserve the e-mail that you send is to *Cc:* it to yourself. That is, in the e-mail header where you address the e-mail to the other person, there is often another header line that begins with Cc:. That means "Carbon Copy," and if you enter your own e-mail address on that line, you'll get a copy of the e-mail you've sent, which you can then save for your records.

The rule of the day when making Net-deals is to be explicit (the same is true on IRC, but for a different reason). The more communication between parties, the better, because it increases mutual trust and keeps everyone in the know. I find that keeping the other party informed of progress through the steps of the transaction helps. That means dropping them an e-mail when you send out a check, receive the product, send out the product, and so forth. Such hand-holding keeps both parties in line and no one in the dark. Of course, if the other party *does* keep you in the dark against your protests, it might be a good idea to drop the deal and find someone more trustworthy.

It's worth repeating: Most Net-deals with other individuals go very well, and both parties benefit. Speaking personally, I've engaged in many Net purchases over the past few years, and only one of them ran into problems. Frankly, I've had more problems with store purchases than with deals on the Internet. Most people are fairly trusting, and if both parties trust each other, behave, and keep the doings aboveboard, the deal will be a happy experience.

By Land, Sea, and Air

When cooking up a deal with someone else, consider the distances involved. The Internet can easily blur the lines between someone who's next door and someone who's a continent away. For one thing, shipping costs skyrocket when you're talking about international delivery. For this reason, many people choose to limit sales of heavier goods to their own country. Even with smaller goods, if they are common, a buyer can probably find them within his own country and save the high shipping costs. Of course, if you're selling an item, and someone overseas wants to buy it and is willing to cover the shipping, then fine. Speaking again from personal experience, I once offered a hard drive and external case for sale, asking about $200. Someone in New Zealand wanted to buy it. After investigation, I found that shipping (from the United States) would cost $35 for the item (which didn't weigh more than 3 pounds) and would take six to eight weeks by sea to reach New Zealand. Air shipping was over $90. I made this explicitly clear to the buyer, and he nonetheless agreed, and the transaction went without a hitch (and he kindly sent me e-mail some five weeks later to let me know that he received the hard drive and it worked perfectly).

Don't overlook proper shipping insurance. It's usually rather inexpensive compared to the rest of the shipping costs, and it can save a great deal of hassle if anything becomes damaged (when the brownsuits use your package to play Frisbee). From the buyer's perspective, it's probably safer to make purchases from within your country whenever possible; if you have any problems, resolving them internationally can be very difficult.

Either way, it has to be clear between parties how shipping costs will be covered. Some people choose to split shipping, on top of the product's selling price. Often, the seller asks the buyer to cover all shipping costs in addition to the purchase price. Lastly, sometimes the purchase price will include shipping costs. Yet another reason to be explicit!

He Pays, She Pays—Exchanging Moolah

Until this point, I've referred to "terms of payment" and "arrangements" without elaborating on the possibilities. I wasn't being miserly, I was just waiting until now. And here we are. Speaking within the realm of "traditional" options, there are a handful of possible payment arrangements. Each has its ups and downs, pros and cons, Laurels and Hardys, Bonnies and Clydes, blah blah blah.

One common form of payment is the regular ol' personal check. You want to buy a certain VCR from Mr. Guy, so you send him a check for the cost and Mr. Guy sends you the VCR. Potential caveats: Your check may be no good, or Mr. Guy may never send you the VCR. To prevent a bounced check, the seller would want to wait for the buyer's check to clear before sending out product. But that puts the buyer at risk for never getting the product. For low-value products, however, a certain level of mutual trust can be stronger than this risk. Since this method is easy, it's common on the Net, especially for parties who trust each other.

There is a sometime-variation on this type of transaction that isn't such a good idea: the "pay half, receive product, pay other half" method. This is most risky for the seller. If the buyer pays half, the seller ships the product, and the buyer doesn't pay the second half, how can the seller get the money or the product back? One possibility is to keep good, explicit records. If you can prove in court (if the circumstance is worth that) that the buyer only paid half of the initially agreed-upon price, you can win the other half. Without excellent records, you've got a problem: if you've deposited the first half-payment, you have no way of proving that said payment wasn't the agreed-upon total. You won't win. Even keeping good records can't avoid the hassle of court, so it's best to stay away from "half-and-half" deals altogether.

Similar to the regular check is the money order. The difference is that the money order is pre-paid, so it can't bounce. That provides the seller with enhanced confidence, and he can ship the product out to you upon receiving the money order. The buyer has no further assurance that the seller will ship, though. Sometimes one can stop payment on a money order, as with a check, which is again hassle-territory. Given levels of trust similar to those we've mentioned, the money order is often the slightly better payment because it lacks the clearance issues of the regular check. Some commercial vendors who won't accept personal checks will accept money orders, and the same is true for some individuals. On the other hand, money orders cost money to get, usually a few dollars. That has to be considered in the total cost-and-payment agreement.

There's a reason all those cheesy ads on TV for "MiracleMops" and "Buns of Aluminum" say "Sorry, no CODs." It's because they want the money up front before they send you anything—which is exactly why COD is a *good* way to make Net transactions. When using COD, the seller ships the product out to the buyer, and the buyer pays the delivery person. The seller then receives a check from the delivery company for the specified cost of the product. This way, neither side can avoid the exchange. That's better than either of the methods discussed earlier. Nothing's perfect, however, and neither is COD. The major delivery services *do not* allow you to examine the contents of a package before paying the delivery person. Which means you may have been sent a box of sand rather than a VCR. That's one downside. Secondly, it can take a while for the delivery company to get the payment to the seller. If the seller doesn't need the money in a hurry, then that's not a factor (the risk of being ripped off by UPS or Federal Express is minimal, so getting the money *at all* isn't the real concern). The seller has the option of specifying what forms of payment the delivery person may accept from the buyer. Normally, personal checks are not allowed as payment on COD. Money orders and certified checks are usually acceptable. Note that some delivery companies have a strange definition of the word "cash." That is, you may be told you can pay for a COD in "cash," but "cash" does not mean actual paper money. They don't allow delivery people to accept "real money," probably for security reasons, so when paying for a COD, "cash" basically means a money order for the exact amount. Be sure that in your explicit communications, the seller notifies the buyer of the exact COD total once he has shipped it, so that the buyer can get a money order in advance. Because shipping by COD also carries an additional surcharge (usually several dollars, but nothing extraordinary), both parties should understand how that cost will be covered.

Private individuals, of course, can't accept credit cards, so even though that is effectively the safest payment arrangement, it's not applicable to the peer-to-peer market.

The Lowdown on Credit Cards

Safe as credit cards are for protecting your transaction, a lot of people worry about the safety of revealing their credit card information. The Internet compounds this potential problem, because secure methods of communication (such as public-key cryptography) have not yet been implemented widely.

Although many people believe there's unanimous consensus on the danger of transmitting credit card numbers insecurely, that is not quite true. In fact, there is some disagreement on the matter. The traditional argument is that if you (for example) send your credit card number via e-mail to a vendor, someone might intercept that message. From there, who knows what array of unauthorized purchases might appear on your card until your friendly service representative calls you out of deep human concern. It is true that in the scenario just mentioned, someone could steal your credit card number—if it were transmitted in plaintext over e-mail. Similarly, if you enter a credit card number into a World Wide Web forms entry, that may also be transmitted over the Internet in plaintext. Note, however, that there is some decrease in risk when the transaction goes over the Web, because your data takes a more direct route to its destination than does e-mail. Nonetheless, your card number can be intercepted, sniffed, or whatnot in either case. Two concerns arise, especially from those who argue that Internet transactions are neither more nor less safe than those in the "real world." Let's look at both.

First, consider the information that's already out there. When you slap your credit card onto the counter at many stores, a carbon copy is made and thrown into the trash. When you order a product by common mail order, you speak your credit card number over the phone. And regular voice phone lines are even more insecure than the Internet. Your credit card number resides in the computers of many a company that you've dealt with in the past, and who's to say someone won't break into them and steal entire customer lists? The argument being proposed here is that the level of credit card insecurity on the Internet—even over plaintext e-mail or the World Wide Web—is really no greater than not-on-the-Internet. Credit cards, the argument continues, are an inherently insecure implementation, and you automatically accept that level of insecurity by using credit cards at all, anywhere. In addition, within the United States you are only liable for the first $50 of charges illicitly rung up on your stolen credit card. None of this is to say that everyone should therefore reveal their credit card numbers with wild abandon—after all, having it stolen and abused is at the very least a real pain, leading to lost time and higher blood pressure. On the other hand, it's probably true that the Internet isn't markedly more insecure than the rest of the world in these regards.

Some companies on the Internet, however, have tried to accommodate consumer concerns; they offer alternative methods of communicating credit card information. One possibility is to fill in your entire order over the Internet—except for the credit card information, which you send via a voice or fax number that the company provides. Whether or not you deem this a safer practice is a subjective decision, having heard the arguments we've made here. Another workaround that some Net businesses offer is the *purchase account*: you can set up an account over the phone in which you reveal your credit card information, and are then assigned an account number. From then on, you can use that account number in online orders, so that the entire order can take place online without the transmission risk.

In the end, I'm not going to offer the simplistic admonition, "Never transmit your credit card number over the Internet!" I consider this another personal-risk issue. I personally find the argument that credit cards are an inherently insecure implementation to be fairly on-target. If you want to avoid plaintext transmissions over the Internet, however, an increasing number of Net businesses do offer alternatives.

The Least You Need to Know

There's a lot to buy on the Internet, and plenty of opportunity to sell. Old asbestos potholder, begone! The thing is, you want to make sure you get what you pay for, and vice versa. This takes a combination of heads-up, insight, caution, and voodoo. In this chapter we looked at the first three of those.

- Be as confident as possible in the reputability of the business or individual that you want to buy from. Look for honesty, forthrightness, solid contracts, and explicit policies. Communicate with either the individual or business about a given product to get a better feel for their integrity. Avoid the deal if there are any signs of shadiness.
- Keep detailed and accurate records of a transaction. This includes the agreed-upon terms of payment, shipping schedule, and total costs (including shipping issues). Saved e-mail messages on both sides of the conversation can back you up later if ugliness should arise.
- Choose a payment method that you feel safe with based on the value of the item, distance between parties, and trustworthiness of the other party. Credit cards, aside from transmitting the number, are the safest when dealing with companies. COD or money orders are popular between individuals; COD is moderately safe for both sides.
- Transmitting credit card information over e-mail or the World Wide Web in plaintext can be a risk. Some companies provide alternative means of communicating the information. Some people argue that the risk over the Internet is neither more nor less than it is over the phone, via fax, or anywhere else. Using a credit card anywhere is automatically insecure, in that sense.
- A properly trained monkey can shell peanuts at a rate of 1500 per hour, and shrimp at a somewhat lower 980 per hour.

Chapter 18

Under This Roof—Parenting and the Net

In This Chapter

- Freedom can be ugly
- Where the dirty pictures are
- Blue news
- IRC awareness
- What (little) you can do
- Healthy kid fun

Normally, one would begin a chapter like this with a platitude such as "There are so many joys to being a parent... ." But hey—what the heck do I know? I do know it's a joy being a kid, and some parents may be concerned that the Internet can make it too much of a joy. The Internet is the only society on Earth today with true freedom of expression, and although some are warbling about trying to end that, it hasn't happened yet. The big media have feasted on lurid Internet tales, and have gotten far more calories out of it then they deserve. As a parent, you might wonder just what sort of stuff is out there on the Internet, and what, if anything, you can do about it.

NC-17: Big Bird and Friends Didn't Do That...

Now, I'm not in the business of telling other people what is and isn't appropriate for them or their children. As a parent, you may have no problem with any of what's discussed in this chapter. But in our current society, the big to-do is all about sex—parents and sex, children and sex, Madonna and sex—ah, but that's the stuff of another, better-selling book. There are other topics, too, that may be of parental concern. We'll cover those as well. It won't be pretty.

Since every third news report these days is about pornography on the Internet, let's get it over with. Is there pornography on the Internet? There certainly is. Is there a lot? I guess that really depends on what one considers "a lot." There's more than none, that's for sure. On the other hand, there's less than any "adult" store has at any one time. The more relevant question is this: Where on the Internet is all this pornography? The answer is, "a few places." Let's look (figuratively, that is) at some of them.

There is something of a de facto regulatory mechanism on the Internet, in regard to pornography. Because every computer connected to the Internet has a limited amount of resources, owners of those computers want to distribute those resources fairly. If a computer connected to the Internet is known to have pornography on it, it will be swamped with incoming connections so quickly as to nearly paralyze it. Conclude what you will about human nature or Internet users, but that's the simple truth. So, even with issues of morality and legality aside, the overwhelming majority of owners of computers on the Internet do not want pornography on their machines. When we're talking about retrieving files from others' computers on the Internet, we're usually talking about FTP, and sometimes Gopher and the World Wide Web. It's not likely that many young people will find pornography at many of these types of sites, for the reasons just explained.

Now, there are some sites that are called "private." That means that not just anyone can access them; only people who know the special username and password can get in. There are some private FTP sites specifically set up to carry pornography, but someone has to have some moderate Internet experience before they'd be able to find and use these. Which means that pictures of people doing unnatural things with pears are not going to pop onto the screen when your five-year-old son logs in. On the other hand, a bright adolescent can probably find some of these sites if he's determined enough. They'll find out about them from friends or others on the Internet, in pretty much the same way that we all found out about this sort of stuff as kids.

On the World Wide Web, it takes the least amount of know-how to view pictures. Because graphical WWW browsers only require the use of a mouse, even a small child could theoretically "surf" the Web and come across unsavory pictures, with no real computing knowledge. The Web, however, is subject to the same resource constraints as FTP; therefore, most Web servers are not going to want to make pornography available.

Doing so would inevitably lead to the host computer being swamped with connections, and it would become useless for any other "real" purpose. Nonetheless, there are some Web pages with such pictures, but once word gets out about them, they don't last long (they get swamped, and the owner or provider has to remove the pictures). In the end, it's certainly possible for a child to easily view erotic images when using the Web, but it's not highly likely that he or she will encounter very many of them.

The biggest source of publicly available pornography on the Internet is Usenet news. There are several newsgroups that carry explicit pictures and text. The most popular ones begin with "alt.binaries.pictures.erotica," upon which there are a few variations appealing to audiences with more specific interests. A picture in visual form cannot be posted to Usenet. Usenet can only carry ASCII text. So the binary files that make up graphic images must first be converted to ASCII characters before being posted to Usenet. When and if you look into one of these newsgroups, you'll see lots of postings that claim to be a picture of something-or-other. But if you read the contents of that post, you're not going to see the actual picture, you'll see a lot of random gobbledygook. To see a picture, that mess has to be saved and then decoded into a binary file. The binary file then has to be loaded into an image viewer on your computer. For someone reasonably comfortable with their computer, this isn't a particularly difficult process, and it can be automated with the help of numerous programs. Having to go through all that to see a picture, however, does mean that it's difficult to "happen upon" an explicit photo on the Internet. You pretty much have to know what you want and how to get it first.

There are some other newsgroups, such as alt.sex.stories, which carry "blue" stories, often written by other Internet users. These don't need to be specially encoded since they're already text, so they can be read directly from the newsgroup. Many, I may as well point out, are quite strange and deviant, often for the sake of being deviant. The subject lines of a story often carry abbreviations telling you what "type" of sex the story contains. For example, "M/F" or "Vanilla" means "normal" male-female sex. But like I said, people seem to enjoy being more deviant than the next deviant, so many of the stories are more like "Mmmmmfffffff pedo horse cat sub dom" (which means one adult male, 15 children, a horse, and a cat, with submission and dominance). I apologize if this offends any readers, but it's simply true—these kinds of stories exist on Usenet and they're not uncommon. Whether you choose to dismiss them as silly fluff or find them deeply disturbing is a personal reaction.

> **We're Not All Depraved**
> There are plenty of newsgroups that post ASCII-conversions of binary files that are other than pornography. Many newsgroups carry pictures and sounds of general interest, or specific interest in other areas, so all of this encoding-decoding stuff *hasn't* been developed for the sole purpose of porn.

Sex, however, is not the only topic that receives explicit treatment on the Internet. There's plenty of talk about drugs, too (hey, when you're not having sex you gotta do something). Newsgroups such as "alt.drugs" contain very open discussions about drug use, similar to the type of discussion about any other special interest topic in any other newsgroup. Remember that since there's no "authority" on the Internet, anyone can (and does) say anything he or she wants. In addition to specific subject matter, just about any newsgroup may have language that you don't prefer.

Yet other newsgroups contain content which, while not what you classically imagine taboo, is on the "alternative" side. Consider "alt.binaries.pictures.tasteless," for example. This group is for exchanging images meant only for those with iron stomachs. Gruesome scenes of anatomy, injury, and death are not uncommon here. Perhaps it's a shock to some people that others find this sort of thing interesting and want to share it with each other, but hey, "freedom" is a big word. Just know it's there.

Beyond Usenet, many young people are drawn to IRC, the Internet chat service. There are definitely many benefits to being able to converse with people anywhere in the world, any time of day. Unfortunately, much of the popular press coverage about IRC has focused on the possibility that child molesters may try to use IRC to talk with children and "lure" them somewhere. There may have been one official case of such an event, and thus it's been seized upon. Let it be known that IRC is not filled with child molesters. IRC is mostly filled with college and high school students.

Of course, it's true that you can't *really* know who you are actually communicating with on IRC. The concern is that someone might allege to be someone else, strike up a relationship with a young person, invite him or her somewhere, and so on. I suppose this is possible. On the other hand, one of the advantages of virtual communications is that nobody can actually harm you in that moment. So the real issue lies in the mixing together of the virtual world and the real, physical world. Whether the Net user is a child or an adult, this is something to be wary about in any circumstance, and handled with caution if you're going to handle it at all. Parents are probably best advised to be very cautious about having their children meet unsupervised with anyone they've met on the computer.

It's easy to read such a warning and recoil in horror. But this is really just another illustration of how the Internet is much like the real world: it's a big place, and every imaginable thing can go on there. In this respect, the issues that a parent faces regarding what a child can come across are similar to those same issues in "real life." Admittedly, however, there are a few complications in the digital medium. The biggest one is that a parent who isn't on the cutting edge of technological understanding may not have the resources (or opportunity) to monitor the child's experience. Presumably, however, you *do* have some Internet savoir-faire if you are a reader of this book—so the concept of Usenet news shouldn't be utterly foreign. Even if you have a working understanding of the Internet, how can you monitor and/or restrict the tidal flow of information that crashes upon you and your child?

Restricting Usenet

If you want to get into restrictions, matters of degree are very relevant. At one extreme, you could disallow your child from using the Internet at all. That's probably the only sure way to maintain control. Once you've established that your child can use the Net, it gets much mushier from there.

Very few interfaces to the Internet offer any sort of parental controls. Some of the proprietary online services do have such features, and for a very concerned parent, it might be better to switch from "true" Internet access to a major online service. Parents who access the Internet through the common UNIX shell, menu, or graphical SLIP/PPP interfaces (which we've been discussing throughout this book) have far more limited options. A classic catch-22 situation becomes evident: to truly restrict a portion of the Internet from a child requires a certain amount of ignorance on the child's part. Yet, most parents would be proud for their son or daughter to learn as much as they can about the computer and computing. Armed with that knowledge, however, any bright child will be able to circumvent any parental blockades. This isn't only true of the Internet. Especially in the early days of cable TV, a bright child knew how to "fix" the scrambled-signal obstacle.

There are no useful software implementations of parental controls for the Internet. If your child has access to FTP, for instance, you cannot regulate where he does and does not connect to. Remember, however, that FTP is not the likely route through which someone will come across this chapter's sort of "information." Similarly, the Web is a vast place, and there's really no way to regulate where someone links to. As with everything in this chapter, you can ban its use entirely, but short of doing that, there aren't any simple parental controls.

Usenet consists of many thousands of newsgroups. You can only access the newsgroups your Internet service provider carries. That means the single best way to prevent your child from accessing the sexually explicit newsgroups is to subscribe to an ISP that does not carry them. Of course, this also means that you, the parent, cannot access said newsgroups either. That may or may not be of concern to you. Your choice of ISPs will depend a lot on where you live. Some regions have a wide selection, others do not. Usenet newsgroups such as **alt.internet.access.wanted** and **alt.internet.services** can help you find regional options. When calling potential ISPs, ask them about what Usenet newsgroups they carry and about the sexually explicit groups specifically. Some ISPs may have implemented other sorts of parental controls, too, such as giving you password-based access to newsgroups. That's not very common, but it's technically possible (of course—again—a whiz-kid with enough smarts and persistence can also circumvent it).

Clever Sneaky

On a technical note, it's still possible to circumvent a restricted newsfeed. Children—look away. If your child can find a "public" news server, he can tell the newsreader to use that server's newsfeed rather than your ISP's. If the public news server carries a full newsfeed, then the child will have access to the explicit newsgroups. The catch is that public news servers are extremely rare and difficult to find, especially those that do carry uncensored feeds. One might ironically say that you should be proud if your child manages to find one—some people on the Internet make posts begging for them. So, while I want to point out that it's technically possible to use a newsfeed other than your ISP's, it's by no means an easy matter.

Down the Stream The whole pile of newsgroups that your ISP carries is called a *newsfeed*. If your ISP claims to have a *full newsfeed*, that means they carry all newsgroups, including the explicit ones.

Let's say, though, that your ISP does carry the "blue" newsgroups. Of the thousands of newsgroups your ISP carries, you can choose to "subscribe" to only a few of them. This means that the contents of the newsgroups you have subscribed to will be transferred to your computer, and you won't get the contents of newsgroups that you've "unsubscribed" to. When you launch your newsreader, be it in a UNIX shell or graphical interface, you'll be presented with a list of newsgroups you have subscribed to. However, this isn't as good a solution as it sounds: viewing the full list of all newsgroups, subscribed or unsubscribed, isn't very difficult; most newsreading software provides an easy way to do it. The intent is that you can choose new newsgroups to subscribe to this way. This also means that anyone over age 8 can probably figure out how to subscribe to newsgroups on their own. So, the subscription solution is useful only if you have very young children who won't be able to manipulate the newsreading software beyond what you have configured. But older children, especially those who are interested in the off-limits material, are going to figure out how to subscribe rather easily.

Of course, if they're not skilled miscreants, they may forget to unsubscribe after reading the newsgroup, in which case you'll see it on your newsgroup list upon running your newsreader. That'll be a tip-off that it's time for *the talk*.

Some have made the analogy between the Net and the "Wild West." In some ways, that's correct; many social institutions haven't been established yet. In other ways, though, the Internet poses many of the same situations as the real world. The common mistake people make is to assume, for some reason, that the Internet—a human creation—is *not* going to reflect human beings in the same way any society does. The Internet represents the birth of a new communications era, but it's still a little baby, and it's quite immature.

Maybe as the general population uses the Internet more and more, their social institutions and values will be reflected on the Net. Maybe the technology of the Internet will have an impact on the values of society. Probably both. Of the total amount of information flow on the Internet, only a very small amount is socially controversial. There is no guarantee that you can regulate 100 percent of what your child sees, be it on the Internet, daytime talk shows, or on the playground. At present, because Usenet news is the most voluminous source of explicit data, a very concerned parent's best bet is to find a service provider that offers limited or restricted newsfeeds. While some of the proprietary online services offer more advanced parental controls in their software, bright kids are still going to learn ways around them.

Rated G

There are certainly some areas on the Internet that you may *want* to promote to your children. On Usenet, check out the newsgroup **alt.kids-talk**, where younger people can have a forum for discussion. If your children like pictures, there are plenty of pictures posted into newsgroups such as **alt.binaries.pictures**, **alt.binaries.pictures.animals**, and **alt.binaries.pictures.cartoons** that are not of the "adult" variety. I can't guarantee that everything in those newsgroups is entirely G-rated, but they tend to attract more "general interest" pictures than the alt.binaries.erotica newsgroups.

While I can't go into all of the resources on the Internet oriented toward kids (because that's not the focus of this book), parents can take up residence in newsgroups such as **misc.kids** to consult with other parents' Net-wisdom. While the Internet can be a great educational tool, it can be even better for children who aren't left to just wander around the Net completely undirected.

The Least You Need to Know

The Internet is not the seething, bubbling den of perversion that some big media reports would have you believe it to be. There is, however, a certain amount of explicit material available on the Internet, which some parents may be concerned about.

- While there is some material available by way of FTP or Gopher, finding such sites is not easy. They are not the type of thing that a youngster will accidentally "happen upon."
- The World Wide Web is the only Internet resource that can lead to images popping up on the screen of even the youngest user. Even so, the amount of taboo matter available on publicly accessible WWW sites is very low, as it burdens the host computer too much if many people know about it. Unless someone is determined to look for it, overly explicit Web pages will not be happened upon easily.
- Usenet news is the public resource with the highest volume of explicit files made available daily. Some proprietary online services offer parents the capability to restrict Usenet access, but most readers with "true" Internet access don't have software-based parental controls.
- If you want to restrict Usenet access in your home, the best solution at this time is to use an Internet service provider that carries a censored newsfeed, so the explicit material on Usenet is not even available to a user of your Internet account.
- Find resources on the Internet for kids, which will keep them directed and less likely to just wander around the Net aimlessly. Older children and adolescents will probably have self-directed goals on the Net, but the younger ones need some direction.

Chapter 19

This Time It's Personal: Net Harassment

In This Chapter

- Hey, don't shove
- Oh, a wiseguy, eh?
- The art of the flame
- When it's time to snitch
- Line in the sand

In this final part of the book, we've looked at a couple of issues that tie together the "real world" and the Internet. In this chapter, we're going to look at the very pleasant topic of harassment. It happens, because people do that sort of thing (don't ask me why). They eat breakfast, they read the paper, and in lieu of a good novel, they start harassing. I've tried to stress throughout this book how personal security issues on the Net mirror those in the real world. In this case, the argument could definitely be made that harassment is worse on the Net than on the street—because people feel empowered by keystrokes. In a sense, I feel imbalanced because so much of this book has focused on the bad things people can do to one another. In fact, people do many nice things for one another, too, and that's true about the Internet as well. But that doesn't tend to sell so well. You also don't need to protect against kindness. Enough about me—on with the chapter.

How It Happens

Usenet news is filled with thousands of discussions in thousands of newsgroups daily. IRC is filled with thousands of people in at least hundreds of channels daily. So, it's going to happen that people will rub each other the wrong way (and in some channels, they rub each other the right way, nudge-nudge). The Internet adds an extra layer of fat between combatants in a debate, and behind the cloak of keyboard, swords swing more readily. Given the opportunity to hide their faces and names, some people are just downright mean.

First let's consider the typical Usenet situation. As a new reader of "rec.music.misc," you ask people about their opinions on Eric Clapton's new CD. A few people write some honest answers, but one person argues that you must be a real old-timer to still be listening to Clapton. Somewhat taken aback by this personal slight, the new Internet user might feel a need to defend himself. "I think Clapton has matured, sure, which has brought along with it a softer sound," you post, in defense. But, this person who suffered a lack of protein as a child, attacks back—"A softer sound? A wussier sound! You are completely lame. Listen to some %!#$* good @%#!! music." If you're not too familiar with the Internet, you may read this and think, "Why would someone just attack like that out of nowhere?" It happens, though—people pick fights. Often, the problem is that most newsgroups involve topics that bring along many opinions. A lot of folks out there haven't yet figured out what opinions are, and when faced with differing ones, they start having conniptions and "flaming" those who disagree with them.

Flame On the Net, it refers to when someone writes a vitriolic message to you, either in e-mail, or as a follow-up post in Usenet, or in IRC, and so on. A lot of very immature people (whose numbers appear to multiply by the day) find delight or solace in flaming; once hidden behind their mouse and keyboard, they bar no holds and take no prisoners. Some consider "flaming" an art form, and they take pride in the "wit" with which they put down others. It's all quite an impressive display, and one only hopes that such clever, useful people remain behind their keyboards. But maybe that's just me.

Flaming is not limited to Usenet. It can happen on IRC, in live real-time action. It can happen in e-mail, usually when someone you've been sparring with in public postings on Usenet really loses it and tries to flame you privately. Flaming exchanges can get quite intense, filled with naughty language and bodily references. The real danger to a new Internet user is how easily they can get caught up in these no-win situations. After all, it's a natural reaction to want to defend yourself. If this all sounds a little like the first grade, that's because a lot of people never left it. The best thing to do if you get caught in the crossfire of a flamewar is to ignore it. (Remember: Fighting words are nothing more than a traditional way to start a fight. Any fight.)

Alas, hot fiery vitriol is only one possible form of Net harassment. In some cases, whether beginning with flames or not, messages from other users can claim to threaten you in "reality." Some users have been known to threaten lawsuits against others (Chapter 21), or when really worked up, some have called their enemies on the telephone. In most of the stories I've heard, the telephone calls have been anonymous pranks, since that's about as far as many cowards get. Nonetheless, none of this is very pleasant, to say the least.

Women, the sad tale goes, have had a particularly difficult time on the Internet. It should come as no surprise that many of the individuals who find joy in preying upon others have had limited success in the mating game. Because there has been a general sociological bias that favors males being more computer-literate than females, women are definitely in the minority on the Internet. I stress, however, that this shouldn't dissuade any women who are reading this book—more women have been using the Internet, enjoying the Internet, and damning the sleazeballs. It does work; there are plenty of males on the Internet who are very happy to have women join in the conversation. People are (for the most part) quite affable to one another online, though some women have had a hard time participating in interesting discussions on sexual topics without having low-lives bother them. Since this is especially true of sex-related newsgroups, some women have chosen to hide their identities as women in such newsgroups; that is a personal decision.

Being Mr. or Ms. Nice Person

The single biggest mistake that people make when flamed, or otherwise challenged in a personal way, is to attack back. It's hard not to, and that same keyboard anonymity that empowers the flamer feels pretty good in your hands, too. There are both personal and ecological reasons to avoid flamewars, however. For one thing, a newsgroup or IRC channel with excessive personal attacks very rapidly becomes quite uninteresting to other participants. More than one Usenet newsgroup has been rendered utterly useless after people turned it into a mudpit. For the network's sake, remember that on Usenet, a copy of everything posted is stored and forwarded to many thousands of computers all over the world. For one thing, this takes communications resources and storage space. There is a finite amount of both, and flushing one's spite down these tubes really doesn't contribute to the Internet as a whole. I've seen some threads (conversations) on Usenet that consisted of nothing more than "Oh yeah? Well you're a ****!" which received the rebuttal, "Yeah, right, you stupid ****!" Admittedly, the first time they're worth a good laugh (in a pathetic sort of way), but a laugh I wouldn't mind missing out on in the first place.

If you're involved in any of these situations, the first step is to ignore it. Don't fire back or try to defend your position in a rational way—just ignore it. Some new users make the mistake of taking a flame's content too seriously, being easily offended by the language used. But remember: It's very easy to type things that someone would never be brave enough to say in a face-to-face situation, so the expression of certain sentiments doesn't necessarily convey the same motivation threshold on the Internet as it would on the street.

Some attacks are aimed at entire interest groups rather than specific people; these are sometimes called "trolls" (the attacks, not the attackers, though it's tempting). A *troll* occurs when a joyrider posts an offensive message to a special-interest newsgroup, trying to get their hair up. For example, it has happened that someone will post to the newsgroup "soc.support.fat-acceptance" a message such as "You're a bunch of lazy whales who don't get off your couch. Try moving a muscle one day or beach yourself." Inappropriate to a newsgroup where people are sharing their experiences about being fat in an anti-fat society? Certainly. Offensive? Therein lies the catch. The newer user, less accustomed to the obvious troll, might take the bait and actually try to compose a response—which is, of course, just what the troller wants. He wants to get people mad. Sometimes trolls are called *flamebait,* which obviously has similar connotations. Ignoring this sort of flamebait is the only way to thwart the poster. Furthermore, responding to him can not only get you involved in a personal flamewar, but the newsgroup then becomes filled with discussion about this garbage, thereby perpetuating the damage of the troll.

There is a small group of extremely determined flamers and trollers who don't recede if you ignore them. They push, and persist, either with continued personal attacks in public or in private e-mail, or they continue to troll a newsgroup without cease. Some problem-people resort to "mailbombing" if you ignore them, or incense them enough. On the Internet, to *mailbomb* someone means to send them a huge amount of e-mail so that their mailbox overflows. This may get the mailbombing victim in trouble with his sysadmin, because if the system's entire mailbox is filled up, other users' incoming e-mail will not get delivered properly. This is, in short, an act of digital terrorism. In these cases, the nice-guy approach has its limitations.

Time to Tattle

Because the Internet lacks any central authority, there aren't any police to call to report a bothersome individual. Left to their own devices, netizens have come up with a few ways of dealing with harassers. None of them involve salt shakers with caps unscrewed just enough so that all the salt will pour out when used. (Learned that at summer camp, I did.)

Perhaps the single most likely-to-be-effective way to deal with a harasser is to contact his service provider. Most providers have someone called a *postmaster*, who may or may not be the same person as the sysadmin. The rightmost two segments of someone's e-mail address should give you a good idea of who the service provider is, be it a school or a business or a private service. For example, if you've been harassed by someone whose address is "markm@naughty.boy.to.org," then "to.org" is probably your best bet for reaching someone in charge.

If sending e-mail addressed to **postmaster** doesn't work, try **root** or **admin**; those will usually work. Your e-mail message should be courteous—remember, it's not the service provider who's been harassing you. Keep in mind that no one has any obligation to help you at all, but a responsible provider should frown upon such behavior coming from his system. However, sending an angry, rude e-mail to the ISP may just turn them off to your cause. It's best to explain to them what's been happening and include what you've been sent by the harasser. If they care about their business and reputation, they have the jurisdiction to cut off the harasser's Internet access, at least from their service. Of course, nobody can stop the perpetrator from finding a new provider.

OOOOOOH...

Who Will Police the Police?

On the Internet, perhaps the better question is "Who will admin the admin?" Consider this incident: About a year ago, there was a user who was posting extremely inappropriate material to many newsgroups. The content was of a religious nature, preaching to the unconverted. Not heeding user requests to stop, people began to send e-mail to his sysadmin. This proved fruitless. And soon it became known why—*he* was his sysadmin! He was in charge of his own system, which he ruled in a department at a school. Once realized, people had to circumvent his computer system and department, and go to the head of the school, which eventually worked; he was removed from his position. That'll teach 'im. Of course, if he were the dean... or the provost...

Taking It Public

When all else fails, there's always the tried-and-true vigilante group. The real question at hand is, when is it appropriate to make your grievance with an individual a matter of public record? There is some degree of mixed opinion on this, not unlike that surrounding the Miracle-Whip-versus-mayonnaise controversy. The crux of the matter is whether it serves any useful purpose to publicize your cause, or if it just clogs the Net with more sparring.

In this section, we put aside the issue of publicly posting private e-mail, because that's better dealt with in Chapter 20. But should you make a public post saying "So-and-so is really harassing me and I can't get him to stop" (or words to that effect)? If you've tried everything else discussed, it seems there's little other choice. One real possible benefit of announcing your cause is that others may be having (or may have had) similar problems with this person. That, in turn, could precipitate a thread of discussion about this individual, something that I have seen happen. Whether that only goads him on or serves to shut him down is not entirely predictable. Given enough people in concert, however, it may then be possible to launch a more powerful complaint against the villain's service provider, or whatever higher-up you can find at their organization.

As with e-mail to postmasters, it's best to be rational, reasonable, and calm when presenting your case to the public. Angry venom will probably only invite more flames and could start a real war. You want to make other people sympathetic to your problem, not alienate them.

The Last Resort

While it isn't frequent, it can happen that a harasser crosses the line from the virtual world to the physical world. Threats of physical encounters or communications by telephone, postal service, or other "real world" methods shouldn't be taken lightly. Even most of the crazies on the Net aren't going to go this far, but we're a diverse species.

Fortunately, the fact that the Internet has no policing body in and of itself becomes immaterial in these cases. Real threats are real threats, and there are real-world institutions set up to deal with them. In cases where someone has stepped over the virtual line, you have every right to contact "real" authorities such as the police (or the post office, if threats have taken the form of physical mail). There haven't been very many cases where this principle has been tested (thankfully), but anything's possible, so it's best to know your options in advance.

The Least You Need to Know

People aren't always nice to one another. In some cases, once they latch on, they're hard to shake. Net harassment often grows out of disagreements, but sometimes it's targeted at specific demographic groups (often women).

- Resist the urge to defend yourself on the Net against spurious personal attacks. Countering flames with more flames only leads to flamewars.

- Resist trolls or flamebait posted to newsgroups simply to offend and disturb. They're a form of public harassment, and your attention would only goad them on.
- If you really get someone's goat, he may haunt you in e-mail. If it gets serious, try to contact his system administrators or service providers. Often, **postmaster@*their.address*** will do the trick. Be calm and reasonable in your complaint, because nobody is obligated to help you.
- You may sometimes want to bring your case to public attention. If others have had problems with a user, you could band together and approach that user's service provider. Save for evidence any harassing messages that you are sent.
- In very rare—but serious—cases in which threats grow beyond the bounds of the Internet and into voice phone calls or the postal service, take it straight to the proper authorities. At that point, the flamer has lost what he hides behind on the Internet—his relative anonymity and the lack of a controlling authority. Out here in the physical world, there are existing institutions that can deal with such people.

Chapter 20

Everybody's Favorite Law: Copyright

In This Chapter

- The copyright crisis
- Don't infringe on me
- What's mine is mine
- What's yours is yours, but I can excerpt

There sure is a lot of interesting information to be had on the Internet; which poses quite a new and interesting dilemma for our personal-property-protectin' society—who owns it? Copyright law has been an attempt at forming a legal answer to this question in the pre-Internet society, but it's facing a mighty challenge in the roaring, wild wires of the Net. In this series of pages that makes up Chapter 20, we'll look at how copyright law and the Internet stack up. This is definitely an "issue-in-progress," with much precedent left to be set, but there are a number of things to keep in mind when… sharing goes too far.

On the Net?

In those halcyon days of 1985, when about eight people were using the Internet, they exchanged information as if it were a big coffee klatsch. "Hey, Frank, take a look at this interesting article I read in the paper." "Joe, here's a sample of that new CD I got, take a listen." "Sue, look what Frank sent me." They were happy and free. But then more people got onto the Net, and some of those people had heard about something called "laws." And here we are now, having to read this chapter.

The Internet straddles two worlds: people can exchange information and ideas as if it were a social club down the block, yet those ideas can reach millions of people around the world. One is called "chatting," the other, "broadcasting." Where the exchange of information tickles the underchin of broadcasting and publishing, things become a bit sticky. After all, if you read Ms. Lane's column in the *Daily Planet* on Sunday and showed it to people at the watercooler, Ms. Lane would probably be pleased. On the other hand, if you make a copy of her column and distribute it to two million people, such that they don't have to buy the *Daily Planet* to read it, she may lose her enthusiasm. Problem is, on the Internet, the watercooler and the two million people are the same thing.

This problem has raised a lot of questions, and many people are thinking hard about them. Some of them even use the Internet. Many lawyers are opening new bank accounts as we speak. The truth of the matter is that there are thousands of copyright violations taking place on the Internet daily. From scanned images out of magazines to reprinted articles from newspapers, millions of people are sharing information without acknowledging, or purchasing from, its source. Whether there's any way to stop this is something for the suits, both law- and three-piece, to figure out (unlikely)—and our societal definition of copyright's purpose may be forced to change. By the same token, the Net can't be a completely lawless land, for some laws do have their uses. Trying to preserve the useful notions behind copyright laws in the face of public mass-distribution systems will be an interesting struggle. We'll begin our look at the current state of things, and what impact they have on your behavior, in a few moments.

One... two... three... four... okay, I'm ready now.

Infringement—It's Easy and Wrong

First, we should cover some of the major aspects of copyright law; although I'm speaking from a U.S. perspective, some of these principles are applications of the Berne Convention, which is an International agreement. (Or so I'm told. I've never actually seen it.) Since I'm not a lawyer, I may be completely wrong about all of this (I have to say that or they'll hit me with a briefcase), but I charge much less.

Don't assume that something isn't copyrighted just because it doesn't say so. In fact, it works the other way around: *unless* a work explicitly, specifically states that it is in the public domain, a work is assumed to be copyrighted. The cute little © symbol isn't a necessity, but it can help if a case should go to court. When and if someone infringes on a copyright is usually for a civil court to decide. To receive any real damages, a plaintiff will have to establish that the infringement has in some way led to false profits or has damaged the commercial viability of the original work. One meaning of this is that to have committed infringement, you do not necessarily have to charge others for the use of a work you've wrongfully made available.

Because most day-to-day copyright issues on the Internet involve Usenet and/or e-mail, we'll consider these in our discussion. Imagine the following scenario: You're kicking back in the warm afternoon sunlight, reading a provocative Dear Abby column, in which a grandmother wants to know whether she should confront her daughter about the fact that she never received a "thank you" card in return for her wedding present. Inspired, you know that this is just the thing your friend Margaret in San Francisco would find interesting. So, since the article is only 500 words or so, you type it into your computer and send it off as an e-mail to Margaret. BZZT—infringement! Worse, imagine you posted it to a newsgroup to incite discussion—BZZT—infringement! Then someone on that newsgroup reads it and chooses to forward it to their friend Tom, in Guam—BZZT—infringement! Tom sends it to Willy in South Africa—BZZT! Willy sends it—BZZT! BZZT! BZZT! As you can clearly see, the Internet makes it trivially easy to commit a good 20,000 copyright infringements per minute, and that's without stopping for a cool drink. Throw a digital scanner into the loop, and you can have people exchanging copies of multi-page magazine articles.

Even worse, think of copyrighted online information services, such as ClariNet. ClariNet is a service that your ISP has the option to subscribe to—which provides you with a whole new hierarchy of Usenet newsgroups. They're not discussion groups, but rather AP newswire reports, hot off the, er, wire, and into your newsreader. You might read an interesting ClariNet article, hit the **F** key in your newsreader, and forward it to a friend. BZZT! Or worse, you might cross-post the ClariNet article to another newsgroup, which everyone receives, thus undermining ClariNet's whole point as a subscription-for-pay service (*stealing*, it's called). BZZT! For their part, the ClariNet people have been known to send happy little e-mails to people they find doing this, warning them first of the wrongness of their actions, and then threatening with eternal damnation.

It's a Fact
Actually, something like this did happen, sort of. The popular, self-admitted booger-joke-columnist Dave Barry's column had begun to be carried by ClariNet. While this entertained many, some couldn't resist forwarding copies of the weekly column to other people, thus infringing on ClariNet's copyright. Ultimately, ClariNet chose to stop carrying the column, as the only effective recourse. The lesson being that only a few million bad apples can spoil it for everybody.

The problem, though, is evident. And if you've read Usenet for any period of time, you've no doubt seen many such infringements. Some people preface their crime with the phrase "Reprinted without permission." For the most part, that really doesn't help, even though it looks nice. It's still a big BZZT! There are some exceptions, of course—one of those being called "fair use," which we'll look at momentarily.

Notice that in the examples just given (except for ClariNet), I never said you'd actually get in trouble for these infringements. That's another stuffed-tamale-with-cheese-and-jalapeños altogether.

The Whole Truth and Nothing But

I said earlier that damages for a copyright infringement are dependent on the effects of the deed. If you wrote a beautiful poem and e-mailed it to a friend, who then posted it under his name in twelve newsgroups, you would have a difficult time winning damages against him. Perhaps if you are a poet, and can show that you reasonably expected that poem to be used commercially, you'd get an award, but otherwise it's not going to happen. So, infringement alone is not going to result in punishment. How you act with that knowledge is your own decision. Even arguably damaging infringement may be difficult to prosecute in the age of the Net. For instance, imagine a famous columnist wrote a piece that was then spread widely on the Net, in blatant infringement. It may very well have reduced the profits and commercial viability of the work, since many thousands of people may have read the column without ever having paid for the newspaper. But who are the newspaper publishers going to go after? This is still an unresolved situation on the Net, so enjoy it while it lasts... er, I mean, take non-involved interest in it while it lasts.

Who's to Say What's Fair and What's Fair Use?

What complicates this whole mess about exchanging copyrighted work is something known as *fair use*. The wise old copyright people realized that it would be impractical and detrimental to disallow any and all usage of a work. For example, parody relies strongly on an original work, and in fact earns its commercial viability on the back of the previous work. Yet parody is not a form of copyright infringement. In addition, using small excerpts of a copyrighted work in a relevant situation may not take away any profit or credit from the original, and in some cases may contribute to it. Thus, the concept behind fair use is that one can use portions of a copyrighted work without prior permission, as long as one doesn't use "too much." Vagaries like that are what give the legal profession its livelihood, and you can imagine that it has resulted in no end of controversy.

On the Internet, and in Usenet news in particular, it's considered acceptable to try to practice fair use. So, if you read an interesting piece in a newspaper, retyping a paragraph or so that is relevant to your specific commentary and citing the paper in which the entire work appears is a reasonable way to go. Readers interested in the whole article may then seek out the original newspaper on their own. It is so tempting on the Internet to bypass that seemingly bureaucratic obstacle, but to do otherwise would truly undermine many of the mechanisms that brought you the article in the first place. Authors, for instance, have to make a living, thus they write for a paycheck. Easy as electronic redistribution may be, you can see how it can put a writer out of business, thus eliminating the source of the product that you felt strongly enough about to redistribute. Until procedures are implemented that can somehow maintain the integrity of this system in the face of public mass-distribution systems, Internet users are going to have to work largely on the honor system. Again, this is another issue that has yet to mature into full, uh, issue-hood.

There are two common bonds between the examples discussed so far. One is that they are works that were only available to a select (paying) audience before the Internet got hold of them. There are many articles intentionally available on publicly accessible areas of the Internet—such as the World Wide Web, which anyone can access. Yet this doesn't negate their copyright—remember that they are not in the public domain unless they explicitly say so. However, even if copyrighted, they may very well be "freely distributable," which means that you may send and forward copies to anyone you like. Usually it's asked that the work be kept intact in such cases, with appropriate credits. Works written for and posted to public outlets such as the WWW or even some Usenet newsgroups will contain a disclaimer to the effect that they are freely distributable if that is the case. Otherwise you cannot assume such.

If I Don't Say This, a Lot of People Will Get Annoyed with Me

There is a difference between Usenet and the Internet, one that I have purposely blurred when referring to them. The Internet is a *communications medium*, like the technologies that broadcast television programming. Usenet, by that analogy, is a "show." It is a body of content that can be transmitted by the medium of the Internet. Usenet, however, is not restricted to transmission via the Internet. There are other ways to transmit data between computers; Usenet, in various places around the world, is carried by a variety of media. The overwhelming majority of Usenet readers, though, do access it by way of the Internet, and so the distinction is often overlooked. Technically, I admit, it shouldn't be.

What About My Own Postings?

A common thread between our previous examples has been that they're all "professional" works by outside-the-Internet sources. But copyright isn't limited to the commercial venture, and many Net users wonder whether copyright applies to their Usenet postings. And if so, how? Are there actually black squirrels in some cities? Yes, Virginia…

Exactly how copyright law interpretation, especially the fair use clause, affects Usenet postings is definitely a matter of spirited debate. The heart of the debate lies in what you consider to be a poster's implied consent. That is, by making a posting to Usenet, one could argue that a poster is knowingly requesting that his work be copied, because the way Usenet works *is* to make copies of posts and send them on to another Usenet site. On the other hand, if that is interpreted too widely, then one could never post an original creative work to Usenet without giving it up entirely. Others believe that posting to Usenet definitely implies permission to quote and re-copy within a broad spectrum of uses. One common Usenet practice comes into play immediately here, which is "quoting."

If you've read any Usenet at all, you've no doubt seen "quoting." It is when someone follows-up a post with one of their own, including portions of the original post that they want to comment on. Like this:

```
On Tuesday, March 16, Teddy Z wrote:
>I, too, used to believe that the concept of a maximum wage was
>good for society. But one thing I've learned in my age is that
>it isn't the case at all. Society, as far as I can tell, is much
>better off now that I have three cars and a horse.

Well I only have a horse and no cars. Perhaps if there was a maximum wage, I
could have a car and a pony, and you'd have a mare and a car and a motor-
cycle. That would be fairer, I think.
```

In the example just given, the second poster only quoted the relevant portion of the original work. Technically, this is a proper adherence to fair use. But if you're a more experienced Internet user, you may be sitting there reading this thinking, "What is he, crazy? Why is he telling people this? Everyone quotes like mad on the Net." And it's true—nobody gives a hoot about fair use in dealing with other people's posts. Sometimes you'll see somebody quote the entire 200 lines of someone's long philosophical rant, and then add the classic, "Me too." You won't hear protestations about fair use violations, although you may well hear people complain about *wasted bandwidth,* since that entire original post did not need to be re-sent over Usenet for the short input at the end. I don't have a particularly solid nugget of advice in these matters. Whether or not quoting an entire post for no good reason is a violation depends on what you think a poster consents to by the mere act of posting.

In practice, I wouldn't worry too much about this whole matter in the course of common Usenet exchanges. It's most applicable, and important, when talking about commercial works that have a real, calculable value outside of a particular informal discussion. If that weren't true, discussion of any sort on Usenet would probably grind to a halt as everyone tried to protect their ideas from anyone else—except for alt.binaries.pictures.erotica, of course (which, by the way, is a newsgroup composed almost entirely of real copyright violations).

Dirty Laundry, Private E-mail

Sometimes it will happen that you or someone else wants to, or chooses to, publicly post private e-mail that they've received. You might, for instance, be taking a grievance against another user publicly, and want to show some of the harassing e-mail he's sent. Or possibly a friend simply sent you some very interesting thoughts, and you want to share them with the world. Posting e-mail from other people has generated some arguments (and flames) in and of itself. You won't find a clear consensus of opinion across Usenet, but here's this book's perspective.

It is believed to be the case that the author of an e-mail automatically holds its copyright. The act of sending that e-mail to another party does not affect the copyright status. It's just as if I sent you an article that I wrote; you don't now hold copyright over it (unless I specifically allowed for that transfer). On the other hand, there's nothing that says you can't tell a third party what someone wrote to you in e-mail. If Bob tells you that he has a crush on Jane, and you tell Penelope (Jane's best friend, who's going out with Martin, whose brother is Bob's teammate), Bob hasn't a legal leg to stand an objection on. (Of course, he may find it socially unacceptable and spit mud at you.) So, you may certainly make a public post about what someone has written you privately. Furthermore, since we're arguing that an e-mail's author holds its copyright, you can even quote relevant excerpts of it under the protection of fair use.

If you want to maintain the moral (and legal) high ground in a dispute, then discuss content and quote within reason, rather than posting an entire private e-mail in a public forum. It should be noted, however, that posting an entire private e-mail may well be a copyright infringement, but there's not much the infringed can do about it, practically speaking. Remember that civil damages are only going to be awarded in cases where Very Important matters are at stake. The truth is that a judge isn't even going to take the cotton out of his ears for a Usenet dispute over who plays the best slide guitar, even if the two of you infringed each other until your shoes were tattered.

In the case of friendly e-mail you'd like to post, you may as well just ask the original author for permission, and note that in your post. It'll keep everyone happy, and that really is the goal of this whole book: to be happy, rainbow-colored, lollipop-sucking folk.

Lastly, remember above all that "none of the above" applies if the e-mail you received *was* a copyright infringement itself. That is, if a friend sent you a transcribed article from the *L.A. Times* (BZZT!), his permission to you to post it doesn't wash, since he doesn't hold copyright on it in the first place. Never speak to him again.

It's in the area of forwarding and posting actual commercial works that the truly serious nature of copyright infringement comes into play. While it hasn't happened in a spectacular way yet, someone is going to get sued, probably to be made an example of, and you probably don't want to be that person. (It'll be fun to watch, though.)

The Least You Need to Know

The Internet, and Usenet in particular, is the land of a thousand copyrights. Copyright law can be your friend, at least if you produce anything worth money, anyway. Otherwise it's just sorta boring. Read on, anyway; it's good for you.

- Don't transcribe articles from commercial sources and send them to people on the Internet or post them in Usenet. You're not supposed to do that; it is copyright infringement. It is, of course, very easy to do, which poses many interesting philosophical issues for society and the Internet.
- The *fair use* clause of Copyright law allows you to excerpt relevant portions of a copyrighted work (without prior permission) to use for your own purposes—as long as you don't use too much and you use it relevantly.
- It may seem a minor act to e-mail one copyright infringement to another person, but on the Internet, information spreads like wildfire. One person can rapidly become hundreds or thousands of people. Such an act can undermine the original creator's ability to continue to create.
- Your own Usenet postings are automatically copyrighted by you, but expect to see them quoted and mangled widely in some cases. The mere act of posting means you consent to that, but even in the case of creative or intellectual works of your own, you still own copyright over them. Posting to Usenet *does not* make your work public domain, although it may be difficult to prevent people from treating it as if it were.
- An e-mail message's author holds its copyright, thus you would commit an infringement by posting an entire e-mail message to Usenet without the author's prior permission. Revealing details about the content of the message, along with "fair use" excerpts, is allowable.

Chapter 21

The Great American Pastime: Lawsuits

In This Chapter

- Suing our pants off
- Free? Speech?
- A whole heap of libel
- Scamming for dollars

The more people use the Internet, the more likely it is that someone is going to sue someone else. In fact, they already have. Which, in and of itself, is not necessarily a bad thing—when and if justified. This isn't going to be a very long chapter because there's a limited amount to say on this topic that's relevant to this book's theme. Nonetheless, we do have a few things to note, comment on, scribble, and otherwise bandy about. Some interesting things have happened in the area of "net.law," which at the very least will make stories to delight friends and family alike. Some may even set precedents.

Sue Happy

There are three basic sources of lawsuits and legal entanglements that have been munching on the Net: computer-illiterate government lackeys, computer-illiterate-but-greedy businesses protecting cash cows, and normal people.

Some related major lawsuits have been launched by the government, the U.S. government specifically (since that's the one I live under). In one case, the government tried to prosecute an MIT student for distributing copyrighted software over the Internet. It's a case they probably should have won, since what he did *was* illegal, but their fervor to make a bigger example of him than was warranted led to a judge dismissing the charges. In another case, some government people in Tennessee got some naughty pictures from California, and so they dropped a basket of charges on the couple who made the images available (actually, this wasn't on the Internet as such, but it was still "online"). In this case the government won convictions on 11 counts of "transmitting obscenity on the interstate phone lines," although the case has been appealed. (Note, regarding the content of Chapter 18, that no one actually cares. The smut flows on.)

Closer to the Internet, and the common user, there's a hefty case in progress involving a college student's fantasy life. Specifically, "Jake Baker" (a pseudonym) wrote a fantasy story that he posted to the Usenet newsgroup alt.sex.stories. The story was not exactly Mother Goose material. It involved a variety of sexual acts of an extreme nature—violence, death, that sort of thing. What's more, a fellow student of Baker's was the featured "protagonist" in the piece, even though he didn't actually know her. An alumnus of Baker's school saw the post, looked down at his diploma and realized that he was a lawyer, and then it all hit the fan (not that I'm implying that his being a lawyer had anything to do with it, not at all, uh-uh). Admittedly, though, there is a valid issue here, one that may well affect Internet users: Does freedom of speech and press allow for Baker's use of a classmate's name in a violent fantasy story distributed for public reading? One argument is that the story can be considered a threat against the woman. Another argument is that, no, you can use anyone's name you want in your work—people don't "own" their names. Ultimately, it seems that this case will rest on whether it can be proven that the story was an actual threat against the woman. However, she could sue Baker for libel, if she can prove the she's been injured (not necessarily financially) by the story's distribution and if Usenet can be considered "media."

The outcome of the Baker case could well have an impact on such issues as free speech and the Internet, the Internet as a publishing medium, and the liability that users take on. This case hasn't even gone to trial yet at the time of this writing, though it's certainly possible that it may be in process—or concluded—as you're reading this.

Moo

Under the heading of "cash cows," there are a couple of noteworthy happenings. Once, an Internet user wrote a computer program that simulated the television game show *Jeopardy!*. He set up a topic channel on IRC called "#jeopardy" that users could join and play his game. All of this was entirely free; no money was changing hands. The real *Jeopardy!* people got wind of it, and they weren't happy at all. They threatened the user with Big Bad Legal Things. Although they would have had to prove that his work could have had a realistic impact on their product (or could have confused people), you can probably understand why he chose to back down rather than fight them.

There have been several instances of businesses (or businesses' lawyers) getting hot under the collar about the usage of a word or image by net users. One person got a little heat about using *Simpsons* images made of ASCII characters in a signature file. Another user was distributing a "fanzine" for lovers of the television show *Mystery Science Theater 3000*, when she got word that her use of a certain phrase (which I won't repeat here so I don't get heat, too) was not allowed without permission. "Cease and desist," as the story goes. Often these events are precipitated by private interests who don't understand the Internet or Usenet, and merely hear about the use of a certain symbol, character, or trademark.

Again, however, the "watercooler-versus-broadcasting" issue arises. What is the limit on what you can say in a conversation with other people and the world, and how many people does it take to turn a group conversation into a form of publishing? (I say eleven, but we'll see.)

Libel! Slander! Fire!

In Chapter 19, we looked at harassment and similar interpersonal battles getting out of hand on the Internet. One of the ways they could really get crazy is by ending up in court in the form of a libel suit. With all of the personal attacks that take place on Usenet, should someone win a libel settlement in such a situation, there may be a sudden and severe shortage of judges to handle all the new suits.

There is, for example, the case of one Brock Meeks, a well-known journalist who has covered many online issues. In investigating a "too-good-to-be-true" solicitation that he ran across on the Internet, he dug up some shady business practices by a particular company, and a particular head of said company, who seemed to be involved in those direct-marketing-style scams. When Meeks wrote and distributed a criticism of this company's practices in his own online "newswire" service, he was faced with a libel lawsuit from the head of said company. Meeks' contention, of course, is that he did not commit libel. Though some have argued that this case has nothing to do with the Internet as such, the Net's ability to allow anyone—established journalist or not—to disseminate critical views seems clearly involved. Certainly the outcome of this case (whatever that may be) will affect the flow of opinion on the Net.

Combatants on the Internet may be prone to claim that false statements by one about the other are in fact damaging (because of the scope of the Internet). Whether or not they can make it stick will depend a lot on how the "publishing" power of the Net is considered by the courts. Equally important will be the content of the alleged libel. If someone makes a post with information about you that is patently false, and you can prove that the information harmed you in some way—if, for example, the newsgroup were populated with potential employers—you have a better chance of pursuing a libel claim than if someone just wrote that you were stupid and wore ugly sweaters.

Whenever possible, of course, the best course of action is to avoid such battles in the first place. It does you no good to get wrapped up in flamewars to the point of lawsuits and court battles. But there are legitimate instances where your person may be attacked publicly and wrongly, without your having fanned the flames.

Fraud and Other True Crimes

Fortunately, you can't punch, kick, or kill someone on the Internet. It's certainly conceivable that someone could try to defraud other people (after all, it happens all the time offline). The most common instance of this in Usenet involves people who participate in the second-hand-market newsgroups, offering to sell items with no intent on delivering once money is received. While it doesn't happen frequently, there have been a few instances of individuals making names for themselves by ripping off a series of Net users.

This is one of the reasons why it's a good idea to read through any marketplace newsgroups you're shopping in, to see if any posts are complaints about some fraud-monger. Like a spare tire in the middle of the road, it's better to swerve and miss these situations than to run right into them. Finding and prosecuting someone with whom you've never even had any physical interaction can be very difficult. Especially when you're talking about relatively small sums of money, such as a couple hundred dollars (small in the grand scheme of things), authorities may not go to the ends of the earth to help you track down this person.

As the Net grows, there are bound to be marketing scams, fraud, and the like, just as there is by phone and postal service. An increasing number of posts to Usenet advertise sheer miracles. Did you know that you could save over 50% on long distance calls, lose 50 pounds a week with an amazing new herbal diet, and meet women? All at the same time! Exactly—this type of stuff should be relatively easy to avoid if you have an IQ above that of a newt. Carry that healthy skepticism into many of the ads you see in Usenet. Remember the issues raised in Chapter 17, especially about trustworthiness and netiquette? These types of scams almost always violate both.

Without a central regulatory agency, it's hard to say who will be the point of contact for reporting such abuses. However, since the Internet does operate largely over phone lines, that would be a good place to start.

Deliberations

You might have the impression that this was a rough-edged chapter without a lot of solid facts or solid advice. Well, the laws of the land often have to play catch-up with technology, and the Internet has pulled way out ahead this time. As society and its laws struggle to catch up, we Internet users are left with a lot of muddy questions about behavior and consequences. At one end of the spectrum, if you don't break any laws while using the Internet, you shouldn't have any problems. Of course, one also hopes that nobody breaks any laws against you. At this point in time, it's certainly possible to get away with things on the Net that you could not pull off so easily in traditional society—sort of like hockey.

None of this is made any easier by the fact that the Internet transcends national borders. What's pornography, or even child pornography, in one nation may not be in another. The Internet doesn't know about nations, and it doesn't care. The same is true for laws regarding libel, trademark, copyright, and so forth. It's just a big mess. For the time being, however, it seems reasonable to assume that nations will try to exert their force on the Internet—and they'll base the attempt on their pre-existing laws. Only when those attempts fail (wanna bet?) will all these issues have to be re-evaluated from scratch.

The last thing we need—for the Internet or the society as a whole—is a flood of new lawsuits precipitated by Net use. Unfortunately, lawmakers who don't understand the Internet itself may help bring about this scenario. On the other hand, it is necessary to preserve freedom as best we can without restricting it. These are questions we faced as a civilization, as a birthing nation, and now as a global population. Some would say we didn't answer them right the first two times, so the prognosis isn't too good. I'll keep mum on that for the time being.

The Least You Need to Know

The law and the Internet have not fully met eye-to-eye yet. A ton of precedents are waiting to be set, and most readers are going to want to stay far away from them. Common, everyman Internet use should not get you into any legal frays, but there are a lot of fringes.

- Those looking to launch lawsuits against Net users are governments looking to make examples of people, business trying to protect profits, and users with gripes against other users.
- Sexually explicit material is going to be a target of a number of sources, so be warned. Birds do it, bees do it, but you're not supposed to.

- Issues involving libel are likely to be the most common arising on the Internet. The line between freedom of speech and infringing on someone else's rights is a thin one, and the Internet's mass distribution doesn't help matters. Be careful about wandering into libelous territory, especially while there's still so much that remains unresolved.
- Don't buy miracle creams. Net scams are often easy to spot, although they will grow more sophisticated with experience. It takes so little to get onto the Internet these days that an alleged company's "presence" is no guarantee of legitimacy.

Chapter 22

The Earth Is Flat and Other Net Myths

In This Chapter

- Nobody's fool
- The virus that wasn't
- No new taxes
- Shootout at the Myth Factory

Without a healthy influx of rumor and innuendo, there would be no evening news. And high school would be even more of a drag. Relationships wouldn't be psychotic. And Hollywood would cease to exist as we know it. But alas, even the digital sophistication of the Internet has not squashed the human proclivity for tales of fancy—more commonly called *lies*. So we'll close out our look at the Good Society with some lies—but no statistics.

The Clueless Newbie

There is a contingent of people on the Internet who forget that they weren't born there. Given what experience they have, they take any and every opportunity to exploit or ridicule the inexperience of new users. There is at least one valid problem they're addressing: with so many new users bootstrapping onto the Net, many questions are directed repeatedly at more experienced Internet users. Many mistakes are made over and over. There have been two general camps of reaction to this by veteran netizens. Some try to help educate the new users, most especially with the creation of Frequently Asked Questions (FAQs) documents, which attempt to answer the questions that many neophytes have on a given topic. Usenet newsgroups such as **news.announce.newusers** should be mandatory reading for the novice. Unfortunately, many new users don't bother with any of these amenities, which does not endear them to the incumbent Internet crowd. "Clueless newbies," they're called, because they stumble around like 10-minute-old baby giraffes. Consequently, other users find great joy in poking and laughing in response.

For example, a common question newbies ask is for somebody to tell them a site for such-and-such material. Not having learned how to find sites on their own, the mischievous but experienced netizen may offer this piece of advice: "You should type 'telnet 127.0.0.1' and then log in with your own username and password. Then type 'rm -r *'." Now, this may *look* like meaningless cryptobabble, but it is in fact very funny to adolescent geeks. Because "127.0.0.1" is the IP address for your own account—it's self-referential. Therefore, the instructions above tell you to telnet to your own account, log in, and then execute the command that would delete everything. Get it? Pretty funny stuff, huh? Well, in the right places, you can see this several times a day, as users with just enough experience to think they're being clever push this counsel onto users with even less experience. So watch out for that, and *don't* telnet to 127.0.0.1.

Here's another one: you are on IRC, chatting away as a newbie, and someone says "I'm offering a cool file for anyone who wants it." Not knowing much about IRC, you don't know how to get a file that someone is offering (putting aside the issue of accepting programs from strangers). So you ask: "How do I get that file?" The response: "You type /si filename to get the file." See, that's hilariously, hysterically funny. Because, of course, "/si" means "sign-off." If you typed that you'd be logged out of the IRC channel, and everyone else there would have a hearty laugh. Thus is the fate of the clueless newbie, when faced off against the pimply netgod.

If all this reminds you of when those two bullies at the bus stop used to take your shoe off and throw it around to each other until the moment the bus came, leaving you to frantically attempt to get it over your foot as the bus driver began to pull away, it's not at all dissimilar. Or maybe that was just me. Velcro only made it worse, really.

You can't avoid being a newbie, so the best solution to this problem of innocent gullibility is to avoid being clueless (or at least, avoid looking that way). Certainly you can't learn everything there is to know about the Net *before* using the Net. Read FAQs posted to newsgroups that you're interested in. Read everything posted to **news.announce.newusers**. Then, when you speak up in Usenet, you'll sound like a clueful newbie, and much less likely to attract the ire of a hungry prankster.

And He Had One Big Eye Right in the Middle of His Head

I suppose these quirks just mentioned were more tricks than myths. Each of the following is a combination of both. As a society, the Internet has its share of myths and legends. Often these are foisted upon new users, who sometimes take them seriously and make well-intentioned moves to inform others. Of course, they're all lies. Bald, shiny, one-hair-wrapped-around-the-entire-head lies.

Good Times

One such recent example of this was the "Good Times Virus." As the story goes, there is supposedly a new virus floating around the Internet, much more dangerous than any before, yadda yadda yadda. What makes this virus particularly virulent, the legend continues, is that it can hide in an e-mail message. And if you read an e-mail message with the subject "Good Times," the virus will "go into your computer." From there, untold destruction and havoc will be wreaked upon your system, blah blah, so forth so on, President Johnson, etc., etc. Now, how is the new user supposed to know whether this is true or not? Certainly viruses are a problem, and it is important to be vigilant about them, especially on the Internet. (Thankfully, you've got Chapter 11 on your side, if I may make such an egregiously arrogant self-reference.)

If you were a close reader of the aforementioned chapter, you may well be looking at this little story and thinking, "What a bucket o' crap!" Which is exactly what the Good Times virus is. Oh, sure, somebody *could* e-mail you an executable program that contains a virus in it. But the mere act of *reading* an e-mail message certainly does not execute any program within it. There is no such virus, and if you see anybody warning others, kindly advise them that it is a big fat hoax. No need to be rude about it, as they may very well be sincerely trying to help. A little education goes a long way. And reading is fundamental. Only you can stop forest fires. I'd like to teach the world to sing.

Even Hallmark Asks You to Stop

There once was a little boy whose name was Craig Shergold. He was dying in a hospital bed somewhere in England. He made a plea for get-well cards, and once the story made the press, well-wishers everywhere began stamp-licking like mad. Soon Craig realized he was getting quite a lot of cards, and decided he'd go for the gold—the *Guiness Book of World Records*. "Send more!" So word spread far and wide across the globe to send this young, suffering child more cards. And it worked—tiny Craig made the Guiness record.

This story is actually all true. And you may see a story somewhat like it, in more detail, posted to Usenet from time to time. It encourages you to send more cards—keep 'em coming. Except for one minor detail: it all happened many years ago. Craig, fortunately, survived his illness and lived. He didn't want any more cards. However, "STOP!" doesn't seem to travel as well as "GO!" So the cards keep on coming, years later, and frankly, nobody really wants them anymore. Getting the influx to stop has been a real problem. It's one of those ironic things—you can't really criticize people for acts of kindness, but the people they're being kind to genuinely don't want any more cards. So, if you see the story of young Craig Shergold, let it warm your heart, and then remember that he's not little anymore, he's not dying anymore, and he *doesn't* need any more cards!

Breaking News! The FCC Modem Tax

There's a lot of concern among netizens that one day the government will try to step in and squash the beautiful Internet like a fruit fly. In this book, we've talked about a number of situations where they may well try to get an arm in somewhere. It is in that spirit that you may see an alarmed poster warning about the "proposed" FCC modem tax. This tax would penalize Internet users in an attempt to create an expensive disincentive against online communications. An appropriate call to arms is suggested.

Well, put down your weapons. There certainly are real threats from the State to be concerned about. The FCC modem tax, alas, is not one of them. There is no such proposal, and there hasn't ever been one. There was a proposal a long time ago that was similar in nature, but it's not on the table now and nobody predicts that it's going to be. So, while it's great to be a concerned and active citizen, this isn't the cause to lick the quill about.

As I write this book, there is a real proposal in the works that *may* be very dangerous to the Internet. It should not be confused with the "modem tax," and it deserves a *lot* of quill-licking. In short, it is called the "Communications Decency Act of 1995," and it seeks to expand current FCC regulations concerning "indecency" to all forms of electronic media. The major plank of concern is that the bill makes service providers criminally liable for the content of information passed through their system. That's right—if you send obscene e-mail, your service provider can be held accountable. There are about 25,432 (at last count) hideous implications of this, not the least of which being possible service-provider censorship and monitoring of user activities. The proposed bill is U.S. Senate Bill 314, and the full text of it should be easy to find on the Internet (ironic, that). While I'm not going to preach about it in more detail here, I do urge readers to at least read the content of the bill and make their own evaluations. Although this book is about protecting yourself on the Internet, it may be necessary to protect the Internet itself, at least in its current form. I do want to emphasize that while the "FCC modem tax" is a Net legend, don't dismiss any and all warnings about government proposals. Soapbox speech over.

"Make Money Fast" and Friends

Lastly, there is the ever-ubiqitous Usenet post that is all of myth, trickery, and fraud rolled into one. There are a number of variations on this theme, not unlike Goldberg's, but they're all recognizable.

The post in question is a friendly letter, written by the self-identified Dave Rhodes, who I suspect has never been born (although there are probably other Dave Rhodeses who are none too pleased that this ersatz Dave has tarnished the name). Mr. Rhodes—er, Dave, tells of how he made megajillions of dollars, and how you can, too. How did he do this? With an illegal "pyramid scheme," that's how, not that it ever happened anyway. The basic text of the post describes how to participate in this brilliant plan to rake in millions (which it is not), in a manner that is simple and completely legal (which it is not). What you do, see, is send each person on the given list one dollar, and then add your name to the bottom of the list, and send the post on to a specified number of people. They, in turn, do the same, and by the time your name rolls to the top of the list, thousands upon thousands of people are sending you money. It's called a "pyramid scheme." It's illegal, and it probably doesn't work anyway. (What's to stop you from just passing it on without sending out the money? Wouldn't everyone do that? Wouldn't *no one* get any money?) It's also a chain letter, which is illegal, too. This thing is bad news. Yet you'll see it posted all over Usenet. The subject line is often "MAKE MONEY FAST," but there are variations.

As I said, new strains are popping up daily. Some aren't even written by Dave Rhodes. This post has been the single most popular piece of crap ever spread on the Net. And those who think it's funny, take note: Almost every service provider will give you the boot immediately if they find out that you posted this somewhere. Other users, sick of it, will be quick to e-mail your sysadmin, and your sysadmin will be quick to say "Hasta la vista, username."

And—need it be said—don't send anyone any money. You won't make money fast. It's that simple. Better yet, e-mail the postmaster of the person who posted the message. Perhaps this is like one of those "kill the mole" games where no matter what hole you fire at, the mole will just pop up somewhere else. But like kudzu, we can at least try to keep it under control.

For Further Rumormongering

If these aren't enough to sate your thirst for baseless rumors, there are newsgroups dedicated to this sort of thing. For example, take a read of **talk.rumor**, in which you can see people propose all manner of absurd stupidity before it hits the streets. Or catch up on the latest falsehoods from Hollywood in **alt.showbiz.gossip**. Actually, 90 percent of the chatter in there is of the "Is so-and-so gay?" variety. But since there are no reports of said celebrity posting, "Yes, I am," the group seems to lack a real element of suspense.

Alt.folklore.urban hosts discussion about myths and legends old and new, from the classics of your grandparents' days to the latest of today. And there are several spin-off groups, focusing on legends related to college, computers, and science. So if the yarns in this chapter didn't move you, something of sure interest is floating around the Net somewhere.

Seriously, and more relevantly, you can use these newsgroups in your defense, too. If, for example, you run across a post that may be a myth, but you're not sure, check in on one of these newsgroups. Perhaps you'll find discussion about it. If not, start a discussion yourself. If anyone can spot a legend, it's these people. Not only can you save yourself from being suckered in by something, but you'll save others, too, by not spreading it. And you'll have the knowledge to dispel the myth for others.

The Least You Need to Know

Trick or treat, every day is Halloween on the Internet. From users wanting to exploit the latest clueless newbie, to ghost stories to scams—where there isn't any news, people will make some.

- Don't be a clueless newbie. Being a newbie is fine, it's the clueless part that causes problems. Educate yourself before asking questions that will make the Net snicker. Otherwise people will be telling you to telnet 127.0.0.1 and to /si from IRC. Don't do either.
- A virus cannot be spread simply by reading an e-mail message. Any rumor that a virus is spreading this way, such as the "Good Times Virus," is a stick of baloney, or a half-pound of bologna, or both.
- The FCC is not proposing to tax your modem, no matter what the post claims. If there is a realistic government scare, any post warning Net users about it will contain a lot of official information, such as proposal identifications and so forth. Fakes are not terribly difficult to single out.
- Stop sending cards to Craig Shergold. He doesn't want any more. He's grown up. Leave him alone.

- Pyramid schemes are probably the biggest scourge of Usenet. They're easy to spot once you know they exist, and they are rampant. "MAKE MONEY FAST" is the grandfather of them all and still sees quite a bit of airtime. Ignore them all, or better yet, alert the admins of the user who posted it because it's serious Net abuse, and he'll get his backside properly whupped.
- You can wallow in more Net rumor in several Usenet newsgroups. However, you may also use those groups in your defense, if you question the validity of a post, seek help there and they will know.

Further Reading

Imagine—you've read this entire book, and you have actually found some of it interesting! In some really warped cases, you might even want to read more about a topic. Fear not—I did a lot of reading to write this book; you can share my pain. While I can't reveal all of my top-secret sources due to their extremely high level positions and involvement with national security (I'm talking about my dog, of course), here is a chapter-organized breakdown of some things you may want to roll your eyeballs around on.

I've avoided many Internet site-specific addresses in this book, to keep it from becoming obsolete two months after release. All the further reading I will offer is on the Internet, however, so I must give you specific sites. If any of these don't work by the time you read this, don't blame me. I suspect many will work, and if they've been moved, you'll probably find a notice telling you where to find them. All links to documents on the Internet are given in URL format. That's the format that Web browsers (such as Netscape and Mosaic) like. If you select **Open URL** in your Web browser, you can enter the address exactly as printed here (in the special "command" typestyle) to get to the document (assuming the document's still in the same place on the Internet). Enjoy, and happy geeking—er, reading!

Introduction

Since this book assumes that you know at least a little about the Internet, you may want to learn more. There are plenty of good books out there, but there are also some pretty comprehensive guides for free, available right on the Internet. Like these:

EFF's Extended Guide to the Internet
`http://www.eff.org/papers/bdgtti/eegtti.html`

Zen and the Art of the Internet
`http://www.cs.indiana.edu/docproject/zen/zen-1.0_toc.html`

World Wide Web FAQ (Frequently Asked Questions)
`http://sunsite.unc.edu/boutell/faq/www_faq.html`

Glossary of Internet Terms
`http://www.matisse.net/files/glossary.html`

User's Guide to Netiquette
`http://www.fau.edu/rinaldi/netiquette.html`

Chapter 2: Getting to Know All About You

Here's a link for locating people on the Internet, as per the "Online White Pages" section in this chapter:

Finding People on the Internet
`http://alpha.acast.nova.edu/phone.html`

Chapter 5: Taking the Direct Route

Learn how to set up SLIP/PPP on your computer. This document contains many links to documents that will teach you how to set up a Mac or PC with SLIP or PPP:

`http://www.charm.net/pip.html`

Microsoft Windows users can stay on top of the latest SLIP/PPP applications and utilities for their PC here:

`http://bongo.cc.utexas.edu/~neuroses/cwsapps.html`

A warehouse of information for everything networked and Macintosh:

`http://rever.nmsu.edu/~elharo/faq/Macintosh.html`

The Firewall FAQ:

http://www.tis.com/Home/NetworkSecurity/Firewalls/FAQ.html
or
http://www.cis.ohio-state.edu/hypertext/faq/usenet/firewalls-faq/faq.html

Chapter 6: Passwords

Information on the S/Key password technology:
http://www.yahoo.com/Science/Mathematics/Security_and_Encryption/S_KEY/

Crack—The Password Cracking/Testing program (for UNIX):
file://black.ox.ac.uk/src/security/crack41.tar.Z

Chapter 7: Encryption

Cryptography FAQ:
http://www.daimi.aau.dk/faqs/cryptography-faq_toc.html

An introduction to PGP:
http://www.mantis.co.uk/pgp/pgp.html

Some information on Macintosh encryption:
http://www.utexas.edu/~grgcombs/htmls/crypto.html

Data encryption and social issues:
http://www.cs.umbc.edu/~mohan/Work/social-issues

That Funny Clipper Chip:
http://draco.centerline.com:8080/~franl/clipper/about-clipper.html

Further information on the beslighted RIPEM:
http://www.cs.indiana.edu/ripem/dir.html

Chapter 8: PGP

PGP Hypertext documentation:
http://www.pegasus.esprit.ec.org/people/arne/pgp.html

Chapter 10: E-mail

Anonymous re-mailers information:
http://draco.centerline.com:8080/~franl/crypto/remailers.html

Anonymous re-mailer list:
http://www.cs.berkeley.edu/~raph/remailer-list.html

WWW interface for sending anonymous e-mail:
http://www.c2.org/remail/by-www.html

Your electronic privacy:
http://draco.centerline.com:8080/~franl/privacy/

Chapter 11: Viruses

Virus FAQ:
http://www.cis.ohio-state.edu/hypertext/faq/usenet/computer-virus-faq/faq.html

Computer Viruses and Security:
http://www.einet.net/galaxy/Engineering-and-Technology/Computer-Technology/Security/david-hull/galaxy.htm

Chapter 12: The World Wide Web

The WWW security mailing list archives (this is technical stuff, for people running servers):
http://asearch.mccmedia.com/www-security.html

WWW Authentication (more technical stuff, bring a pillow):
http://www.w3.org/hypertext/WWW/AccessAuthorization/Overview.html

Chapters 13–16: UNIX, UNIX, and Sysadminning

Comp.security.unix FAQ:
http://www.cis.ohio-state.edu/hypertext/faq/bngusenet/comp/security/unix/top.html

BUGTRAQ Mailing List archive: UNIX security holes:
http://crimelab.com/bugtraq/bugtraq.html

The COAST Security Archive: everything a sysadmin needs to know:
http://www.cs.purdue.edu/coast/coast.html

SATAN Security Scanner:
http://www.cs.purdue.edu/coast/satan.html

Chapter 17: Capitalism

Buying and Selling in Misc.forsale FAQ:
`http://www.cis.ohio-state.edu/hypertext/faq/usenet/misc-forsale-faq/buying-selling/`

Posting Ads to Usenet FAQ:
`http://www.cis.ohio-state.edu/hypertext/faq/usenet/misc-forsale-faq/posting-ads/`

Chapter 20: Copyright

The big detailed Copyright FAQ:
`ftp://rtfm.mit.edu/pub/usenet-by-group/comp.answers/law/Copyright-FAQ`

Actual Copyright Law:
`gopher://marvel.loc.gov/11/copyright`

Chapter 21: Lawsuits

Legal Beat: covering net-related legal cases:
`http://www.wired.com/Staff/justin/dox/law.html`

Some Goodies (Neat Files and Things)

I've made vague, fuzzy references to "major FTP distribution sites" and things like that in this book. That's because there are some places on the Net that have a lot of files for certain platforms. Both the Mac and PC have these, and I recommended that whenever possible, you get programs from these sites. Of course, I didn't tell what these sites were. Now I will. Funny how that works out... .

For the PC People

Users of PC "clones" commonly use either MS-DOS, Microsoft Windows, or both. There are a few main sites for software for these operating systems. Each site has what are called *mirrors*—other sites carry the same software as the main site. Each evening, they check in with the head honcho site for anything new, and they retrieve it. The point of this arrangement is to spare 5 million people from having to FTP to just one machine to get files for their computers. So I will list both the main sites and the mirrors. The general rule of thumb is to use whichever is geographically closest to you. That keeps transglobal traffic down, and the Internet is happier that way.

When you're looking for MS-DOS programs, consider that **garbo.uwasa.fi** contains a massive archive in Finland. Of course, you can crawl over to a closer mirror such as these:

ftp.cdrom.com (California)

ftp.netnet.net (Wisconsin)

Users of Microsoft Windows can find hordes of programs at **ftp.cica.indiana.edu** in Indiana—better yet, check one of its many mirrors.

Some U.S. mirrors are:

ftp.cdrom.com (California)

gatekeeper.dec.com (California)

ftp.dataplex.net (Texas)

mirrors.aol.com (Virginia)

archive.orst.edu (Oregon)

mrcnext.cso.uiuc.edu (Illinois)

Some international mirrors are:

ftp.funet.fi (Finland)

ftp.uni-paderborn.de (Germany)

info.nic.surfnet.nl (Netherlands)

src.doc.ic.ac.uk (UK)

ftp.iij.ad.jp (Japan)

Lastly, have a look at "Simtel" for another motherlode of files for both MS-DOS and Windows:

oak.oakland.edu

ftp.netnet.net

When You're Feeling Macintoshish

Mac users needn't fear. Your goldmine of software awaits at *Info-Mac*, the head site being **sumex-aim.stanford.edu** (California). Mirrors, please:

grind.isca.uiowa.edu (Iowa)

mirror.archive.umich.edu (Michigan)

ftp.funet.fi (Finland)

ftp.lth.se (Sweden)

src.doc.ic.ac.uk (UK)

nic.switch.ch (Switzerland)

archie.au (Australia)

ftp.u-tokyo.ac.jp (Japan)

Another big repository is "Mac.Archive" at **mac.archive.umich.edu** (Michigan). Try connecting to this site using Gopher; it often responds better to Gopher than to FTP.

None of the above are exhaustive lists by any means—and you can find software for both platforms at a bunch of different places. The above are the biggest, largest, best maintained sites, though. Once you're wheeling around the Net, it's pretty easy to find more details, like specific sites. Any of the above will carry the programs I've mentioned in this book for their respective platforms. If not, sue me. (On second thought, *don't* sue me. I said it in haste and I'm sorry.)

Glossary

Speak Like a Geek: The Complete Archive

account Your access to the Internet. If you sign up with a service provider, be it a school or private company, you will get an account. Your account is your "home" on the Internet, and must be protected as such.

anonymous FTP A service with which anyone on the Internet may exchange files on a particular computer. Extremely popular, but poses risks to someone inviting the public onto their machine (that is, to those running an anonymous FTP server) unless configured properly.

anonymous re-mailer A voluntary service provided by some Internet users and organizations. You can send messages to the re-mailer, and it will strip away all identifying information and pass on Usenet posts or e-mail messages to their proper destinations. Recipients can even respond to you without knowing who you are, and their identities will be hidden as well.

anonymous server The same thing as an *anonymous re-mailer*.

archive This word has several possible meanings; as used in this book, it means a collection of files bound together into one bigger file. When you retrieve programs from the Internet (often by anonymous FTP), they are usually in the form of archives. Once you've transferred the archive, you split it up into its component files by using various unarchiving (or de-archiving) utilities.

ASCII Basically, one computer "alphabet." It consists mostly of readable, printable characters; it's the alphabet used in most e-mail and Usenet posts because it's meant for human users. Files that need a more extensive alphabet use "binary." See *binary*.

attachment Sometimes, you will "piggyback" a file onto your e-mail. You may want to e-mail somebody a pre-existing file, such as a word processing document. Often you can send this file as an e-mail attachment. It's distinct from the text you type directly into an e-mail message body.

authentication Any means by which a system can verify the identity of a user.

backdoor In computer-ese, this refers to a nonobvious feature of a system or program that can be exploited to gain access. If someone sneaks into an account in an other-than-normal way, he has used a backdoor. Some programs purposely include backdoors, which allow certain people access that everyone else can't have.

BBS Stands for *bulletin board system.* Often privately owned, run by a single individual (or small group) on a single (or small group of) computer(s). Some BBSs offer access to Internet capabilities, but they are not the Internet in and of themselves.

binary Whereas ASCII is the alphabet for human computer users, binary is the alphabet that the computer understands. Anything not human-readable (such as graphic files, sound files, executable programs, and so on) probably needs to be in binary format.

browser The application one uses to access the World Wide Web. Examples include Mosaic and Netscape. Although very capable, browsers are *not* used to access anything and everything on the Internet (such as your account information). They are merely one application out of many for Internet use, just as a word processor is one application out of many for desktop publishing use.

Cc: (carbon copy) Usually, when you address an e-mail message, you have the option of filling in a carbon-copy destination. If your account does not automatically save the e-mail you send to others (as *sent mail*), you may want to Cc: e-mail back to yourself so you have a record of what you've sent to other people.

channel In this book, this term refers to IRC (see *IRC*). A channel is essentially a group in which people gather and hold discussions, often around a particular theme topic. Discussion in channels is live and in real time, like a CB.

ciphertext What you get after encrypting text. It's gobbledygook. It's meant to be. If some-one intercepts a file that you've sent in ciphertext, they can't make heads or tails of it. A very important security term.

cleartext Sometimes used instead of *plaintext* to describe data before it's encrypted, such that anyone can see it. When someone transmits data to you in "cleartext" or "in the clear," it means someone else can intercept the data and make sense of it, hence it is vulnerable.

client A computer program that sends requests for information and receives or retrieves it. For example, a program that asks another computer for a file, and then receives the file, is a client. A program that asks another computer for the number of home runs that Babe Ruth hit is a client. Common clients that you probably use include Telnet, FTP, Gopher, and a World Wide Web browser.

Clipper Chip A proposal/fantasy of the United States government to include a computer chip in all digital communications devices that will encrypt data in such a way that other people can't "listen in" on your communications. Trick is, it has a backdoor that will allow the government itself to listen in, should they want to. The chip is meant to establish a popular form of security that won't lock the government out, as opposed to the alternative—a form of security that is *truly* secure.

Crack A popular program that attempts to break passwords using dictionary algorithms. Though it's a fave of hackers and crackers, system administrators can also use it to check the solidity of their own users' passwords.

cracking The act of breaking into a computer with illicit or malicious intent. Anal-retentives should note that this is different from hacking (see *hacking*).

Craig Shergold He doesn't need or want any more get-well cards. You'll see his story on the Net, with an accompanying plea. Ignore it; he's fine now.

cryptography The art of encryption. Anything that falls under the umbrella of methods, procedure, or theory behind hiding information from others' eyes.

decrypt The act of converting a hidden, gobbledygooked (encrypted) file into a readable, useful file.

digital signature A combination of authentication and cryptography that allows you to "sign" a computer document in such a way that the recipient can verify that it truly was you who sent it—and that the document has not been modified in any way since the digital signature was applied. Very useful, and very resistant to forgery.

directory In our usage, a "drawer" or "folder" of files on a computer.

disinfect The act of removing a virus from a file and attempting to restore the file to its original state before it was infected. You should do it when you've found a file to be infected with a virus, and you do not have a "clean" backup of that file.

Disinfectant A specific program for the Macintosh that takes care of most anti-virus needs.

distribution Very similar to *archive*. Someone might tell you to get "such-and-such distribution," which means to get the archive that contains all the files necessary for some program.

dot file In UNIX, a filename that begins with a period. The normal UNIX directory command ("ls -l") does not show dot files, hence some people call them "hidden files." You can see the dot files by using **ls -la**.

download The transfer of a file from a remote computer to the local one. That is, when you are transferring a file *from* somewhere else *to* the computer you are using, that is a download. See *upload* for the opposite.

dumb terminal A simple way to access a remote computer. The computer you're using doesn't process any commands; rather, it simply sends whatever you type to a remote computer for processing, and the results are sent back to your screen. Cheaper Internet accounts (often those that are UNIX shells) are accessed using dumb terminals. Commonly, you use a terminal program (or "communications program," depending on the lingo near you) to control your modem.

dynamic IP Your IP is the address of your computer on the Internet. Only users who have direct (Ethernet) or SLIP/PPP connections are lucky enough to get such an address. If you get a different IP address every time you connect to your service provider, you have dynamic IP. If you always have the same IP address, you've got static IP.

e-mail folder A file or directory in which you store a bunch of e-mail messages. You may have separate e-mail folders for different types of messages (if you're that organized)—such as a folder for messages from Sue, a folder for work-related messages, and a folder for junk.

encryption The act of obscuring information from the eyes of anyone who cannot decrypt it. The stronger the method used to encrypt data, the less likely that someone who doesn't know how to decrypt it can figure it out. A major tool in protecting security and privacy. Sort of fun, too.

/etc/passwd A file on a UNIX machine that contains the encrypted passwords of user accounts. Hackers and crackers will try to steal this file and run Crack on it, in an attempt to break user accounts. Quality passwords reduce their ability to succeed.

/etc/exports A file on a UNIX machine that contains file system mounting permissions. In short, the entries in this file tell the UNIX machine what other computers are allowed to access what portions of the machine.

Ethernet Technically, a piece of hardware, including cables and interface cards. Practically, it's often used to connect computers to the Internet directly. Supports TCP/IP and very-high-speed communications. Only found in businesses and universities—you can't get an Ethernet connection from your home, at least not unless you sell your home first to get enough money for what it would cost.

Eudora A particular e-mail program that uses a graphical interface. Very popular on the Macintosh and PC with Windows.

execute When you execute a program, you tell the computer to begin interpreting the instructions within. Same as "running" a program. A virus can only be launched when executed, hence a virus can only be launched when it resides in another program that is executed.

F-PROT A specific anti-virus program for MS-DOS. Supports virus scanning and disinfecting. Very popular and recommended, available on PC FTP sites.

file ownership Determines which user on a UNIX system owns, and thus has control over, a particular file. Only the root user on a UNIX system can change file ownerships, but users other than yourself and possibly root shouldn't own any of the files within your UNIX account (in most circumstances).

file permissions Determines which users on a UNIX system may have access to a file or directory, and what they may do with that file (or directory). Very important to have permissions set properly, otherwise users on a system may be able to access your important files without ever having to break your password.

finger An Internet client program that requests information about a user from that user's system. Can reveal a lot more than many people realize.

firewall A digital "moat," which very security-conscious organizations may choose to install as a buffer between the Internet and their internal computer network. Can be used to filter what types of communications go in and out of the organization.

flame When a user on the Internet sends a scathing, personal attack to another user. Often takes place on Usenet, but also on IRC. It's nothing more than bullying; being suckered by one can lead to a flame war.

flame war When users begin hurling attacks back and forth against one another, and thereby looking like fools to the rest of the public. Can take place in private e-mail, too. Serves no real purpose, and can easily lead to harassment.

flamebait Usually a Usenet posting meant to annoy readers of a newsgroup intentionally. Often the poster doesn't even believe in or care about the content of what he posted; rather, he just wants to "get a rise" out of everyone in the group.

forged e-mail When someone tries to alter the header information of an e-mail message so that you think it's from someone else. Poor forgeries are easily traced by looking at the full header information. Better forgeries may be more difficult to track back. Suffice it to say, if you receive e-mail from a deity or other unearthly presence, it's probably a forgery.

forms Elements of Web pages in which you can enter information or choose options among several. The information you enter is then sent back to the server, often "in the clear," so be sure you don't mind risking that someone might see what you've sent.

FTP site A computer that allows users to connect to it for the purposes of file exchange using the FTP protocol. A private FTP site requires that the user have a preexisting account on that FTP site. Public FTP sites, which anyone can connect to, are called *anonymous FTP*.

FTP A computer protocol for transferring files between computers on the Internet. "File Transfer Protocol" is what it stands for, funnily enough.

Gopher Another computer protocol that supports more complex communication between computers than does FTP. Often used for providing information services and searches, it can also transfer files.

graphical interface The use of windows and icons and the like to control a program, rather than entering commands with the keyboard. Controllable with a combination of mouse and keyboard, it tends to be easy-to-use and user-friendly.

hack In the sense that I used it in this book, a hack is an "addition" that someone sticks onto a pre-existing computer program. It's like grafting a branch onto a tree. Some hacks provide useful new features to a program; others can be *Trojan horses*.

hacking Very similar to cracking, except that a hacker is said to "explore" (break into) other computers for the purposes of learning only, and not for destruction. Nonetheless, the act of hacking itself, whether motivated by malice or not, can still cause damage.

home page On the World Wide Web, a user who has his own Web page has a "home page."

home directory The subdirectory within your service provider's computer where your account resides. In the UNIX command line, you can use the tilde (~) followed by your username to refer to your home directory.

host A host is the computer that is accepting an incoming connection for a given purpose. When you connect to your ISP's computer, that is the host. It makes sense if you think about it—it is "hosting" you.

HTTP The protocol for hypertext communications, used on the World Wide Web. Probably stands for "Hypertext Transport Protocol."

hypermedia The ability to hop, or jump, from one piece of information to another is what "hyper" refers to. On the Web, one can jump from text, sounds, or images to any of these media.

hypertext Used more commonly than "hypermedia," in practice it means the same thing.

infect When a virus inserts itself into a file, be it a data file or an executable program, that file has been infected. The virus can only spread from an infection in an executable program—infections in a data file will only lead to a damaged or corrupted data file.

Internetting The act of using the Internet. I don't know if it's a word (I made it up), but I'm sure other people have made it up, too. It's not all that clever, really.

IRC Internet Relay Chat. The CB-like service where anyone in the world can get onto the Internet and engage in live, real-time chatting with one another by entering thoughts on the keyboard. Users join topic-related channels and fritter hours away.

key management An umbrella term of issues involving public and private *keyrings*. Removing keys, adding keys, verifying keys, and so forth are all aspects of key management.

keyring Used in reference to *PGP*, a keyring is a file that contains cryptographic keys. Your *public keyring* contains any users' public keys that you have added to it, and a *secret* (or *private*) *keyring* contains your personal key(s), used to decrypt files.

local The local computer is the one you are using. Pretty logical.

mailbomb An act of anger or a prank, when someone sends you so much e-mail that it overtaxes the capacity of your service provider's hard drive, overflowing the incoming mailbox and causing all manner of havoc on your ISP's computer. Your sysadmin will not be happy if you are mailbombed.

menu-based interface Some service providers offer UNIX accounts, but, to alleviate their difficulty, provide simple-to-use menus that offer you a list of possible actions to choose from. Similar to a graphical interface (you must choose your action from a provided list of choices), and far easier for the beginner than a UNIX command line.

message body The "body" of an e-mail message, which is where you type its actual content. Most e-mailers separate a message into a *header* and a *body*; the header contains addressing information, and the body contains the message. Additionally, an e-mail message may contain an attachment (see *attachment*).

MIME A protocol for transferring binary files through the ASCII-based world of e-mail or Usenet news. Applications that support MIME encoding don't need users to convert files to ASCII first. Only users with MIME-capable applications, however, can receive MIME messages from other people.

mount A way of sharing another computer's storage space, or a portion thereof, on your local computer. In UNIX, the "/etc/exports" file determines which computers can mount which portions. Don't let people mount parts of your system that you wouldn't want them to have access to.

multiuser An operating system that supports sharing a computer's resources by a number of different people. This means that there must be mechanisms in place that prevent the users from looking at each other's stuff.

native A program written specifically for the operating system it is running on is said to be "native." The alternative to running a native program is *emulation* or *remote access*, both of which are always slower. For example, if you run the e-mail application PINE on your UNIX shell account (and therefore on your ISP's computer), you are running PINE remotely. On the other hand, if you actually had the PINE program (or Eudora) on your PC, you'd be running it natively (and much faster).

netizen A citizen of the Net. Since there aren't any citizenship requirements for using the Net, I suppose every Net user is automatically a netizen.

newsfeed Your service provider receives a certain chunk of all of Usenet news. They may receive the entire thing or only a portion of it. Whatever they receive is called their newsfeed. You, as a subscriber, can only access newsgroups that are carried by your ISP's newsfeed.

newsgroup A topic area on Usenet where people discuss issues within a certain interest area. There are many thousands of newsgroups, with every conceivable topic, some of which you may find disturbing or offensive.

online When I use this word, I mean that your computer is using the phone line/modem, or in some other way connected to another computer (or the Internet, which equals other computers). For many people, being online costs money.

packet On the Internet, information is transmitted from computer to computer in little teeny chunks for technical reasons. Each little chunk is called a packet. So any time you do anything on the Internet, your computer is sending and receiving lots of little packets.

pass phrase PGP's version of the word "password." Used to protect your secret key. Rules for password selection all apply equally to pass-phrase selection.

password The secret series of characters that allow you access into something, often used in regard to accessing your Internet account. It's like a lock on your front door; the weaker it is, the easier someone can walk right into your home.

PGP "Pretty Good Privacy" is a program used for encrypting and decrypting data. Although there are strange and convoluted legal issues involved in the field of encryption, PGP is widely used on the Internet and is the de facto standard for encryption and decryption of data.

PINE A commonly used e-mail program under UNIX. Another popular UNIX mailer is called "Elm," which is similar to PINE, but I like PINE better.

plaintext The opposite of *ciphertext*—data that has not been encrypted and is therefore naked to anyone's eyes.

plan A little blurb that you can write about yourself. Other people will see the contents of your blurb when and if they *finger* your Internet account.

platform Different computer systems are referred to as "platforms," and each has its own set of programs, interfaces, and everything else. For the most part, your platform is defined by the operating system you use. Mac users use System 7, while PC users often use MS-DOS/Windows (though some PC users use OS/2 or Linux, which are different platforms). *UNIX* is a software operating system that can be run on a wide variety of hardware systems, most of which you've never heard of (although there are some versions of UNIX that can run on Macintosh or PC hardware).

post A post is a message that someone places in a newsgroup on *Usenet*. Very similar to the idea of tacking a note to a communal tackboard. When you read Usenet, you read people's posts, to which you may respond (follow up) with a post of your own.

postmaster The person to complain to if a user is misbehaving terribly. Send e-mail to **postmaster@*bad.users.address***, nicely explaining the problem. The offending user may then be dealt with, although the postmaster has no obligation to do anything.

private key (secret key) Your personal, private file used to decrypt data that someone encrypted for you using your *public key*. Very important that you keep it maximally secure—never let anyone get your secret key!

process In UNIX, a program that's running is called a process. Because UNIX can run multiple programs at the same time, there are often many processes running simultaneously on a UNIX machine.

program file Same as an *executable* file—something that can be "run," or executed.

proprietary online service Commercial service such as America Online, CompuServe, or PRODIGY. These are not the same thing as the Internet, even though they may offer certain types of access to the Internet. These services are regulated by their owners; each has its own set of rules and uses its own interface.

protocol A mini-language that computers use to talk to each other. Both computers need to speak the same protocol to accomplish some task, and different protocols are written for different tasks.

public key The key that you use in PGP to encrypt data for someone. You use the intended recipient's public key to encrypt data for him, which he can then decrypt using his private/secret key.

pyramid schemes Attempts to make money by inviting people to send money to other people. Although they promise riches, they are illegal, won't bring in riches, and are posted to Usenet with extreme frequency.

quoting Repeating a portion of a previous post in your own post, usually to respond to it, so readers will know what you're talking about. In theory, you should quote within relevance to comply with the "fair use" clause of copyright law. In practice, you should quote within relevance to save Internet traffic. Fair use in regard to other people's posts is pretty wide open, but when and if you quote actual commercial works, be much more prudent.

remote The remote computer is the one far away from you. Actually, it could be anywhere, but it's the computer you connect to with the computer you're using.

.rhosts A configuration file in the home directory of your UNIX account that can control access into your account without a password. Configure it properly or (better yet) don't use it at all.

rlogin A UNIX program that can be used to connect from one UNIX account to another, without being prompted to enter a password. Regulated by the *.rhosts* file in the remote home directory. Very dangerous if you don't know what you're doing. Use *Telnet* instead.

root The head cheese on a UNIX system. The root account has access to any and everything on a UNIX system, including everyone's directories, e-mail, files, and so forth. Hackers and crackers often try to break into root and play digital god, which can be very dangerous.

rot13 A quick and simple form of encryption that is easily decrypted by anyone. It's used to hide information from immediate reading, in case you might want the option of not reading the text. Not for securing information by any means, just a quick "delay" for offensive jokes, plot spoilers, and so forth. Sometimes used in Usenet news, but seems to be losing popularity.

server The machine that processes requests from a client. The server sends out files, information, data, or what not at the request of a client. So, when you use FTP, Gopher, or a Web browser, you are connecting to an FTP server, a Gopher server, or a Web server (respectively).

service provider The people who give you Internet access. For some, this is their workplace or school. Many others pay out of pocket, just as they would for electricity, water, and telephone service. There are thousands of service providers, and the number is growing daily. Quality of connection and customer service varies widely, so it's wise to shop around in your region.

shell/shell prompt The UNIX interface, wherein a user is faced with a blinking cursor and a blank screen. You must enter commands, many of which don't seem to have any relationship to the English language. Steep learning curve, but once you've climbed it, you've got a very powerful interface that can offer much more flexibility than any graphical or menu-based interface.

signature A little tag line at the end of an e-mail message or Usenet post that you may add. Some people use it to identify their workplace or phone number, others brag about how big their hard drive is, and yet others draw pictures using ASCII characters.

SLIP/PPP Both are ways to communicate using *TCP/IP* over a modem, rather than with direct Ethernet connection. This allows your computer to have its own *IP address* and get the gaggle of benefits that come along with that. While purists will point out that SLIP and PPP are very different things, they both serve to accomplish the same thing, so it really doesn't matter for your purposes.

source code The instructions that make up an executable program, written by a programmer. A special computer program converts source code into binary, which that particular operating system can understand. Examining the source code before executing a program is often the only way to effectively spot a Trojan horse, and very few people have the know-how to do that.

subdirectory A directory within a directory. A folder within a folder. And so on.

subscribe When you subscribe to a Usenet newsgroup, the contents of that group are available to you. When you unsubscribe, they are not. This would be an effective way of preventing a child from seeing newsgroups you don't want him to, except it's usually pretty easy to subscribe and unsubscribe, even for a ten-year-old. Still good for real little kids, though.

System administrator (sysadmin) The person in charge of the system your Internet account is on. He has *root* access. You bug him for any problem you have. If you are a sysadmin yourself, you probably wish you were the captain of a single-hulled oil tanker instead.

TCP/IP The computer language of the Internet. When a computer can speak TCP/IP, it can communicate with other computers on the Internet. If your computer cannot speak it (such as if you don't have a *SLIP/PPP* or direct connection), you have to rely on some other computer to speak it for you. Hence you have to use a *dumb terminal* to connect to a remote computer.

Telnet A *client* used to log in to a remote computer. Preferred over *rlogin* whenever possible (which is almost always).

terminal Originally, this meant a keyboard and monitor that were connected to a real brainy computer that was somewhere else. Now, your home computer may be your terminal and your ISP computer is the brain computer located elsewhere.

Trojan horse A secret "feature" of a program that the user doesn't know about. Can wreak all kinds of damage, and can be hard to protect against.

troll Similar to *flamebait*—a post in a Usenet newsgroup trying to get angry responses, for no other purposes than to elicit angry responses. Best ignored.

tty Your host computer—probably your ISP's UNIX machine—has a finite number of incoming connections it can handle at any one time. When you dial up, you are assigned one of these connections, which is called a tty.

UNIX An operating system, like System 7 or MS-DOS, but far better, as well as far more complex and powerful. Actually, most machines don't run "UNIX" as such, but a variant of it, of which there are quite a few. They all try to sound something like the word "UNIX," such as Ultrix, HP/UX, Irix, Linux, Minix, and SunOS (okay, well, that last one doesn't have an x, but it's still a UNIX variant).

Usenet The global "message board" of the Internet. A tackboard the size of the Earth. This is where millions of people post messages with anything they want to say—divided into appropriate (sometimes) topic groups.

UUEncode A common way to convert binary data into ASCII. Not really a form of encryption as such, though it could be used that way for very insecure purposes. More commonly used to post binary files such as pictures and sounds to Usenet, or to send them through e-mail.

virus A computer program which, when executed, will try to stick itself into places on your system in such a way that it can infect files and spread itself as far as possible. May or may not be programmed to inflict damage as well, but the mere act of infection and spreading will probably cause damage.

Web page Anything on the Web, really. When you use your browser to navigate the Web, you move from Web page to Web page. The document you see in your browser's window is the current Web page.

World Wide Web The "network within a network." A loosely organized and dynamic set of computers on the Internet (which itself is loosely organized and dynamic) that can exchange *hypermedia* documents. All the rage nowadays, and very useful. Exploring the Web , however, is an easy way to waste one's life away.

Index

Symbols

A

B

C

D

E

M

N

O

P

Q-R

S

T

U

V

W

Who Cares What *YOU* Think?

WE DO!

We're not complete idiots. We take our readers' opinions very personally. After all, you're the reason we publish these books! Without you, we'd be pretty bored.

So please! Drop us a note or fax us a fax! We'd love to hear what you think about this book or others. A real person—not a computer—reads every letter we get, and makes sure your comments get relayed to the appropriate people.

Not sure what to say? Here's some stuff we'd like to know:

- Who are you (age, occupation, hobbies, etc.)?
- Which book did you buy and where did you get it?
- Why did you pick this book instead of another one?
- What do you like best about this book?
- What could we have done better?
- What's your overall opinion of the book?
- What other topics would you like to purchase a book on?

Mail, e-mail, or fax your brilliant opinions to:

Barry Pruett
Product Development Manager
Alpha Books
201 West 103rd Street
Indianapolis, IN 46290
FAX: (317) 581-4669

CompuServe: 75430,174
Internet: 75430.174@compuserve.com